Out of the Chrysalis

A personal journey through World War 2, Agoraphobia & Spirituality

the autobiography of
Marjorie Shepherd

Copyright © 2007 Marjorie Shepherd. All rights reserved. No part of this book may be reproduced in any form or by any means without *written permission* from the author.

This book is available to purchase from www.lulu.com

Cover design & inner typography by Dave Shepherd — www.ethos.uk.net Text faces used are DeepDene REGULAR, ITALIC & SMALL CAPS at 18/12/9PT

Revision 2 : 02/12/2007
ISBN 978-1-84799-223-9

Other books by Marjorie Shepherd.

Tomorrow's Promise — *Growing up in Hull through* WW2
Under the Blanket — *My Life with Agoraphobia & Fear*
The Healing Journey — *Overcoming Agoraphobia & Fear*

The trilogy above come from sections of 'Out of the Chrysalis'

HULL LIBRARIES	
01283062	
Bertrams	05.04.08
942.837	£11.95

Dedicated to

my children & my family

without whose help and encouragement

this book would not have been written

Table of Contents

INTRODUCTION	page 6
PREFACE	page 8
CHAPTER ONE · *WW2 & my Childhood Years*	page 12
CHAPTER TWO · *Finding Independence*	page 46
CHAPTER THREE · *The Adventure Begins*	page 79
CHAPTER FOUR · *Stepping out of the Comfort Zone*	page 88
CHAPTER FIVE · *Out of the Frying Pan?*	page 110
CHAPTER SIX · *A Brand New Start*	page 147
CHAPTER SEVEN · *Dramatic Change*	page 181
CHAPTER EIGHT · *A Completely Different Life*	page 213
CHAPTER NINE · *My Healing Journey Begins*	page 256

INTRODUCTION

I FEEL AS IF I HAVE BEEN HIDDEN under a blanket of fear (of people and situations), all my life with just glimpses of normality now and again. Now, at last however, I know the blanket has been lifted off me completely and I am just amazed by the way I have changed in my outlook and my confidence.

Throughout their lives, I used to tell my children snippets of my life and they were so interested that they would ask me to put the details into a book which could be handed down in the family. As well as recording my experiences, it would also tell them a little of their history (as far as I know it) and what life was like, from my point of view, as a child growing up in *Kingston upon Hull in East Yorkshire*, during and after the Second World War.

The book also charts the traumatic events which occurred during my two marriages and the upbringing of six children.

As the work progressed I, realized that it was mainly my on-going battle with and eventual victory over *Agoraphobia* and *Fear*, one minute feeling elation when I had a success and the next plunged deep into despair, when I chickened out of something I had set my heart on doing. It turned out to be a therapeutic exercise, enabling me to understand how and sometimes even why, I had attracted these experiences.

The big turning point of my life was finding the *Spiritualist Church*. It is also the story of the highs and lows on my Spiritual Pathway and my happiness at being able to help a great many people through my mediumship.

I did bring one gift with me when I started this life's journey though, for which I will be eternally grateful. It is something that my whole family, from my parents down to my youngest child possesses. That is our ability to laugh at ourselves and see things from other points of view. I am sure that this has helped carry us all through the rough times and will do so forever. Of course we get annoyed with each other sometimes, but the feelings never last long because we have a very strong bond, that I feel sure will *always hold us together.*

PREFACE

IN FEBRUARY 1934, in a small terraced house in Grange Street on Fountain Road in Kingston upon Hull, I, *Marjorie Dixon*, was born. My father (born 1910) was George, and mother (born 1908) was Ellen, (Nellie). I had two elder sisters, Joyce who was five years old and Brenda just over two and a half years.

My maternal grandparents, John and Alice Abram also lived in the terrace with my Aunt Jean and Cousin June. June had been born nearly four months after me but her mother – Violet – had then developed milk fever and was taken to *De La Pole Hospital* in Cottingham, where, about a year later she sadly died. Granny and Granddad Abram then brought June up as their own child. They also had three older boys, Jack, Fred and Bob. Granddad worked at Ranks Flour Mill until he retired.

Before serving with the 8th *Army* in the Middle East, Uncle Jack worked at *Castle Hill Hospital*. When he was away he would send us letters, which were only on one sheet of card with glue all around the edges. The writing had to be very small to fit a lot on. He wasn't allowed to tell us exactly where he was. After being demobbed he became an Ambulance Driver.

Uncle Fred was in the also Army but after losing his wife, Violet, he wanted to be by himself, and became a very solitary person. That was why he left June in the care of my granny and granddad.

Uncle Bob was a window cleaner, working down Fountain Road. In his spare time, he entertained the crowds at the Hull Rugby Club matches with his fancy dress marching band. They were known as *Bob and his Ragtime Band*. All the members dressed as different characters and all played different instruments. Bob played a Bazooka and they raised lots of money to take the children from his local – the Brunswick Pub on day trips to Withernsea. I remember that as the bus approached Withernsea the band would get out and march in front of it, playing till they arrived at the Spread Eagle Pub, where they would have a meal. Bob would give each of the children £1 to spend and on the way back, they were all given a stick of rock to take home. Once people got to know about Bob's band and their outings, he had lots of requests from other pubs to take their children also. I later found out that my brother-in-law was one of the children taken from another pub in East Hull. Sadly in 1954 Bob committed suicide by drowning in Barmston Drain. It turned out he thought he had cancer. A post mortem found that he had an ulcer but no evidence of cancer. His death was a great shock to all his friends as well as his family and a great many people attended his funeral at Eastern Cemetery.

Granddad Abram was a good singer and would entertain at the music hall in Fountain Road. Mam also had a lovely voice and from an early age she would often sing with him.

Mam had worked in 'service' from leaving school and had worked her way up to becoming a Head Cook at *Rockliffe home for the Blind*, which was on the same site as the Blind Institute. It was here that she met and later married dad.

My paternal grandmother was Ada Dixon who lived with her two sisters, Alice Dixon and Lilly Walham in Walcott Street on Hessle Road. Dad was an only child. Alice had a son Wally and Aunt Lil had two daughters Freda and Nora. Granny Dixon never married and I never met granddad. Aunt Lil's husband was a fisherman who, I think, was lost at sea.

My Granny Dixon and Great Aunt Lil worked for the Trawler Company *Lord Line* in charge of the net-braiders (making nets for the fishermen to use at sea). Granny Dixon was the Forewoman and when she retired Aunt Lil took her place. To the girls at work they were known as *Aunt Ada* and *Aunt Lil*.

Aunt Alice stayed at home and ran the house and was also a home worker making the nets, which hung from bars on the front room wall. After her retirement Granny Dixon also made the nets at home. When I went to visit, they would let me help to fill the wooden *needles* they used for making the nets. I loved the smell of the twine. My sister Brenda also did net braiding from home whilst her children were young.

Soon after he was five years old, and had started school, my father's eyesight deteriorated rapidly. He completely lost the sight in one of his eyes and had very poor vision in the other. Dad was sent to the *School for the Blind* in York, where he learned to be independent. Although the regime was very strict he mostly enjoyed his time there. After leaving, dad started work at the *Blind Institute* on Beverley Road, where he stayed for most of his working life. In later years, dad told me that had passed his exams to be a teacher of the Blind. After he left, he was always kept up to date with teaching procedures by a monthly newsletter / report sent from the school in York. I am not sure why he did not pursue a career in teaching.

Dad really enjoyed working for better conditions for Blind and Disabled people as their Union Representative and Branch Secretary (He was still Yorkshire and North Eastern representative for the RNIB right until his death in 1986 at the age of 76).

Dad also played the Saxophone in what was at that time referred to as *the Blind Band* and then changed to the drums, so we always had lots of music in our lives. He used to sit on our bed, practicing the Saxophone, before my sisters and I went to sleep. I loved the velvet softness of the notes in the tunes he would play.

CHAPTER ONE

ww2 & my Childhood Years

For the first 6 months of my life I was a sickly baby, having serious problems with my digestive system. I was operated upon to cure 'twisted bowels' as the condition was called at that time. I know now that this is called *Malrotation* and *Volvulus*. This happens when the bowel does not coil up into the correct position at ten weeks of pregnancy, causing bands of tissue which block the first part of the small bowel. This then causes the bowel to twist so the blood supply to that part of the bowel is cut off. My mother told me years later, that I had been *asleep* for three months after the operation (Looking back from a distance I believe I was lucky to have survived at all, surgery 73 years ago being not at all like it is today). I've always believed that I had to *hang on* in this world because I was needed to help and comfort many people later in life.

My memory of the first few years of my life is sketchy to say the least. I can still however vividly recall my first experience of *fear*.

In my mind I have a picture of myself standing at the window of an upstairs room, looking down and seeing gypsy ladies with big baskets on their arms knocking at all the doors. They knocked so loudly that it frightened me (at that time, Gypsies were ignored by most people, who never answered their doors to them, yet all they wanted to do was sell their home made wares to be able to buy food for their families). No one answered the door and no one came in to comfort me. I thought my mam had left me by myself and I was crying. I remember clutching an unopened block of chocolates in my hand, it was made up of five thin squares of chocolate; each wrapped in different coloured silver paper piled up on top of each other and all held together with coloured metal type ribbon. I made no attempt to open this chocolate although I really *loved* the taste. I cannot remember anyone talking about this so I never learned the truth of the situation.

When I was about two and a half years old we moved into No 12 Alexandra Crescent, Alexandra Road on Newland Avenue. The houses had no front gardens making the crescent a lot wider than normal; providing a safe place for the children to play. Everyone knew everyone else and they were all very friendly. Despite growing up during the *Second World War* (I was five when it started) my childhood was very happy.

My first memory of the war was walking with my family down Goddard Avenue to a large house on Chanterlands Avenue, which was being used as a government distribution centre. Here we collected our gas masks and were shown how to put them on. I remember feeling as if I couldn't breathe when the straps had been tightened behind my head and under my chin by one of the staff. If there was even enough room for a finger between the masks and the chin they had to be taken off and refitted. All I could smell was rubber – it made me feel a bit sick and I nearly pulled it off again. The gas masks had to be carried everywhere in a little cardboard box which had a piece of string for a strap. My parents two elder sisters and I had ordinary black ones but children under five years old had what they called a `Mickey Mouse` mask. I thought it was *grotesque* with a long red flap instead of a nose. This made a noise and flapped up and down when it was breathed out of – I supposedly so that the child did not get frightened. My sister Barbara had been born in August 1939 so she was given a sort of fully enclosed carrycot. Air had to be pumped into this all the time the baby was inside. I'm quite sure that if the enemy hadn't finished them off these baby masks would have *frightened them to death*! Thank goodness they were never put to the test.

At Sidmouth Street Primary School I was in the baby class and was taught by a kind quietly spoken lady called Miss Young. She was everyone's favourite and even when we moved up in later years we all remembered her with love. It was during this time that I heard my parents talking together about having to send us away to keep us safe. I did not know what *evacuation* really meant though.

Arriving at school one day I saw that buses were parked in the playground and we all had to climb onboard. I didn't know where we were going and it must have been like an adventure to a five year old. Our parents were able to go with us onto the buses which then made their way to the town centre, eventually stopping at the Bus Station on Ferensway. There, leaving our parents behind we boarded another bus which would take us to the end of our journey. The only thing I remember about the ride was stopping somewhere and being given a carrier full of groceries; there was a packet of biscuits on the top but we were not allowed to eat them. I held on to that carrier tightly. (I still remember to this day the awful feeling I had when it was eventually taken from me.) I was not told at the time why we were given the carrier. I know now that it was intended for the person who kindly took us in to help feed us until other arrangements could be made.

At the end of our journey which was in Scarborough, we were all taken to a big hall and people came in and chose the children they were to take home with them. Later there were only a few of us left when a lady called Mrs Knott came and took my friend Peter and I to her house at 36 Raleigh Street. (I didn't remember how traumatic it must have been for a five year old child, until years later in psychotherapy).

The first night I was there, I remember dreaming that I was in the toilet and felt very ashamed of myself when I found out that I had wet the bed. As I shared a bed with Mrs Knott, I felt awful but she was very nice about it and from then on until I was given my own bed in her room I slept on a rubber sheet. I settled down happily after that. Mrs Knott had a daughter called Trixie who owned a hairdressers shop at the other end of the street and she would sometimes take Peter and me there. I enjoyed my visits. I also remember going to the school and having lessons in the playground. Whether this was all the time or just for one day I do not know. I don't remember meeting any of my friends from Hull whilst I was there. On my sixth birthday I caught Chickenpox and had to stay in bed for a few days (I was in one of my own by then). One of my presents was an alphabet book full of the adventures of *Bengo the puppy*. I liked it so much that to pass the time I learned the alphabet backwards as well as forward.

Mrs Knott would take us to the promenade but we could not go onto the beach because of the rolls of barbed wire that had been placed there to stop any invaders from coming ashore.

Mam brought my baby sister to see me one day. I remember that we had our photographs taken. Although I was happy to see them I was quite content to stay where I was when mam went home again. Mam loved knitting and made us girls 'jumper suits'. She brought me a new one that day. It was red wool flecked with white and had a pleated skirt which had been sewn onto a vest type cotton top. Over this was a ribbed jumper made from the same wool. I felt very proud in this and still have the photo. My elder sisters Brenda and Joyce had been placed one near Goole and the other near Withernsea. They were not allowed to visit me (I did not know why) and with dad working, I didn't see him either. As a five year old I just accepted everything I was told and knew I couldn't ask questions either ('Children should be seen and not heard' was what I had always been told).

After about a year and a half, mam could not stand being without us any longer and took all three of us home. My sister Joyce didn't like it where she was staying so she was pleased to go home. I, on the other hand was *devastated*. I can see myself now in the corner of the kitchen, crying and clinging to Mrs Knott's long dark skirt because I had grown to love her and did not want to leave her. I was so settled and happy living in Scarborough with her, Trixie and Peter, so I didn't want the upheaval of being taken away again, even if it was back with Mam, Dad and my family. I cried all the way back home on the bus. My Auntie Jean told me in later years that Mrs Knott had wanted to adopt me. No one ever spoke to me about Scarborough again but as I've grown older I wish that I had been able to keep up contact with them both.

Whilst we had been away, Mam, Dad and my baby sister Barbara had moved from the terraced house in Alexandra Road to no. 4 x 10th Avenue on North Hull Estate. The thing I liked about it was the long garden with grass. I remember the winter when the garden was full of snow and the water butt was frozen over like a little lake. We had a lovely time there. Something strange happened one night. Joyce, Brenda and I were in our big bed when we saw something like a hand coming round the door. We were all frightened and screamed loudly making it disappear. Joyce thought it was Dad but we found out that he had been in the garden at the time. We were allowed to keep the light on that night and were never given an explanation for what had happened. Unfortunately mam couldn't settle in the house and we moved back to the corner of our old terrace in Alexandra Road. It was there that we felt the full force of the war.

I was too young at that time to understand much of what was happening so I think I just accepted it. Children in those days were not usually told about things and we just followed our parent's instructions.

One night we were awakened by the *Air Raid Warning Sirens* and had to go to the shelter which had been built in the middle of Alexandra Crescent. This was a long brick building that had an entrance at each end and one in the middle. It was separated into three rooms but as there were no inner doors, everyone could walk right through. To me, it had the smell of cold concrete which I can still call to mind today. The shelter had a thick grey curtain at each entrance and one separating the rooms. There were bunk beds made of wood with strong mesh bases along each of the sides. We took our own pillows, blankets and coats to sleep on as well as to cover up with, I was always put up onto the top bunk which was very near to the ceiling. From this vantage point I could see thick black wires fastened to the brickwork on the ceiling and small lights fastened in by metal guard wires to stop anyone burning themselves on them.

Although I was very tired, it was exciting to me to be there with all the grown-ups instead of being asleep in my own bed. I remember that one night, when the *all clear* sounded; we weren't allowed to go back home because a bomb had dropped in the fish shop near *Monica Picture House* on Newland Avenue (which backed on to our crescent). The bomb hadn't exploded but we might have been injured if it had gone off when we were at home.

We were told to go to the church hall at the corner of Brooklyn Street on Beverley Road. It was strange and a little scary to be walking out in the pitch-blackness but I knew my family would protect us and it only took a few minutes to walk up Alexandra Road.

Arriving at the hall we found that mattresses had been placed side by side round the edges of the room. After being given soup from a massive big pot, the children were all put to bed lying *top to toe* and it wasn't long before I fell asleep – in spite of all the excited chatter coming from the older ones.

The next morning we were given tea with bread and jam. Standing back from the road, the church hall was surrounded by a large area of grass. Not being aware of the seriousness of the situation, my friends and I were really happy to be *exploring* the site. Later in the morning we were all allowed home.

A few nights later the same thing happened again, this time the unexploded bomb was nearer, at the other corner of our terrace. Once more we made the trek down the street to the church hall and almost fell onto the mattresses with tiredness.

For the third time in two weeks the sirens awakened us. I was getting used to this now so I wasn't frightened. This time though, when we all left for the shelter, mam stayed behind in the cupboard under the stairs with my baby sister. Mam did not want to take her out into the cold, as she had measles and under the stairs was then thought to be the safest place in the house. As soon as Mr Wardle our local air-raid warden found out, he went to our house and made her come out. As mam got to the door of the shelter she turned round and saw what she later described as 'a ball of flame on a basket'. It was a landmine and it had fallen on the other side of Alexandra Road flattening three terraces and the houses in between, killing everyone in them.

It was very frightening for everyone to be walking up the street that was littered with glass and items from people's houses. There was a large empty space on the left side of the street and the bits of rubble strewn around were the only indication that peoples' homes had recently filled the gap. An *indescribable* smell filled the air. My Uncle Bob carried me on his shoulders so I wouldn't cut myself and the grown ups didn't talk to each other. They were all in shock that this awful thing had happened to so many people.

I have since been told of other parts of the city which suffered heavier bombings than our area. A friend of mine – George – tells of the Clifton Terrace, Day Street, Adelaide Street, Goodwin Street and Anlaby Road which experienced much damage and many casualties. He remembers a land mine being dropped on Walker Street causing extensive damage. A soldier was helping the search for the injured and dead, when he came across the body of his own wife, who he thought was safe with relatives in another part of Hull. George was evacuated at Garton-on-the-Wolds with his family and when darkness fell they could see the redness in the skies over Hull and the surrounding areas, due to the fires started by the bombings. This sight must have caused quite a lot of concern to the loved ones who were watching. Even the wedding celebration of George's Uncle John and his fiancé Violet (at the Barkers Arms), ended in tragedy. The sirens sounded and as everyone made their way to the shelters, his Grandfather – who was an Air Raid Warden, went on duty. A number of Bombs were falling along the main road with one or two falling near the pub. Coming out of the second shelter, after checking everyone was safe, he was hit in the chest by flying shrapnel and killed instantly. There were many casualties in the pub cellar and George's future Auntie Violet was one of them. She was pierced through the thigh by a table leg. When the wedding finally took place, some of the guests wore black out of respect.

This time we couldn't go back to our house. The blast from the mine had broken all the windows at the rear. The back door was off its hinges and the roof had caved in. We had had a bird in a cage in the front room window, but it was nowhere to be seen. The door-knocker had somehow been *wrenched off* and pushed through the letterbox. It had travelled down the passageway and had ended up on the sideboard in the kitchen. After we moved to our new house we found the birdcage but not the bird <u>inside</u> the piano behind the lower front board. Someone was *definitely* looking after us that night.

When we left the church hall the next day we stayed for a short while at a wool shop on Beverley Road owned by the friend of one of our teachers. Dad had organised temporary places for us. My elder sisters and I went to stay with Granny Dixon. I can't remember where the others stayed, it was hard to find accommodation for all our family at one place now that there were six of us. After a couple of days dad came to bring us home, telling us that we now had a new house to go to. This was at 87 Edgecumbe Street Newland Avenue. My Granny and Granddad Abram, Jean and June, moved in with us for a while until they were given a house on the opposite side of the street. Mam's cousin Elsie also lived down there and she had asked the landlord if we could have the houses.

We were lucky with ours and I was really excited; instead of a tin bath on the wall outside, our bath was in the kitchen! It had a strong wooden top which would lift up and clip to the window when the bath was in use. This top also served as a workspace, so that we had plenty of room to prepare food for our family.

Some of the houses in the street still had gas globes for lighting. On the evenings I used to love running across the road to Granny Abram's house to watch her light hers and pull the side chains which controlled the level of light. It made the room *fill with shadows* but it felt really cosy. Although our house still had its gas mantles on the wall, ours was powered with electricity. It was good not having to carry candles and night-lights up the stairs when we went to bed.

Life then settled down into a routine. I enjoyed being at school; my favourite lessons were Arithmetic and English. We were taught our tables *parrot fashion* with the whole class reciting them together. Words were given as homework and we had 'mini tests' once a week to prove that we knew how to spell them. I loved reading and Friday afternoons were favourite times when we would have stories and poetry read to us. Sometimes we would rehearse for concerts or plays which we would put on for our parents and friends. I had grown into a tall slim child with blue eyes and blonde hair which despite my protests was always cut straight just above the bottom of my ears at the sides and into a fringe above my eyes. In school plays I was always given the part of an Angel or a Fairy; sometimes even a flower because of my appearance.

At home wide strips of sticky paper were put across all the windows to save the glass from shattering if it was broken in the blitz, and heavy black material was made into blinds for the windows and doors to stop the light getting out. Before any door was opened the light in the room had to be switched off. If any light did show, the *Air-raid Warden* patrolling the street would soon shout "Put that light out" to remind us. The street lamps could not be turned on so when we went anywhere after dark, which for me was hardly ever, we would all have small torches to show us the way. We swung them in front of us so they just lit up a little of the path.

Every signpost in the country had been taken away so that if the enemy had invaded, they would have trouble finding directions. This also made it rather difficult for anyone to find their way in an area not known to them. There was an unwritten rule that if the Air-raid Sirens went after midnight; we would not have to go to school until after lunch the next day (I think most of us children, not realising the seriousness of the situation hoped for that; we thought it was a great adventure).

As my Dad could not join the Forces he became a *Fire Watcher* checking for fires started by incendiary bombs dropped in an air raid. Big silver *barrage balloons* floated high in the sky, held in place by strong wires; these were meant to be traps for the enemy aircraft which flew low over the city.

Although we weren't bombed out anymore, other parts of the city were and fear still hung over us whilst we were in the shelters. Shrapnel – pieces of spent shells – were dropping all over the place, one even hit the side of our shelter and Dad picked it up. We kept it on our mantelpiece for a long time. Lots of people did that and we children used to compare the different pieces with each other. *Doodlebugs* or *flying bombs* often passed overhead. When we heard their droning sounds we would will them to keep going because we knew that when their engines stopped, they would drop straight down out of the sky. Mam and Dad held onto each other and no one spoke until the plane had gone past then everyone spoke at once, even laughing at silly things because we were all so relieved.

My mam started working at *Ideal Boilers & Radiators* in National Avenue on the nightshift, making shells for our aircraft to use, it was strange to see her in her grey overall and dust cap. Her clothes smelled of metal when she came home, I can still remember the smell today.

Men came and took away the railings from around our houses to make bombs and bullets. It was exciting to us little ones to watch them all get loaded onto a big lorry, although it was strange being able to walk through everyone's front when we went to the shop at the corner of our street.

My friend Brian's father got him to dig out the lead that was left in the holes in order to make toy aeroplanes, soldiers and army vehicles which he would sell for Christmas.

Everything was scarce, almost everything was rationed – especially tea and rice. Anything that was normally imported was in short supply, even string was hard to get hold of, so nothing was ever wasted.

We couldn't just go to different shops to buy our food, so mam registered at the Maypole near Lambert Street for groceries and Smythes the Butchers near to Monica Picture House for our meat. Although we could still buy vegetables and fish from different places, it was best not to do so as the shopkeepers attended to their *regular customers* first when food that was scarce came in.

Long queues formed for almost anything we needed. I loved the smell of the fresh bread from the bakers at the corner of Melbourne Street. We had to take our ration books for this also and were only allowed a little for each person which had to last us a week.

Mam would make bread and hot cakes to eke out our bread supplies although the flour was also rationed. She would leave the dough to rise in a big 'panchon' in front of the fire. I'd watch her make it into the big flat cakes and put them into the fireside oven to bake. Dad had an allotment at the bottom of our street and grew all his own vegetables and even Strawberries, Brambles, Raspberries and Loganberries, therefore we didn't need to go to the fruit shop very much. Dad also bred Rabbits for food and after their skins had been stretched out to dry on our pantry door they would be made into gloves for us all or sold to other people.

We also kept chickens for a while and one-day dad had just killed one for dinner when the dustmen opened the back gate. The poor bird escaped and ran out of the gate without its head. I can't remember if or how we got it back, but dad said it couldn't have got far because it was only a nervous reaction that had made it move. I have since heard other people tell this story so I don't really know the truth of it now.

The government *Minister for Food* used to broadcast on the wireless to give our parents tips on how to make our rations go a long way. Marguerite Pattern – a well known cook, would also make up recipes which were very filling when we tried them out even though they didn't contain a lot of meat or rationed items. People also learned to cook with dried eggs. I don't think these went down too well but I got used to the taste and enjoyed mine.

Before going to work Dad would make his breakfast drink by pouring boiling water on the tealeaves from the previous night and although the tea was really weak, we all got used to doing the same. We would eat bread spread with dripping or home made jam without butter, but when things were **really tight** we would use condensed milk. We often had bread and hot milk before we went to bed if we were still hungry.

Being an important port, Kingston upon Hull was one of the *most severely bombed cities* in England, but so that the enemy would not realize this, it was just referred to as 'a north east coast town' in news reports. Even today people do not realize just how much the residents of this city had to endure during *the Blitz*.

Everywhere we went we had to pass empty spaces full of

rubble which we called *bombed buildings* — where houses, which had been loved homes to the families who lived there, once stood. They all had the same damp decaying smell that has also stayed with me all my life.

The dirt from the bombed houses took its toll on the school's cleanliness. One day when we arrived we were told there was an epidemic of Scabies in the town and the only way to combat this was to treat *every child* in the school at the same time. Each class went in turn to the School Clinic which was at 77 Beverley Road. We had to march in a 'crocodile' up Sidmouth Street and Alexandra Road then on to the town end of Beverley Road to the clinic — We usually enjoyed our trips out of school; it felt strangely quiet but good, to be out in the fresh air when everyone else was working. On our arrival, girls were separated from boys and we were told to strip off all our clothes. Next a nurse came with a big bucket of something that smelled like *wallpaper paste* and proceeded to brush us all down with — wait for it — a wallpaper brush! First of all our fronts were brushed and then our backs. I remember it was a very cold day and we then had to put on our clothes whilst we were still wet. It was a very sorry procession that headed back to school that day.

A much nicer surprise awaited us on another occasion though. The teacher asked us to come to the front of the class if we had been 'bombed out' (lost our homes because of the bombing). I excitedly joined the queue but my *heart was in my mouth* hoping that I would qualify. I could have danced for joy when told I did and could pick a present sent to us from the American Army. I chose a box containing strips of different coloured plastercine and wooden blocks which had farmyard animals carved into them. I can still remember the lovely feeling it gave me to make a plastercine farmyard. That was my favourite toy for quite a long time. The Americans also provided us with long oval shaped boxes of sweets. I used to look forward to Fridays when the teacher would come round the class with these, inviting each child to take one, I even enjoyed looking at the boxes – which had a sort of pretty imitation lace patterned paper frill round the edge. The most exciting thing to me though was actually being allowed to eat them there and then.

I was 9yrs old when my only brother was born. I hadn't known anything about this but I remember coming home from school and opening the door to be greeted by the smell of *Dettol* and *Johnson's baby powder* and wondering what had happened. Everyone was very happy. My parents had the son they longed for after four girls. Our house seemed to bulge with people coming and going for what seemed a very long time.

Things weren't always so happy for me though. One day when I was ten years old I was at a fruit shop near to Edgecumbe Street, queuing for bananas when a neighbour of ours from Alexandra Road came up to me. She had been carrying round a letter addressed to me because she didn't know our new address. I can still remember that meeting. She took the letter out of a big dark coloured, oblong shaped handbag. I excitedly took the letter home but imagine my shock when it turned out to be an appointment for me to have my *tonsils out*. The letter also promised that I would be given ice cream, even though it was scarce. In spite of this I felt very nervous about going – asking tearfully if I really needed have the operation. I had had several very painful bouts of tonsillitis over the previous few years, so when my mam told me that I should never suffer from that again I was very pleased and eager to go after all.

We arrived at *Park Street Children's Hospital* and we were shown into a room with lots of other children. A nurse came in and put red rubber capes around our necks, then red rubber, elasticated caps were put on to us as well (We found out later that this was to stop the blood marking our hair and clothes). My nervous feeling came back then and I started to cry, but as mam had already gone home there was nothing I could do but wait my turn. We all had to walk into the operating room in turn and were helped onto the high bed. I fought against the mask that covered my mouth and nose, it reminded me of the rubber gasmask and I didn't want to breathe in it. I dreamt that I was lying on my stomach with something heavy and cold holding my tongue down, it wasn't a very pleasant experience altogether, especially when the girl before me was given the *last ice cream*! I was very relieved to be told — a couple of hours after the operation — that because I was no longer bleeding I could go home. My throat was very sore for a few days and it was difficult for me to eat without it hurting but it wasn't long before I started feeling better.

Another very vivid memory I have of my tenth year was being hit over the head with a hard backed book at school. I had been talking in class and this was the way my friend — sitting behind me — chose to attract my attention. I thought at the time that the blow had been the cause of an abscess which grew on a gland in the back of my head which also needed to be operated on, however, reason tells me that this probably wasn't the cause.

I think it must have cost too much money to be treated in the hospitals at that time, so the operation was performed in our front room (usually used for Weddings, Funerals, Christmases and Births).

My own doctor, Dr Marian Coleman, came to perform the deed. I remember I struggled to get away from the smell of the chloroform phial which she had broken into a cloth and tried to put over my nose. I heard her say to my mam "I dare not give her any more, I've given her three already. I shall have to do it without".

The next thing I knew was that something had pierced my head and cut down. I shouted "Mam she's pouring boiling water down my neck". I saw the doctor remove red towels (which should have been white), and then I must have passed out because when I opened my eyes the room was still; it was getting dark and I was by myself.

A nurse came every day to plug the wound, which always involved a tussle ending with me climbing all over the bed before she caught me – because I had seen the long rope of gauze that she was trying to push into my head. The pain of the plug going in was the worst I had ever experienced. On the last day of my treatment a new nurse arrived, I felt like crying with fear and I wouldn't look at her but she was really kind. She asked if she could just have a quick look. All I felt was a gentle tapping and when I asked if she was going to do it, she told me it was already done. This made me feel so happy and relieved and I wished she could have been my nurse from the beginning.

Peter who had been evacuated with me, had come home from Scarborough and I used to see him at school, although we didn't get together very much. It came as a great shock to me one day however, to be told that he had died. He was only *ten years old*. A few days later another friend lost her 10yr old sister. I was really frightened, I thought everyone aged ten was going to die. I don't remember ever telling my parents or anyone of these fears though, so I just 'pushed' them away.

Going to the shops one morning a few months later, I saw one of our neighbours running out of her house shouting to the whole world "The war is over, it's really finished". When I got to the shops it felt like Christmas. Everyone was laughing and talking together. Some were even crying and hugging each other. I couldn't wait to get home to tell mam. Church bells started ringing and people were coming out of their houses in our street. I had never seen so many out at the same time.

Someone drew a big chalk picture on an empty wall at the end of the street. It was of a man with lines for eyes, hanging from a gallows. Underneath was written "Down with Tojo". I was told later that he was the man in charge of the Japanese people – the war with Japan was not over yet.

Lots of women rallied round to organise a celebration party in the middle of the street, they all had jobs to do. Some came round with a bucket to collect what little money and ration coupons anyone could spare so that they could buy everything that was needed. The street was 'buzzing' with the excitement of making preparations for the best celebration we had ever known. On the day of the celebration, they borrowed trestle tables and long forms for the children to sit at. Some people had been busy baking cakes and buns and making sandwiches, trifles and jellies, some were organising games. A strange feeling came over me when my mam and elder sisters were busy in and out of the house, excitedly getting everything ready. I wanted to hide in a corner by myself – <u>wanting</u> everyone to forget about me, as if no one wanted me. I was very happy when mam found me and told me 'not to be so daft' and to 'come out with everybody else'. I couldn't understand why I felt like this though. Each child was given a paper hat and a fancy dress made out of crepe paper. Our piano was taken out through our front room window and put at one end of the long tables. Someone put another at the other end, the music went on for hours, no one seemed to want the celebrations to finish.

After the little ones had been put happily to bed, the older children were allowed to dance round the bonfire, which had also been hurriedly organised. Grown-ups who had been out celebrating joined in and everyone was very happy. A week or so later my mam won a competition for the *best-dressed window in the street*.

I wasn't old enough to think deeply about the consequences of the war to everyone involved, either in the fighting, imprisonment, the air raids or the horrible atrocities that happened to many thousands of people. Even living with the aftermath caused such a great deal of mental and physical suffering.

I loved putting my arms round my Mam's waist when she was combing my hair; and one day I noticed that she was a lovely round shape instead of being flat – as she usually was – although I was 11yrs old, it didn't really dawn on me to wonder why (no one ever told us anything about the facts of life in those days).

Shortly after that, I arrived home to the familiar smell of *Dettol* and *Johnson's baby powder* – again. This time we had another baby sister Marian. We loved babies in our house and we were all really happy. Once again the house seemed full of people coming and going for a long time. When I was young I always thought that mam and dad must have been so delighted to have a boy after four girls, that they had tried for another one. Even though another baby girl was very welcome, she turned out to be their last child. In later years I forgot to ask Mam if that was the way they had felt.

I always felt important when I went to school to tell the teachers of a new baby. They were really nice, telling the whole class how happy they were for the family.

After the war when the 2nd Eastern Division of the St John Ambulance Brigade (sjab) started up at my school in Sidmouth Street, I joined and really enjoyed learning how to look after people, I also liked working together in a group. The officers in charge were Mrs Hardy who lived down Torrington Street and her second in command, Enid. They were both really nice people and I liked them a lot.

We used to use the school gym for recreation and one night I fell over something and dislocated my shoulder. Although I was in quite a lot of pain, Mrs Hardy knew exactly what to do for me. She took me to a 'bone setter' friend of hers who lived near by and with one *pull and push* my shoulder was back in place and the pain disappeared. I was given a sling to wear for the rest of the night, though really it was just to remind me not to move it for a while. I stayed in the SJAB for five years taking exams in *First Aid, Home Nursing, Child Welfare* and *Toy making*. We went on duty on a Saturday, working at the Park Street Children's' Hospital giving food to the babies and changing nappies. We also sold flags in the foyer of picture houses to raise funds and when I was a little older I took my turn on *standby* in the first aid booth at the Hull Fair. I always felt very proud in my grey dress with white *frillies* over the cuffs of the dress and making it look really smart.

One night we were taken — by bus — into the town centre where we took part in the *Torchlight Parade* with members of the different forces. That was a wonderful experience for me, marching to the music of the military bands and seeing the pitch black night being lit up by *light stick* torches, carried by almost everyone in the whole long parade. I knew it wasn't only happening in our town and it was good to think the lights were showing again after six years of darkness. This was also a new experience for me, being only five years old when the war started and the lights went out all over the country.

My Dad encouraged me to start learning to play the piano. My music teacher lived in Goddard Avenue and I enjoyed going. After about a year or so Dad made me stop, because I just wanted to play the finished pieces without all the 'what seemed to me' boring effort of practicing the scales and learning the theory.

Dad told me that he couldn't afford the lessons if I was not taking them seriously. I still loved playing though and I would buy pieces of sheet music and learn to play them, practicing each hand separately before putting them together. Looking back, I wish that I had been more committed, I have always regretted not taking my lessons seriously.

My next venture was singing lessons. For these I went to *Madame Sharrah*, who lived at the town end of Spring Bank in one of the big houses which had lots of steps leading up to the front door, I really liked this lady. She had been famous when she was young and had a beautiful deep voice. Her house was almost full of cats – the ornamental variety – although she did have two or three live ones. I learned how to breathe correctly from my diaphragm and how to project my voice, opening my throat and forming the words correctly. Although I got a lot of stick from my sisters when I practiced, I stayed with Madame Sharrah for quite a while. The same thing happened again, Dad said I wasn't taking it seriously enough and it cost too much money to waste.

At school I enjoyed *Maths, English* and *Music* – always gaining high marks in those subjects, but I really disliked *Geography* and *History. Drama* was another favourite of mine and because of my colouring I was often chosen to play either an Angel or a Fairy. I was *Angel Gabriel* in the Nativity and *Tinker Bell* in Peter Pan. Oh, and later on at the *High School for Commerce*, I was a flower fairy in Peter and the Wolf. I don't remember how good my acting was though!

I hated PE. I was never energetic enough to vault over horses, climb ropes, or hang from bars. I did enjoy playing Netball and because of my height I was the Shooter or Defence. In Hockey they stood me in the goal because I wasn't fast enough to play anywhere else. I did like to walk though. In those days nearly everyone who was able, walked wherever they went.

At one time we were taken to the *Beverley Road Baths* with school to learn how to swim and I remember the first time that I went. When we were all in the water we were told to move away from the side and *jump* to catch hold of the edge of the baths. I jumped – missed and went under. I saw bubbles of air rising above me and when I hastily got out scared stiff I was allowed to get dressed. To this day I still haven't learned to swim (except once in Singapore I swam with someone holding my chin – until I realized he had let go, but I don't think that can count!). I always said I can swim – with one foot on the bottom.

Sometimes Mam would ask me to take my Dad's dinner sandwiches to him at the *Blind Institute* where he worked and I liked to do this. I went into the main gate, passing the *Knitting Department* on my left and *Rockliffe Home* (where Mam and Dad had met many years before) to my right. Behind the Knitting Department was the big hall where the *Blind Band*, as well as others would provide the music for the dances and special occasions that were held there. Walking on past I smelled the lovely odour from the spray shop on my right, where the cane furniture would be coloured with blue, pink or green, intermingled with gold, paint. A little further on to my left, outside the workshop and office, stood the long 'bath' full of water, for keeping the cane supple and ready for weaving.

Dad worked as a foreman in the Basket department at that time and there was a lovely smell of wet cane in the air. Each side of the room was divided into individual work spaces of about six foot by ten foot and each of these was separated by a nine-inch low wooden partition (I'm not too good on judging size from this far back in my memory). No one ever tripped over these partitions however as having a 'measured tread', the men knew exactly how many strides it took to reach wherever they were going. They would sit at the back of their spaces, weaving their baskets or whatever they were making. It was lovely to hear them shouting jokily to each other. A lot of them knew me and as soon as they heard someone say my name, they would all shout to me as well. I often wondered why everyone couldn't be as happy with each other as they seemed to be.

One day I found my dad in another room. As I walked through, I saw him standing next to a man who was a stranger to me. He seemed to be hitting him on his arms grabbing his hands and pulling on his fingers, this really upset me; I had never thought of my dad as being aggressive. It was a relief to be told that he wasn't being cruel after all – the man was deaf/blind and this was the only way to communicate with him.

Pocket money day was always Thursday, *Dad's pay-day*. This was definitely the highlight of our week as we were each given 6D. Mam would give us our ration books and we would go off excitedly to the shop to buy sweets. On the sweets page, there would be dated coupons marked D which you gave for 2oz and others marked E which were worth 4oz.

These four ounces of sweets had to last us all the week so we thought very carefully before spending our money. When we had used our ration, we would buy sticks of black liquorish or liquorish root to chew on. There were also cinnamon sticks that would help to keep us going.

Sometimes Dad would take us to *Monica Picture House* on a Thursday night. A sloping walkway led to the back of the foyer where we would pay for our tickets at the window in the wall on the right. Walking further on – we would see the curtained off entrance to the cinema. Once inside, if the lights had already gone down, the usherette would shine a torch and lead us down the sloping isle to empty seats in the place of our choice. We would sit in the front row and Dad would buy us *three cornered ice bricks.* I still enjoyed going with him sometimes when I was older. I was always very proud of walking anywhere with my Dad.

I remember one time when Dad had been having trouble with his wrist, it had swollen into a big ball shape. This — he was told — was due to banging down on the cane when weaving the baskets. This particular day he had gone to see the doctor because a red line was creeping up his arm, we all knew that this was blood poisoning. The doctor told him to go home and sent an ambulance to take him to *Beverley Road Hospital.* My sisters and I were upset about this but also because this was THURSDAY — *pocket money day.* No one wanted to say anything, so it fell to me to ask Dad, with the others pushing close up behind me as he was just climbing into the ambulance. We needn't have worried though, because he had left our money with Mam.

Whilst Dad was still in hospital, Mam asked me to take some clean clothes to him but she only had enough money for my bus-fare there. I had never seen Dad ill in bed before and I thought he was going to die. I was so frightened that I dare not go into the ward and I just stood looking through a little oval window in the door. I felt really guilty having to get the nurse to ask my Dad if he had a penny for my bus fair home, Mam hadn't wanted me to walk back because it would be dark before I arrived home if I had done.

Another occasion that sticks in my memory was when my friend Shirley — who lived opposite me — had to have operations on both her feet and for a few weeks was in plaster up to her knees. Shirley had always been strong willed and wouldn't do anything she didn't want to. I used to help her mam take her out in her wheelchair sometimes but she always let us know that she was still in charge. One night we had all decided we would go to *Mayfair Cinema* to see a film that was showing there. Shirley changed her mind as we set off and decided that she wanted to go to *Monica* instead, although her mother was adamant we were going to stick to our original plan. Halfway across Newland Avenue towards Grafton Street, Shirley suddenly got out of her chair and started walking across the road in the other direction towards Monica. I thought she looked like a *zombie*, up to her knees in plaster, striding along with her arms flailing out at the sides in an effort to keep her balance! We could do nothing else but follow her, to quickly get her back into her chair. She was, once again, exerting her authority over her Mam and me. We ended up going to see a film which we had all decided earlier that we did not particularly want to see. I was very glad when the time came for the plasters to come off and Shirley would be back on her 'real' feet.

 I think I must have been a little wilful myself really, but somehow I always *got my comeuppance* as my Granny Abram used to say. Once I was told to 'run straight away' to the shop on the corner of our street, but I decided to call for my friend Mavis who lived down the terrace opposite, to ask if she wanted to come with me. We always went everywhere in two's or three's at that time. I had just stepped off the kerb when I went flat on my face. Putting out my hand to stop my fall, I cut it badly on the rough ground. I went inside to get it bandaged but didn't tell my Mam that I was crossing the road when I fell. If I had done as I had been told, maybe my 'accident' wouldn't have happened. I still bear the scar under my right thumb to remind me.

 Our Street — being a dead-end with allotments across the bottom — was very safe for the dozen or so children who lived there to play out in. Our parents did not have to worry about us. If we weren't playing or watching football with the lads, the girls along with Pat were organising concerts. Shirley and I would pretend we were famous singers and we held our 'shows' in someone's back yard. All the girls took part, either singing or reciting poetry. Our dresses were made out of crepe paper and we charged *one penny entrance fee* which we used for refreshments. Calling ourselves the 'Newland Follies', we made up a signature tune, (which we sang to the tune of 'we are the Ovaltinies').

For our entertainment we bought whips and tops, which we decorated in patterns of different coloured chalk, and would see who could keep them spinning the longest. Marbles was also a favourite, mostly with the lads and they were all very proud of the different sizes and patterned ones they had won from each other. We played *Truth Dare or Force, Rialio, Conkers* (which we then called Hong Kongs), *Can I come across the Golden River? Kick Ball Fly* and other ball games, as well as chasing in teams and skipping. When the lads were playing football and I was the only girl outside. I liked to stand next to one of the lads, Donny, in the goal (I had a secret crush on him).

In the winter we skated on the ice in the gutter under the street lamps, so that we didn't cause a danger to anyone walking on the path or the road. As we were just outside our house, I was allowed to stay out a bit longer. I loved to see the thick snow and glittering white frost, which made the whole world seem quiet and still somehow. I didn't even feel the cold, with sliding up and down. It was a great feeling playing out in the dusk; everything seemed so still.

The lads would show off by jumping across the kerbs at the end of the passageways between the houses. As these were pretty wide it took me a lot of practice to be able to reach. One day I was showing them how clever I was – when my foot slipped over the kerb and I ended up doing the splits, which not being at all athletic, made me really hurt my groin. My 'reward' for this cleverness was to have to stay indoors for a couple of days, which I hated.

I loved reading though, getting lost in a story and imagining I was really there. Dad would buy us comics on a Sunday along with his papers. I would have the *Girl's Crystal*. This had about five stories but not many pictures. I would soon join in the adventures unfolding inside. There was a girl who loved reading so much that she turned into a bookworm and wriggled her way through the pages. I remember she was a small thin girl with dark curly hair and black glasses, I used to think that could be me, because I felt so much like her. There was also a group of girls who went to a boarding school; putting on hooded capes, they had secret meetings and solved all the mysterious 'goings on' at the school and in the surrounding village, I was definitely one of them.

Whenever I got the chance I would escape into a lovely fairy tale land in my mind, where everything was perfect and everyone was really nice to each other. Mam sometimes got angry with me, because when I was reading I didn't hear her calling to me.

I seemed to have my *head in the clouds* when I went on errands too and I was always such a long time. I would meet friends and forget I was supposed to be in a hurry, or I would spend ages looking in shop windows. Once, when I was sent to the shop to buy a tin of peas, I brought back beans. Mam was so angry that she threw the tin across the room at me. I ducked away from the approaching tin and unfortunately my younger sister – who was sitting on a table waiting to be washed, was hit under her eye. She still has a scar where the rim hit her.

Another time I was told to put a tin of beans into the fire oven on the *Yorkist Stove*. It must have been around Christmas time because I remember I was enjoying playing *schools* with my new blackboard and easel. Later on there was a loud bang – I didn't know I should have pierced the tin first! The oven door blew off and my blackboard was splattered with beans! It was lucky no one was in the kitchen at the time.

At Easter we would have special eggs. Mam would hard-boil them and we would all colour them in. Even whilst sweets were rationed, my Mam always managed to save the coupons from somewhere to buy us a chocolate egg in an egg-cup every year. Then we would all go to Pearson's Park on Princes Avenue for the day which was very enjoyable.

We always had new clothes for Whit Sunday and we would be taken to visit my Mam's brother Uncle Jack and his family, who lived in Williamson Street on Holderness Road. The grown ups would go into a nearby pub and the children would stay outside. Uncle Jack brought out crisps and lemonade to us. As there were about seven of us, we always found ways of passing the time. Sometimes people coming out would give us pennies, we enjoyed our visit very much.

Summer was really exciting because, although we couldn't afford to go on holiday, my Granny Dixon and Great Aunts used to take my sisters and me, in turn along with my cousins Leslie and Freda, on 'mystery' bus trips. We went to see different *stately homes, churches* and other places of interest in Yorkshire.

Once or twice the family would go on the ferry across the Humber to Cleethorpes for the day with my Uncle Jack, Aunt Rose and my cousins. It was a bit scary to me, when as we were sat on the deck of the Ferry; the big chimney would erupt into a loud noise which would hurt my ears for a while. I always looked forward to going on it though.

At other times my sisters and I would take a drink and a sandwich to the field near the *River Hull* in Beresford Avenue and because it was so peaceful I felt as if we were in another country. We would walk through the field where the football games were played and sit near the river. I didn't like to go too close however because the steps looked very slippery.

We had plenty of entertainment in our street as well. There always seemed to be something happening to interest us. Early on a Sunday morning the *Salvation Army Band* used to come and sing, stopping at various places down the street. They had one stop right outside our house. I loved to see them in their uniforms and the ladies in their bonnets, I also really enjoyed their brass band and their singing.

One of them would knock on each of the doors asking for donations for the good work they were doing. Sometimes the children, who were outside by then, would *follow the band* as they went on their rounds to hear the instruments playing.

I remember a *Fruit and Vegetable Cart* pulled by a horse would come down the street. Mam would always send us for *William Pears* and *Oranges* which she would roll under her foot to release all the juice.

Another firm favourite was *Atkinson's* (Acko's) ice cream. The seller would cycle down the street on a bicycle, which had a 'stop me and buy one' sign painted on a big white box in the front. I've never ever tasted any ice cream as enjoyable as that one.

Sometimes a *Hurdy-Gurdy Man* would stop at the top of the street. We would all run up to see the monkey, who was holding out a little brass plate for pennies, whilst the man turned a big handle to make the music play. Sometimes a horse pulling a carousel ride on a cart would attract a lot of attention as we came home from school. I never saw many children on the ride though; I don't think any of the parents had any money to spare.

On rare occasions we even had a man with donkeys, giving children rides up and down the street.

When *Hull Fair* came every October, Mam and Dad would take us all there. This was something for us to look forward to at the end of Summer. It would be very cold by then and if the rain hadn't started, it would almost certainly not be far away (Everyone called it 'proper Hull Fair Weather').

At that time it was the *third biggest* Fair in England and it gathered lots of the showmen and attractions from other parts of the country. Early in October they would all meet up at Nottingham for the *Goose Fair* – which was then the second biggest fair – and then most of them would come on to Hull.

Today it is one of Europe's' largest travelling Fun Fairs and is one of the oldest *Charter Fairs* still in existence, the first charter being signed as far back as 4th November 1279.

As our family walked up Spring Bank West towards Walton Street, some people would be coming away tired but happy. Children, who were still trying to hold on to big stuffed teddy bears and other things that they had won or bought, were being carried on their Dad's shoulders. Parents would be trying to carry goldfishes in bags whilst at the same time keeping excited children from straying. The atmosphere was really great, the smell of the cooking coming from the stalls billowed out and made us feel hungry, even though we had already had a big tea at home. I loved this part of the journey, hearing the music and the excited screams of delight and seeing the all the different coloured lights even before we got there.

Walking down Walton Street, we saw vans selling dolls with big flouncy dresses in styles belonging to other parts of the world. There were toy monkeys on elastic bouncing up and down, soft toys of all descriptions and sizes, clockwork toys and other things were all on show to entice the children. Vans selling *tea and cakes, sea food, pomegranates, coconuts, candyfloss and nougat* also filled the sides of the street, as well as others making and selling *hot dogs or fish, patties and chips*.

In the centre of the street several caravans were parked behind each other, their sides adorned with posters and drawings inviting people in to see 'The Real' *Gypsy Petrulenga, Gypsy Rose Lee* and others. If you crossed their palms with silver they would tell your fortune. Each one of these caravans had long queues of people excitedly waiting to see what was in store for them. My Mam always loved going there to have her fortune told. Dad would buy us some chips or candyfloss to eat as we walked round. If it had already been raining we would have to jump over big puddles from the many potholes that littered the ground, but no one cared for once if we put our feet into the water. There were more stalls, near the entrance this time, inviting us to *hook a duck, play roll a penny; knock the coconut off its stand, test our strength* or try our luck on the *shooting range*.

The first rides we came across were the small ones for youngsters. There were *carousels*, some with horses and others with buses, which were safe for the children. Ladies in their skimpy clothes invited us to *come inside to see the smallest woman in the world, the Flea Circus* and *the Boxing Booth* where men had a chance of earning half a crown if they knocked out the champion and the *Ghost Hall of Horror* later called the *Ghost Train*. I liked the *Helter-Skelter, the Waltzers* and *the Bumper Cars*, but my favourite was *the Caterpillar*. When this ride had been going for so long, a big green tarpaulin would come over it and cover everyone. This was always a favourite for courting couples too. Not being at all athletic, I definitely wouldn't go on anything adventurous like *the Shamrock*, or rides that 'flung you into the air'. Even riding the *Big Wheel* was beyond my capabilities at that time. We all liked *The Cakewalk* on which the ground never stayed still. As you came out on to a sort of landing to come back down the slope to the ground, a big whistle would sound and your skirts would fly up if you didn't know that a grating in the ground was pumping air upwards (I didn't think this one would be very good for anyone who had had a big meal or even a drink though). Another favourite was the *Hall of Mirrors*. Everyone had a good laugh seeing themselves in all different sizes and contortions. The fair was always a big talking point at school, some people even went two or three times in the week, but we only went the once.

A week or so later, my Granny Abram would take June and me to another much smaller fair, which consisted of two or three carousels and rides that had not moved on when the main fair went. We would get the Beverley Road bus to Fountain Road and then walk down to Charles Street. We always had a good laugh that night, I think this was granny's way of *doing her bit* for us, because she never went to Walton Street. My granny jokingly called me a 'crab walker' because I kept walking into her. She said this was because I was not allowed to be out on a night after it became dark.

In the beginning of November our attention would turn to *Bonfire Night*. We would go round to all the houses in our street asking for old furniture or anything at all that would burn. We would even go on raiding parties to pinch wood from another street's bonfire when we thought their kids were not playing out — as everyone had the same idea though, no one really benefited by this. A couple of days before Bonfire Night we used to take our Guy Fawkes round to the houses asking for a penny, which would be spent on fireworks mainly *Fountains, Jumping Crackers* and *Catherine Wheels*. A grown up would be in charge of these.

The fire was always lit early, to let the younger children join in the fun before they went to bed. In our house, we all ended up black from the smoke but very happy. Because even our clothes smelt of fire we had to change everything and there was always a queue for the bath in the kitchen.

Sometimes I would to have to go to an off-licence shop in Grafton Street to fetch my mam a bottle of Guinness. I hated doing this because of a girl who lived down there. She would be out playing and would always step in front of me, put her hands on me hips and tell me I shouldn't be down 'her' street. She always kicked me before letting me pass. If she wasn't outside I would breathe a sigh of relief, but just when I thought it safe to pass her house, she would suddenly be there again kicking me on the same knee as usual – I must have been a very wimpish child to allow her to do this. I used to beg my Mam to let me go to the off-licence at Sharp Street corner, or near Walters Terrace but she insisted I go to Grafton Street. I remember seeing this girl when I was older and she just ignored me. I don't know whether this was because of a guilty conscious, or perhaps she had been a 'knee kicker' to everyone smaller than herself.

Often on a Saturday I would go to my Granddad's sister Great Aunt Lizzie's house in Washington Street on Beverley Road, to help her with the cleaning. She had the same kind of deep voice as Grandddad and I loved to hear her talking – even if it was only to tell me what to do. In Aunt Lizzie's kitchen there was a sort of metal table the size of a single bed, which had wire mesh in the front of it and a blanket inside. I was told it had been for protection against the bombs, as there were no shelters in their street. As Aunt Lizzie was a very large lady, I couldn't see how she and her grown up daughter Elizabeth would be able to fit into it when the Air Raid Sirens went. I loved climbing inside to see what it felt like. Aunt Lizzie would make me *cocoa* without sugar and a *strong cheese sandwich* without butter. Although I didn't really like it at first, I got used to it and even looked forward to finishing my work so I could `tuck in`.

Helping our milk lady in the school holidays and sometimes on a Saturday morning before going to Aunt Lizzie's, was something else I looked forward to. Previously, milk had been delivered from a horse-drawn cart containing 2 large churns. The milk had to be ladled straight into jugs brought by each customer, however, this method was being replaced by a bigger cart, carrying crates of bottled milk. The cart had to be pulled along manually, but I didn't mind that (I felt a bit like a horse between the shafts). I enjoyed talking to the customers and getting my pay – 2s 6d at the end of the week, which was a lot of money in those days. I would give this money to my Mam to help her to pay the bills. This made me feel as if I really was growing up.

CHAPTER TWO

Finding Independence

I WAS 13 YRS OLD when I had my first 'big' adventure. Our division of the SJAB decided to take us to their camp just outside Hornsea and Mam and Dad said that I could go. We had a great week but the best thing for me was being asked to sing a song on the *Open Day*, when family and friends had been invited. I felt a bit sad that my parents had not been able to come but I enjoyed the experience. It was the first time I had ever sung in public (apart from when we had had our concerts for our friends in the street). I sang a popular song at that time, called *Forever and Ever*. I thought my heart would burst when everyone clapped loudly for ME. Another highlight was meeting my friend's brother Bernard. He was a couple of years older than me, taller than I was with dark hair and lovely brown eyes. Bernard was an amateur boxer, but to me he was a very gentle person. I was totally in love.

Back home, I started delivering newspapers morning and night. Children had to have a medical and carry a green card to prove that they were fit enough to have a job, as well as doing their schoolwork. At different times I had rounds down the whole of Goddard Avenue and also on Cottingham Road and round Newland Park.

The job I kept the longest and enjoyed the most though, was helping our paper man Joe Chambers, who lived in Melbourne Street. A friend of mine Dorothy also worked for Joe on a Sunday morning. He had a very large paper round and a long barrow fixed to his bicycle. This was filled with papers, comics and magazines and all of his customers looked forward to Joe coming. They would choose different Sunday papers and magazines, as well as the ones they had ordered, but there always seemed to be enough to go round. In the middle of the round we would stop at his house and his wife would give us all strong, steaming tea and hot buttered toast. When we had finished, Joe would give us 2s 6d. I enjoyed the toast and tea so much I would have worked for nothing.

This money also helped Mam with her housekeeping — although I wished sometimes that I didn't have to give it all in. Around September time, Joe would bring lots of books and games to the houses to take orders for Christmas. People would give him so much money each week, till the items were paid for and then we would deliver them. This was a very exciting time for us and we had to promise not to tell any of our friends what they were getting from *Santa Clause*.

A few days before Christmas, my Mam would cut horseshoe and star shapes from card, which she would then cover in silver paper from the inside of cigarette packets. Filling a box lid with cotton wool she would place the shapes into it and then sprinkle silver coloured dust all over it. I would be sent out to neighbouring houses and even onto Newland Avenue, with instructions to ask people if they wanted to 'take the lucky horseshoe in', which they did. When it came out again, it would have some pennies or sometimes, silver coins on it. People always commented how lovely this box looked. The money would be given in at home to help to provide special treats for us all (my friend and I soon got into the habit of paying a visit to *Monica Picture House* to buy a 3D ice cream before we went home).

We were all very excited about Christmas. My elder sisters and I once started making up a poem about how we felt. It went like this...

> *Creeping, Prying, trying to sleep,*
> *All is in darkness; all are asleep.*
> *We hung up our stockings twelve hours ago,*
> *And now we are waiting for the toys we adore.*

I don't remember if we ever finished it; (maybe we fell asleep before we could) but I cannot remember any more of it.

Although money was scarce at this time, (Dad didn't earn very much at work), we always seemed to wake up to a bulging stocking at the end of our beds and little pile of books, games and 'educational' toys for each of us on the settee.

I used to love feeling for my stocking in the dark, trying to guess what was in the different sized packages that filled it. It was such a good feeling for me, that I would put everything back on Christmas night, trying to recapture the same feeling again the next morning – of course I never managed to do that.

The war had taken its toll on my Mam. She had started to smoke and was very short tempered with us. Coping with six children and the stress of managing everything had really got her down. Dad also came in for a lot of flak when he came home from work. Mam used to say to us "Just wait till he (my dad) gets home, I will give him hell" and she did. The minute he stepped

Finding Independence

through the door he would be told of someone's misbehaviour or cheekiness. Often it was me, and Dad was so frustrated that he would start hitting me on the top of my arms. Then Mam would say "The other two were just as bad, you can't see them laughing at you behind your back". Of course, this was not at all true, but Dad didn't know what to do next. In the end he told her he would not *chastise* us anymore. She would have to do it when we were playing her up, not hours afterwards. Funnily enough I never cried when Dad hit me, but if I had done something really wrong he would talk to me in a quiet voice, telling me how I had hurt him and Mam by whatever I had done, this would really get to me. I would break down, absolutely ashamed of myself and would promise to try harder to be good.

Dad decided to try working for himself, so he left the *Blind Institute* and rented an old stable building on Spring Bank. He used to make and repair *Sulphur Baskets* and *Peanut Baskets* for *Jacobs Larvin*, a firm of Stevedores. Uncle Jack worked with him. We children including my cousins – Rose and Doreen, used to go to see them on a Saturday and we would enjoy creeping into the baskets and eating the nuts that had got caught between the lining and the cane. Mam couldn't cope with not having a wage every week however, so after a while Dad went back to the Institute.

Arguments between my parents were very heated. Although they never said a word in front of us children, I used to lie in bed listening to their raised voices, and feel very frightened. I would try to imagine what life would be like if they parted and I would cry myself to sleep because I didn't want to be without either of them.

When Mam and Dad married they had their first three children in five years, and even though Dad went out playing the Saxophone in the Band at the *Blind Institute*, Mam never went out. When we were older we heard a story that Dad had been seen with another woman at his works entrance. Mam found out and took the children with her to confront this person. She told her that if she wanted Dad she would have to take the three of us as well. This liaison finished before it had even really started.

Mam had started to go out to dances a couple of nights a week. Now and again she would take my elder sisters with her. The younger children would be in bed and dad and I would listen to the wireless.

Every week, we would enjoy listening to Valentine Dyall saying 'we invite you to an *Appooointment with Feee-aaar*' and – this is your storyteller; The Man in Black. His voice was deep and menacing. It sent shivers down my spine just listening to it. It was always a horror story with a very frightening ending – to me, at least. After listening one night I went upstairs to my room and suddenly heard a tap, tap, tapping on the bedroom window. For a while I was scared but then I plucked up enough courage to open my curtains. The window was already open a little and as I looked out, there was Dad, in the back yard, tapping the clothes prop against it. I put my hand through and gave the prop a push. As I ran downstairs I could hear Dad laughing outside. I put a flannel under the tap in the back kitchen and for the next five or ten minutes we were laughingly throwing wet cloths at each other whilst also trying to hide. Imagine my horror when, as I saw the kitchen door opening I flung the flannel – *right into my Mam's face*. Of course she was very angry and called us both names. That made me feel silly and *put a damper* on our night of fun.

There were always parties at our house. After a night out with her friends, Mam would bring them back home for supper. Sometimes Dad would be there and sometimes he would be out playing with *Bertram Home's Band*. I used to sit at the top of the stairs listening to all the people laughing and singing to the piano.

Mam was a lovely baker but we children were not able to sample much of it. She used to make big plates of cakes and pastries and then count them before putting them into the walk in pantry in the back kitchen. There was always a big row when the numbers did not add up! My brother told me in later years that he used to go into the back yard, take the pantry window out, lean in, and drink the jelly. One of my sisters used to buy buns from *Mainprize's* shop on the corner of Edgecumbe Street, on her way back to work at dinner time and put them on the shop bill. Another sister used to shut herself into the pantry to eat the pies when no one was looking. I also used to take the pies and wait for the flak. We were always told by Mum "I can't cater for kids"

When my Uncle Jack and his family visited us we were happy. We hung around the table, even asking for the *goodies* hoping that Mam dare not say no. We were all treated to *daggering looks* and a *woe betide you when they've gone* face. The grown ups used to have their meal first whilst all the children looked on, trying not to be noticed and hoping they would save something for us.

Once when everyone was laughing and joking I was carrying something out of the room when I heard my mam say – so everyone could hear – "For goodness sake close your mouth, your bloody teeth look horrible". Despite being an *outgoing* child, I was still sensitive about my teeth, I had sucked my thumb all the time until I was 13 and only stopped when I used to wonder what my husband – if ever I got married – would think of me for turning away from him to suck my thumb. My two front teeth crossed in what was called 'buckteeth', I felt so stupid. For years I could not bear anyone talking about teeth, I thought it was a reference to the way mine were.

Mam spent a lot of her time knitting; she was a beautiful, fast knitter and had told us that in the 1920's she spent her school days in the Staff Room knitting for the teachers because she did not like lessons. I remember a deep red flecked 'jumper suit' she made me when I was evacuated. It had a pleated skirt sewn onto a material bodice, under a ribbed patterned jumper.

Mam had also made these in two different colours for my elder sisters when they were younger. She used to get so engrossed in her knitting that she seemed to be *in a world of her own*. Once when I came home from school, I remember sitting down in front of her and excitedly telling her what had happened to me that day. As I looked up at her, she gave a big sigh; looked up to the ceiling and without even putting her needles down, or stopping her knitting, she said "I wonder what to get for his (my Dad's) tea tonight. This made me feel as if I didn't matter at all. Even when Mam apologized, I still felt awful and wouldn't talk to her. Often she would wait till Dad came in to ask him what he wanted for his tea. Then she would send one of us out to get it. I thought this would make anyone a little angry, especially if they were coming in hungry from work, but Dad never ever said anything to her.

I started waiting till Dad had had his tea, and then telling him about the new things I had learned. It was very surprising to me to find out that he already knew these things and told me more about the subjects also. I loved having these long conversations with Dad, he seemed to know such a lot about most things.

On a Sunday, Mam started sending me with my 2 elder sisters to the *St John's Newland Church* on Clough Road. I remember us going three times in one day (I thought it was a way of getting us out of the way when school wasn't open). My eldest sister used to make us walk very sedately up Newland Avenue, along

Cottingham Road and on to Clough Road on our way to church, but on the way back we would all chase each other and laugh at the one lagging behind (usually me). I loved the Sunday School in the church hall and listening to the stories of *Jesus*, but I couldn't understand the morning and night services. I would often have a hard time keeping my eyes open during the sermons! I used to think God lived behind the big organ at the back of the church because I saw people coming and going into there. I don't think these three times a day lasted very long though, my elder sisters refused to go in the mornings and on the evenings.

Sometimes on a Saturday, Dad would take me to see Granny Dixon, and his aunts in Ireland Terrace, Walcott Street. He took all of us children in turn. We would get the no.62 bus to King Edward Street and cross the town to pick up a tram, which would then take us down Hessle Road. The trams ran on rails set in the ground and were long with a rounded end at the back as well as the front. The seats were made of polished wooden slats, placed, facing each other down both sides of the tram (I used to find it difficult to stay in one place because they were so slippery). There were controls at both ends and after he had reached one end of the road, the driver would just walk to the other end of the tram and control the return journey from there.

I enjoyed my visits and sometimes Granny Dixon would take me across to *Boyes* store. I liked seeing the different items on sale there, Granny would invariably buy me new gloves or a hat for winter, which I thought was great, we didn't have a shop like that on Newland Avenue. Quite often, Aunt Lil would give me pairs of thick khaki lisle stockings, to take home for my elder sisters and me to keep us warm in winter and I remember Mam dying them brown. We all hated wearing these but we couldn't say we wouldn't. I have been told that in later years, the stockings were reddish-brown, although this didn't make them any more appealing.

Later we would all have tea at the big table which dominated the tiny room. This was usually hot sausage rolls and bread cakes with cooked meat, followed by toasted teacakes. Dad would listen to the football results on the wireless. It was always the same routine; A large, patterned oilcloth was placed on the top of the thick dark-coloured tassel edged chenille tablecloth, and whilst one of the ladies put out the crockery, another was warming the sausage rolls and buttering the bread cakes before toasting the teacakes. The third one boiled the kettle on the *Yorkist* stove and mashed the tea. The youngsters who were there would climb onto a long couch that stood by the wall, whilst the grown ups sat round the other three sides of the table on chairs. The timing was always the same. The football results always came on just as we started eating.

After the meal, any remaining food items were cleared away and a big bowl of hot water was put onto the table. One of my great aunts washed up whilst another dried and Granny put them all away. The oilcloth was then washed down and also dried before being put away, and everything once more returned to normal. I always enjoyed watching this routine, and I was really glad when my turn came round to visit. As I got older, Dad would sometimes ask me to go to Granny's on an evening, and I was always invited to stay to supper. Granny and I would go to the fish shop near to where they lived and when we came back the table would have been set again. They all drank shandy and as I didn't like the taste of beer, only a minute amount was put in mine.

Back home, if Mam had anything to go into the town for, she would take my elder sisters and I with her. When she met any of her friends she would introduce us as 'her girls'. This would make me feel very proud. She would then take us to a café in

Paragon Street where we would be treated to oval-shaped buns or tarts. This just made my day.

Our school opened a youth club at the boy's school on Newland Avenue from 7.00 to 9.00PM every evening and my friends and I joined. We enjoyed playing table tennis and dancing. There was even a singing class which I went to. The teacher thought it would be a good idea to enter me for the *Musical Festival*, which was held every year at the City Hall. She had never done this before so she sent off for the rules and the piece that I had to sing. It was called *The Nightingale*. We practiced every time I went to the club and although she had never heard the piece played before she said that we were in with a good chance.

Soon it was the day of the Musical Festival and we arrived at the City Hall. I hadn't been able to eat properly because I was so nervous. There were 42 competitors altogether. I sang my song the way I had been taught, but imagine my dismay when the other contestants sang theirs. We had practiced it slowly and they were singing it fast and jolly (I must admit it sounded better that way). The judges said if the tempo of my song had been faster they would have awarded me more marks. I came seventh and I was so disappointed I could have cried and although the teacher thought it was a good result, I never went to the singing class again.

The Youth Club closed at 9.00PM and I had to be home by 9.15PM, so there wasn't a lot of time to stand and chat. Even saying goodbye to each other brought us to the attention of the *bobby on the beat*, who would take his gloves out of his epaulet, gently waft them at us and tell us to 'move along', which we did without a murmur.

I had passed my scholarship for *Escourt Street High School* when I was 11, but as my youngest sister had just been born,

Mam and Dad hadn't the money for a uniform for me. I was told to wait until I was 13 and take the exam for the *High School for Commerce* in Brunswick Avenue. I passed this and left Sidmouth Street School, a little sad at leaving all my friends behind.

The uniform was very smart, in navy and white. The thing I didn't like though was that instead of a beret, Mam bought me a navy hat like a boater (which was optional) to go with the velour overcoat. There were only a few girls wearing these types of hats and coats and I felt a bit embarrassed and silly wearing mine. This type of school was an entirely new experience for me. The main hall was open plan with a wide balcony, which the upstairs classrooms opened on to. The teachers all wore cap and gowns. We were all treated like adults and were responsible for attending our own particular lessons with different lecturers.

As well as the usual 3Rs, we learned *Shorthand, Typing, Book keeping, Commerce, French* and even *Speech Training*. The latter was to fit us for our new commercial careers.

I enjoyed most of the lessons but I was still a little bit cheeky, (innocently making my friends laugh), with one of the teachers. He was a really nice man called Mr Verity, who had recently become the father of twins. I think his subject was Geography or one that I didn't really like. I would start changing the subject by asking him about the children or one of his other interests. He got a bit exasperated with me on one or two occasions though and I had to spend time standing outside the classroom.

Because the building was on a street, it didn't have any grounds to the front or the rear. We had to go to *Newland High School* on Cottingham Road to use their *Netball, Hockey* and *Tennis* courts. It was great to see all that grass and although I didn't excel at any of the games, I enjoyed playing. The teacher was Miss Webber. She was a friend of Miss French from Sidmouth Street School and told me that she had been asked to 'look after me' although I never found out why and although Miss Webber was very nice to me, I didn't get, or even want, any favourable treatment.

Before my 14th birthday I asked Mam if I could have a few friends from my new school round for tea. I think she must have been distracted because she said yes. I happily invited five girls. On the day before, which was a Saturday I listened to Mam giving the list of groceries to my sister. I timidly said "what about the things for my party?". "What party? I never said you could have a party. I can't cater for kids" was the reply.

I sat in my Granny Abram's window across the street, watching my friends calling at my house and being turned away. I was really upset – especially when I saw they all had presents with them. That is my only memory of that time. I don't know what happened when I went to school the next day.

Another vivid memory I have is sitting down to Sunday dinner with the family. At that time there was a serial on the wireless called *King Solomon's Mines*, about Alan Quartermain's search for a lost city in Africa. This always came on as we started our meal. The beat of the drums, hearing about cannibals and the screeching of the witches filled me with fear, so much so that my food seemed to stick in my throat. I couldn't swallow and I would just go up to my room and lie down on my bed crying, wondering if I would ever eat again. As the weeks went on, I only had to hear the programme start and my reaction would be the same. As soon as the serial ended however, I was relieved to find I could eat normally again.

A short time later, the Youth Club started a Saturday night dance from 7.00 to 9.30pm at Sidmouth Street School and I was given permission to go, but I had to be in by 9.45pm. Another girl, Gloria and I sang with the band on alternate Saturdays. I would always see Bernard there and he would partner me — unless there was someone else more 'forthcoming' than I was! When this was the case he would ask one of his friends, John, (a distant relation of my brother-in-law) to look after me and make sure I arrived home safely. As young as I was, this didn't make me think any less of Bernard. At one of his birthday parties later on, he turned up with one of these other girls and he was told off by his mam — I think his parents thought more about me than he did. He did however, ditch this girl later, in time to take me home, I suspect with 'gentle persuasion' from his father.

Bernard was an ABA champion by then and I went once with his Mam and Dad to *Newland Homes* to see him fight. Everyone was excited when he won his match but I couldn't stand to watch the boxers hurting each other so I never went again. In later years when he was boxing for the Army Bernard was ill and was told he must never fight again. That would have been an awful shock to him because he loved it so much.

My elder sisters and I all had our own jobs to do at home. Mine was the kitchen. The stone floor had to be 'donkey-stoned' (A square of soft scouring stone which was rubbed in rings on the flagged stone floor after it had been scrubbed). I then had to cover the floor with newspapers until it dried. If I wasn't going out, I took my time over this. My dad used to tell me he would buy me a desk and stool in there and I could call it my office!

Mam used to polish the front room furniture and wash the front step. She used to take a real pride in rubbing the donkey stone over the edge of the window ledge as well as the door step and even the flags down to the front gate were washed before being donkey-stoned in rings to keep up the high standard of cleanliness of the street.

I left my senior school at the age of 15 yrs because my parents couldn't afford to keep me there any longer. I wasn't given a choice and had mixed feelings about going. I felt sad that I was leaving behind a part of my life that I really enjoyed, whilst also feeling excited at the thought of working – oh, and the fact that I wouldn't have to struggle with shorthand anymore! As I wasn't able to finish my course I left school without any real qualifications (in later years I was to regret this). I felt that I was 'neither nowt nor summat', because of being only half trained for the commercial world. Even speaking correctly made me feel as if I was trying to be a *cut above* other people.

Before I started work, a hairdresser friend of Dads – Marian – (whose husband Bert owned the band) asked if Mam would let her give me a 'bubble cut perm', which was the latest craze. Mam and Dad both said it would be alright, so I went off to their little shop on Holderness Road. My hair was cut all over, to about two inches, and then strands of it were pulled through square pieces of rubber to protect my scalp. Something like wire was wound round the hair and clipped into place. The whole *set up* was fastened up to some kind of machine in or near the ceiling. I didn't really like the feeling of being *fastened in* but it didn't last long. After it had been permed it was just left to dry. Having my hair straight all my life, the change made me feel so grown up. I felt good with this style and it really suited me.

My friends and I used to go to the dances at *Blind Institute* and *City Hall* sometimes. When we were sitting out between dances, I used to have to gauge a boy's height as he came over to ask me to dance (I was 5'7" by then and I always felt tall, gawky and stupid, dancing with someone smaller than myself),

Another thing my friends and I liked to do on a Saturday morning was to go into town even if we didn't need to buy anything, We would meet lots of people we knew when we were walking down Whitefriargate and would make plans for the evening.

My first job was as a filing clerk at *Ideal Boilers & Radiators* on National Avenue, I worked in the main office. Part of the room was sectioned off and lots of filing cabinets stood round the walls. In the centre stood a long grey metal machine looking something like a low seesaw, which, instead of moving up and down vertically, moved horizontally. Two people would sit facing each other at either end, inside two rows of lettered-flaps. These were marked with A – M on the left and N – Z on the right. We would each take piles of the correspondence from the morning post, first putting them on the fitted trays in front of us and then sorting them into the relevant lettered flaps. These had been made to move backwards and forwards, enabling both of us to reach the whole of the alphabet. After this we would file the correspondence into metal cabinets. In the afternoon the same procedure would happen again.

At lunchtime one day, one of the girls offered me a cigarette, but I refused though being easily led at that time, I was persuaded to try one. I thought this was being very grown up and I didn't refuse when it was finished and she straight away gave me another one, telling me to breathe in the smoke. When I tried to stand up afterwards, I felt dizzy and sick but everyone just laughed at me, I was told that the effect would soon wear off. It wasn't long before I became 'hooked' and sometimes even my dinner money was spent on 5 *Park Drive* or *Woodbines* for sevenpence halfpenny.

Some of my junior school friends worked in what was called the Carbon Room, putting individual sheets of carbon paper between piles of invoices to make copies for typing on. They seemed to have a great time. When I had been on the filing machine for about 6 months and with encouragement from the girls, I asked for a move. The boss told me that it was the first time he had ever been asked to move someone in a downward direction! It was easy work but I found it very boring. We used to take our *Film Star Annuals* and as it didn't take us long to finish our quota of invoices; we filled our time by tracing the different stars on to the discarded cardboard backs of the invoice blocks and then coloured them in. One relief from the boredom was watching an extension to the building being put up right next to our room. We used to talk to the floor layers and painters who were working there.

The enjoyment of the Carbon Room soon wore off – especially when I ran away from a date that I made with one of the painters, I wonder if I had ever known his name? We had made the date for a Saturday night and were to meet outside *Mayfair Cinema* on Beverley Road at 7.00pm. My mam and my elder sisters were really pleased for me and they helped me to get ready. Mam even said that I could be home at 10.30pm.

When I first arrived at Mayfair, I couldn't see my date, then I was shocked when this person came up to me and I realized this was him. He looked so different without his white painter's overalls, (I think that had been the attraction really,) wearing a long camel coloured coat and with his hair slicked back with grease I suddenly thought "this man is OLD". I was only 15 and he was 21!

In the cinema we sat near the back but he didn't seem interested in the picture. At about 8.30pm he wanted to go home and even though I had told him what time I had to be in, he said we needed time to say goodnight – <u>two hours</u>?

He really frightened me, we came out and I ran down the steps before he did and made a dash into Grafton Street. Luckily he did not follow me. I went straight to the youth club dance and told Bernard about it. He was angry with me for going, but we took advantage of my 'late pass' however and enjoyed talking to our friends for longer. — I can't remember if I ever told my mam about it though. When I arrived at work on the Monday morning I was greeted with stony faces. The news had already gone round the room and everyone was angry with me for running out on this man.

I changed my job to work as a Junior Clerk at *Gosschalk & Austins*, a solicitor's firm in Whitefriargate. I enjoyed this, especially when the office juniors of other firms in the city centre used to gather together in Queens Gardens to exchange the office mail.

I was still filing and making tea for everyone, but the work was a lot more pleasant and the people were very nice — even though I was told off one day for singing in the kitchen. I was told that, "This is a commercial office not a music hall." but they were all still very friendly.

My friends and I had started to go on the train to Hornsea on a Sunday, it was strange because we would meet lots of the people we knew there, even those who had set out for different destinations. Hornsea had come to be known as the *Cyclists Graveyard*. Around 4.00PM we would see piles of cycles on the hill outside the Amusement Arcade. Riders always stopped there on their way back home. More often than not, even the so called 'Mystery' Bus Trips ended up in Hornsea!

One day, my friend decided to ride there herself instead of taking the train and persuaded me to go with her. The only bike I could borrow was a *sit up and beg* one from Shirley. I rode fine for the first few miles and then every time we turned a corner I asked if we were there yet (did I say before that I wasn't energetic?) Luckily we made friends with two of the *real* cyclists and one of them took hold of my shoulder and just about *pushed* me home. Needless to say, I never tried that again.

One Saturday morning I was talking to a girl who lived in

Finding Independence

the other half of our street (known as Big Edgie' — I lived in 'Little Edgie'), when she told me of this wonderful job she had just taken. She told me she was expected to start work at *Hornsea Convalescent Home* as a Pre-Student Nurse on the Monday and she would have to let them down.

Without a thought, and feeling very excited, I said she must not worry about it because I would ring the Matron and take her place. I told Mam and Dad about my intention and they both wished me luck. They knew how much I loved SJAB and Dad said it was a good career and he thought I would do well. After quite a bit of persuasion, the Matron agreed to see me the next day. I feel sure that the fact that I had been in the SJAB for five years helped to show her that I was keen to take the post. I almost 'flew' home to tell my parents that I was leaving, to begin my *Nursing Career* the next day.

I was so excited about the thought of actually starting nursing that it never even entered my head to tell *Gosschalks* that I would not be going back to work for them. The thought that I may not get the job did not occur to me for even a second.

The train journey seemed endless, but when I arrived in Hornsea it didn't take me long to find the place. Matron was tall and stern-looking but after she had shown me around and given me my uniform, she smiled at me and said she hoped I would be happy working with the other nurses. I was to share a large airy room with one of the other girls. Even the bathroom was as big as my shared bedroom at home and I fell in love with the whole place and felt really proud as I put on my pink uniform dress with white 'frillies' which covered the end of the short sleeves. A pure white starched apron and small white cap finished the look.

The Convalescent home was a big rambling building opposite the bus station on Cliff Road in Hornsea. Children who had been ill or in hospital, and who weren't quite fit enough to go home, would come here for fresh air, good food and recuperation.

As well as the Matron, there was a Sister, an SEAN (State Enrolled Assistant Nurse) and, if I remember rightly, eight pre student nurses. We worked from 8.00AM to 9.00PM and filled three shifts per day, each nurse working two out of the three, with one half day and one full day off each week. One of us covered night duty for two or three weeks, from 9PM to 8AM, after which we were given three or four days leave. Whilst on night duty, we did not sleep in the home because of the noise from the children. We went to a house in the terrace by the side of the bus depot. It was strange at first getting used to living 'upside down', but I soon became accustomed to it. Mrs Milner was a really nice lady, who enjoyed having the nurses to sleep at her house, I dressed a little doll in a nurses' uniform for her to remember us by. I often wonder if she kept it.

Back on duty, it felt strange going into the quiet house. The sister or nurse in charge would tell us if any of the children needed help in the night and then would go off to bed, saying that she could be woken up if she was needed. I wasn't used to the silence at first and my footsteps seemed to echo as I went to the kitchen. The midnight dinner would consist of something the cook had saved from the staff midday meal. I used to ask her to leave me some mashed potato and vegetables which I would fry with eggs – there was also a sweet for afters, this was my favourite.

The maids' sitting room on the ground floor was our base and as well as carrying out ward rounds throughout the night we would mend any of the children's clothing that needed it. One night I was sitting in the chair reading, when I heard footsteps coming closer and closer. I was really frightened but I couldn't move a muscle. I wanted to pick up a poker or something but

I just couldn't. Suddenly a figure loomed in the doorway and I heard Matron's voice saying loudly. "Are you asleep Nurse?". I assured her that I wasn't and she went back to bed. I was left puzzled by the experience and none of the other nurses could explain what had happened either. Later, at Western General, I was to hear that this is a regular occurrence for people on night duty. Evidently your body is so tired but your mind is very alert. That is why I couldn't move. They called it 'Night nurses Cramp'. I was pleased that it was a well- known phenomena and not just something I alone had experienced.

It was strange, but as it neared the time to get the children up, washed and dressed, I didn't feel tired anymore. When I went off duty, I often went for a walk with one of the other girls, either down into the town or along the cliffs and down to the beach, before going to Mrs Milner's to sleep. I loved to be out in the early mornings.

After making sure the children were washed and had eaten their breakfasts, two of the morning shift nurses would take those who were well enough, down to the beach to play. They were taken for a walk by the afternoon staff also, if the weather permitted.

Whilst they were on the beach, one of the other nurses would set the tables for the children's meals and after their supper we would again set tables and cut the bread and butter (covering it with a damp teacloth) to go with their breakfast. If the weather was bad we would play games with the children in a long wooden extension at the back of the building, making sure they were all happy. We used to wash and iron their clothes each day, I don't think I had ever been so contented in all my life. I had been there a few days when the Matron had a phone call from the Solicitors' office saying that I must return to give 4 weeks notice. I felt as if the bottom had fallen out of my world.

After I had pleaded with her, telling her I definitely wanted to return as soon I could, Matron agreed that I could leave my personal things there. On the bus back to Hull I felt so sad about leaving and I wondered what the solicitors would say to me. I hoped Matron would keep her word to let me come back.

Back in Hull I presented myself at the office – trying to be interested in what I was doing, but all the time my thoughts were with the children I had left behind – when a couple of days later the solicitor took me into his office and told me that he could see how being there was making me unhappy and saying he would not keep me any longer, I nearly cried with delight. He gave me a month's wages in lieu of notice and let me go. I almost 'flew' back home to tell Mam and Dad, and caught the next bus back to Hornsea.

It was whilst I was there that I had my last date with my childhood boyfriend Bernard. He was on leave from doing his *National Service* and he came up to spend a day with me. We hadn't seen each other for a couple of years and whilst we had a lovely day, I think we were both very disappointed to find that I had grown about 4 inches taller than he had. We didn't arrange to meet again and even stopped writing. I only ever saw Bernard once again, it was many years later when we were both married and I had my twin sons with me. He was with his family on the top of a bus. It was great to realize how comfortable we still were with each other.

Off duty I met a girl named Janice and we became friends. On my days off, either she would come to stay at my house or I would stay at hers. We would sometimes go to the *Star Cinema* in Newbegin or to the Amusements on the front. We would also go for long walks and talk to the local boys. I went out with one of them Colin, for a few weeks but whilst I was home on a week's holiday, he started taking Janice out instead. Although I felt jealous and upset, it didn't spoil my friendship with Janice, but it made me a little more wary of men.

It was snowing and freezing hard one night when a group of us went for a walk and had snowball fights. One of the lads was trying to fill my boots with snow when I slipped and fell through a plate glass window. Luckily I did not hurt myself — everyone ran off and left me. I didn't stop to think what the shop owner would do when he found out, but even though I asked the lads later what had happened, nothing was ever heard of the incident.

If we weren't going out on an evening, the other nurses and I would gather in our sitting room, writing letters or just talking of our future dreams. Sometimes I would sing to the others. One girl, Mavis, used to always ask me to sing 'The Lights of Home' and she would enjoy a good cry. Although she loved working with the children she was very homesick.

Whilst I was living in Hornsea, I made an appointment with the dentist because I had been having a lot of pain with my teeth for quite a long time. He told me I would need fillings in my back teeth and at the same time, he would be able to fix a brace to my front ones. This sounded great to me, I would end up looking 'normal' again, with straight front teeth like other people. I had some of my back teeth filled but circumstances always seemed to prevent me from keeping the appointments to complete my treatment.

It was a policy of the Convalescent Home that, apart from the senior staff, they would only employ *pre-student* nurses. The Matron felt it was in the best interest of the children to have as many young people as possible looking after them. As about five of us were now seventeen years, we would have to make way for younger nurses. We were given brochures showing the conditions and career opportunities provided by the different hospitals and we had to choose which one we would like to go to. Three of us decided to go to *Western General*, which is now *Hull Royal Infirmary* on Anlaby Road and the two of the others chose *Kingston General* on Beverley Road. One of my friends, Anne, went to train at the *Hornsea Cottage Hospital*. I had mixed feelings about leaving the children, but I was really excited about starting the newest phase of my life. We all said our tearful goodbyes and came back to Hull.

At that time, Student Nurses had to 'live in' one of the two nurses homes, which were at 198 Anlaby Road or Lansdown House at the corner of Lansdown Street. I think some nurses also lived in the hospital itself. I was to live in Lansdowne House (which pleased me). This had originally been two houses, which were later knocked into one, the big main house having all mod cons and quite a few bedrooms. The ground floor of the other one was taken up by the Nursing School and had just two bedrooms. My friend Faith and I were given one of these, which was reached by going along a corridor on the first floor of the main house and down an iron ladder. There was a bathroom but it didn't have hot water, so we had to climb back up the ladder to a hole in the wall, which led back to the corridor in the main house, when we wanted a bath. The housekeeper – Mrs Taylor – was very strict and gave all the new intakes a lecture, laying down the rules of the house. We all thought she was a bit of a dragon.

We had to go across to the hospital for our meals though and because things were still rationed, we each had to provide two jam jars, into which the Sister in charge put our butter and sugar ration for the week. At first it didn't seem possible that this would last, but we soon became accustomed to eeking it out.

We also had to have a medical to make sure we were fit to do the work. During this, I asked the doctor if I could have time off to visit the dentist, having told him about my unfinished treatment. He looked in my mouth and said "no I won't allow that, there's nothing wrong with your teeth". In those days we just had to comply with people who knew better than us, but I must admit to secretly feeling very upset that the treatment wasn't going to be carried out after all.

There were three intakes of nurses in Lansdowne House, The PTS (Preliminary Training School), Second Year and Third Year students. In the PTS we had to complete three months working full time studying *Anatomy, Physiology, Bacteriology, Hygiene* and *Psychiatry*. On our first day we were given our uniforms which included an oblong piece of starched white material that baffled us. We were shown how to turn this into a 'butterfly' cap, with pleats down each side forming the wings of the butterfly. When this was done correctly it really did look nice, I can still remember how to make this up. I felt very proud wearing my uniform. We also went to the College in Park Street to take *Chemistry*. At the end of that time we had to pass exams in all the subjects before we were allowed on the wards, although we still had to take lectures and sit more exams.

The older nurses were very supportive to us though, and we had some good laughs together. I was pleased to find that two of them, Val and Barbara were the sisters of my school friend Pat. They remembered me from visits to their house and we spent a lovely time reminiscing about our childhoods. One night, my friends and I were bored so two of us started making up our faces grotesquely. I pulled the hood of my navy blue cape tightly round my face, so that the red lining was hidden and we both went downstairs to surprise the older girls; who then dared me to stand at the front gate to see the reaction of passers by.

This I did, asking people for the time. One man looked up startled and pulled his lady companion past as fast as he could. I bet he wondered what we were up to. On returning to the house, we found that the older girls had decided that they could play tricks as well as we could and all our beds and mattresses had been turned over. My room-mate Faith, had not been with us outside and she was rather angry because her bed had been treated the same. They had also locked the door at the top of the ladder so I couldn't get into the main house for the hot water and I had to sleep in my green and black makeup.

After passing my PTS exam, I was assigned to the *Gynaecological Ward* – being told it was for 'diseases pertaining to women'. The Ward Sister, Sister Greenly, was a very likeable woman, who could be stern when she needed to be. I found out that so long as all our work was done and there was no slacking or chattering, we would see her *good side*, and even her sense of humour. I liked her very much and enjoyed my time on her ward, even though she did sometimes tell me off.

The discipline was really strict, in contrast to today. We all had to arrive on time and be immaculately dressed. We were always being told, 'not to run except in the in a case of fire or haemorrhage'. Talking to each other was also not tolerated, except if we were talking about the patients. Sister, or the Nurse in charge, always made sure that we did not stand around with nothing to do. There were always jobs like tidying the linen cupboard or cleaning the sluice that needed to be done constantly, as well as making and tidying beds and lockers. Urine was tested in the ward bathroom with the aid of a bunsen burner, mentholated spirits and litmus paper. Machines for cleaning bedpans were just beginning to be put into hospitals before I left, so the nurses had to clean these themselves.

When a patient had been discharged or moved to another ward, beds had to be stripped, rubber mattresses, pillow covers and every part of the bed frame had to be washed with very strong disinfectant. Even the bedside lockers were disinfected.

Our hands had to be washed constantly, especially between tending to different patients and there were always little tubs of *lanolin* on every sink to help keep our hands soft.

The ladies cleaning the wards everyday had to make sure that, as well as cleaning and polishing the floors; the lockers, window frames, ledges, skirting boards and curtain rails round the beds, were all clean and dust-free. When Matron was due to make her ward round each day, everyone was kept very busy. We had to make sure that not a thing was out of place. Bedcovers had to be smoothed over, patients as well as lockers, had to be tidied up and even the casters on the bottom of the beds had to be turned inwards. We didn't speak to her or to the doctors unless we were specifically asked a question. It was hard work but really satisfying, and although I came off duty very tired, I thoroughly enjoyed it.

At Christmas time the hospital put on a pantomime. One year, Barbara was *Aladdin* and I was the *Fairy Godmother*. I was very happy in that part, as I had to sing three songs. Later, we took the show to entertain the 'displaced' Latvian adults and children who had been sent to Hull. They also enjoyed it and they were such lovely people that we went to see them by ourselves a few times afterwards.

My friends had started going to a club in Midland Street and one day they asked me to join them (I didn't know this place had a bad reputation, because I had never been in any club or pub before). There, we met some boys who worked on the fishing trawlers, and I paired up with one of them, Terry. We went every night for a week and as I was asked to get up to sing on the microphone, I enjoyed my nights out there very much.

On the Friday night I was told that there was a telephone call for me, which was puzzling because no one was supposed to know we were there. Terry came downstairs with me. The caller asked for 'Nurse Dixon' and when I said that I was she, the phone went dead. We all had our suspicions as to who it might be, but this was never proved, and it worried all of us.

The next morning (Saturday) I was called into Matron's Office. My knees shook, I must have done something terrible to be called in to see her. Matron told me it had come to her notice that I had been 'frequenting a club in Midland Street'. She asked if my mother knew that I had been out drinking and I admitted that she didn't. Matron then asked me to promise not to go there again. I willingly agreed to this because Terry was going back to sea that day and I did not want to get into any more trouble. I felt as if I was *walking on air* as I went back to my ward. Later, when I told my friends, they all breathed a sigh of relief. If it had happened to me, then it could also happen to any one of them.

The Monday was my day off. Our housekeeper, Mrs Taylor, had given me a message the night before, that Matron wanted to see me again and told me to bring my Mam in. I didn't sleep much that night, wondering what I had done now to displease her. I told Faith how worried I was about telling my Mam and she said that she would come with me to help me to explain. This we did, assuring mam that I had done nothing wrong. She listened to both of us, but never gave a hint as to what she was thinking. That trip to Western General seemed to go really fast, and my stomach was just in knots all the way there.

My heart was in my mouth when I knocked at Matron's office door, but I was glad that Mam was there with me. After being told to sit down, Matron said, "I understand that you have been singing in this club, and not only that but they have called you *The nightingale of Western General Hospital*". "I can't have my nurses bringing disrepute onto this hospital, so I am going to make an example of you, therefore you will be dismissed". I felt

Finding Independence

as if someone had hit me in the stomach and I felt a bit sick.

Mam asked what was going to happen to the others who went with me. Of course I would not tell who they were so, Matron said her decision stands. She told me that she had nothing against me on duty so I could work my month's notice. Mam was very angry and said that if I had to leave she would take me now. This really upset me, especially when I had studied and paid the fee for my first exam, which was only 6 weeks away and would not now be able to take it. I couldn't believe it – I had been thoroughly enjoying my training and now my nursing career was over! The older nurses at Lansdowne House were also angry. They said they couldn't understand why the others had not owned up to being there also. Nurses were in short supply and Matron could not have sacked 5 of us.

Living at home again was hard to get used to, but I soon found another job in the office at *Burnett & Co*, an import and export company in Mytongate. Whilst I enjoyed this work, I really missed nursing and looked for something else to occupy my time as well.

My eldest sister and her husband lived with us at that time. They were both in the *Territorial Army* and I rather liked their descriptions of what they did, so I joined as a trainee driver and felt very proud when I came home with my uniform in my kitbag. A girl who lived at the top of our street, Audrey, also joined and we went together.

Coming home late from work one night and rushing to get ready to go out, I walked straight into my room and started looking into the wardrobe. As I turned towards the bedroom door I got 'the shock of my life'. I thought a man had come into my room. Of course I screamed. Everyone came running in to see what was wrong. My brother in law had fastened all my uniform together and hung it on the bedroom door — boots, gaiters, cap and all. It even had a stuffed pillowcase for a head. From all the laughter, I realized that everyone else was in with the joke too.

After a couple of weeks training with the TA's we were taken to *Leconfield Aerodrome* to practice driving. We couldn't go very often because of a shortage of qualified instructors. It felt good being in charge of a small truck, known as an Austin 'Tilly'. I wasn't very confident on the narrow country roads though. I wished I could have practiced more.

One day my parents asked me if I would like to go with them to *New Inn* on the Bandstand at Stoneferry. Of course I agreed. This was the first time I had been out for a drink since I had left *Western General*. It was a big friendly room with seats all the way around and tables in the middle. At the back of the room, by the side of the bar, there was a small stage and after we had been there a while, people started to get up and entertain the crowd. Of course I was persuaded and I sang 'The Old Homing Waltz'. Everyone seemed to like my voice and I enjoyed the applause. In between acts the pianist would play all the familiar tunes and everyone would link hands and sway from side to side with the music.

A tall slim man then got up and went into a comedy routine. He kept looking at me and I tried my hardest to make him think I didn't understand his jokes. At the end of the night all the artists crowded onto the stage to sing 'Now is the Hour'. I was standing at the front and I heard a voice behind me ask if he could take me home. It was the comedian. I had been hoping that he would talk to me. My stomach was doing *summersaults* and my legs felt like jelly. To round off the evening most people went round to the fish shop next door. He came with me and told me his name was Ross. I introduced him to my family and Dad was happy to let him escort me (with everyone else, of course). We caught

Finding Independence   75

the NO.30 bus to the station, and then to the 62 bus to Newland Avenue. Saying goodnight, he asked if he could take me out. I felt as if I was walking on air, and found it very hard to sleep that night, or even take the smile from my face. I was going on my first, real, grown up date.

My family and I called him Ross for about a week until he confessed that he had only been kidding and his name was really Joseph Charles Arthur Shepherd., known as *Shep*, to his friends (Ross Shepherd wrote a column in the Sunday People). I think he had expected us all to see the joke straight away. I felt really foolish because I hadn't.

Shep had been with three of his friends the night we met and he told me that they took it in turns to choose where they were going each Saturday. It had been his choice that night and it was lucky that he had chosen *New Inn* on the same night that my parents had taken me. I started going with them to different places and would always be asked to sing. Joe, as I later called my friend, was six years older than me but I never felt frightened with him – as I had done with the painter on that first disastrous date. Joe and I went out quite a lot in the next few months, almost always to different clubs and pubs, sometimes with his friends but mostly on our own. We never seemed to go to the pictures or other places very much, but I didn't mind – for the second time in my life I was totally in love!

Joe would always meet me from TA's, bringing me cartoons he had drawn of the different things we were learning. He was great at drawing and these brought a lot of amusement to my friends at the barracks. On the bus we would laugh all the way home and if he was embarrassed at me being in 'boots and gaiters', when other girls were in nice dresses, he never showed it.

The landlord of the New Inn wanted to put me into the *Artists Federation* where I would get paid for my singing, but my Dad wouldn't agree to this. He said that at 18 I was too young for a life that would entail visiting clubs in and around Hull. I would have to go most nights of the week in order to get known before anyone started booking me. I felt a bit disappointed about this, but soon got over it.

Sometimes I would go to Joe's house and we would go out to his 'local' *The Botanic* at the corner of Derringham Street for the evening, after which he would either walk me home or put me in a taxi. When it was Joe's turn to come round to my house though, I would wait at the bus stop at Goddard Avenue (to be with him longer). I could never sit at home waiting for him to get to me. As the bus rounded Queens Road corner on to Newland Avenue, I always knew if he was on it or not. If he was, my stomach would turn somersaults, Joe always laughed when I told him this.

Things were not always so pleasant though. One night, we had been to Gardeners Arms on Cottingham Road and had a really nice evening. We had eaten our supper at my house and, as it was filling up with people, we had gone onto the doorstep to say goodnight when 'out of the blue', Joe told me that he was going to 'pack me up' saying it was because he was getting to like me too much. He said one of us was going to get hurt and he didn't want it to be him. I felt devastated. Even though I tried to talk him round, because I couldn't understand what he meant, he was adamant. It still took him about 2 hours on our doorstep to 'finish with me' though!

I was really upset and after a few days decided to meet him from work. I walked to the Cottingham Road end of Newland Avenue, knowing that he always took that particular bus back to Spring Bank. I rode with him up to Goddard Avenue. It was only three stops but we had enough time to arrange another date and start going out together again. The third time this happened, Joe changed his route from work and wouldn't answer the phone. I thought my life was at an end, nothing would console me.

A few weeks later, Audrey told me she was having trouble at home and was going to join the WRAC. After asking her all about it, I decided that, as Joe no longer wanted to know me and my Mam and I were not getting on very well, I had now nothing to keep me in Hull, and I would enrol with her. The night Audrey had to go for her test was the same night as our TA meeting, so it was easy for me to get away without awkward questions. The Recruiting Officer – Joan, was a friend of my eldest sister. When she saw me she said, "you had better go on Marjorie, your friend will be quite a while". I told her I wanted to join the WRAC also. Joan was quite flustered and asked if my Mam knew, to which I replied, "I was hoping you would tell her". Having passed the initial test, I arrived home feeling happy and yet very apprehensive. I said to Dad, "A few of the girls at TA's are joining the WRAC". Dad told me he knew one who wasn't and I felt really guilty – but not enough to make me change my decision.

When Joan called at our house a few days later to tell me the date of my medical, Mam thought she had come to see my sister, who was not home yet. Afterwards, Joan told me that she had had to make Mam a cup of tea to calm her down.

Our next-door neighbour (who we called Auntie Olive) told me later how upset Mam and Dad were. She said that I had broken their hearts. Looking back on this, over the years I have felt ashamed of the way I treated Mam and Dad. I must have been really selfish and wilful when I was a teenager.

Audrey and I were due to travel to Guildford in Surrey for our three months training in the October and my parents organised a farewell treat for me at New Inn. A week before this happened I found a way to get in touch with Joe and rang him to say that I had joined the WRAC and we were all going out for my last night, saying that I would like him to come – if he wanted to. He was really shocked to think I was going away (although he had made no attempt to contact me for weeks). My *heart was in my mouth* for the next few days. I didn't hear anything else from Joe and I couldn't stand the thought of him not being there.

There was a thick fog that night and I kept my fingers crossed that everyone would get there. Our party set off; Mam, Dad, Granny, Auntie Olive and me. As we walked down Newland Avenue and Clough Road, I couldn't help praying that Joe would be there also. I didn't need to have worried; he was there, looking just as good as he always did. He had always made my heart 'turn over'.

During the evening Joe took me outside and asked me not to go. By that time however, I was really looking forward to the adventure and told him I had given my job up and couldn't change my mind now. He even said that he would pay Mam my board money until I got another job, but I told him that my parents would be horrified to think someone else was giving me money (I was glad to have an excuse though because I had already received the 'Queen's Shilling' – the money given for joining – and my travel warrant). Besides that, I was really looking forward to the idea of a different life. Joe told me that he still wanted me to be his girl and that he would be waiting for me when I came home. It took us a lot longer on our doorstep that night, neither of us wanting to say goodnight.

As I later tried to sleep, I was a little apprehensive as well as being excited. What new adventure was round the corner? This wasn't just Hornsea 17 miles away. It was Guildford in Surrey, right at the other end of the country. I couldn't just get a bus home in about half an hour if I didn't like it. On reflection, I wonder if I would have been so eager to go if I had known what lay ahead of me.

CHAPTER THREE

The Adventure Begins

THE FOLLOWING MORNING I woke up feeling really excited. The day had finally arrived. I made sure that everything I needed had been packed. On an earlier visit to see my Granny Dixon and Great Aunts Alice and Lil, I was presented with a tin box full of toiletries to save me having to buy any for quite a while. They seemed pleased that I was going to start a new phase in my life, although they said they would certainly miss my visits.

As well as lots of sandwiches, buns and my favourite peanut butter for the journey, I took a bottle of *Owbridges Lung Tonic*, a local medicine. This was the only thing that cleared the catarrh that seemed to plague me when I was away from Hull. All I could do that morning was drink tea and smoke. I just couldn't face eating anything, which was not like me at all. I spent the time checking over and over again to make sure I had not left anything behind. At last the time for departure came. Dad took me to *Paragon Station*, where we met up with Audrey and her family. I usually loved the smell of the steam engines, but this day I just felt sick with anticipation. A few tearful goodbyes later, the train pulled out and we were on our way.

We sat in silence for the first 5 minutes or so. I was thinking of how I would miss Joe and my family. Suddenly I started to feel starving hungry so Audrey and I had a long awaited meal of sandwiches and buns.

At *Kings Cross* we left the station and travelled across London to *Waterloo*. The train from there would take us to Guildford in Surrey. We had absolutely no idea what life would be like in the camp and could only try to guess, what was to be our 'home' for the next 5 weeks, would be like. Having been in the TA's for a few months, I did have a very slight idea but it was nothing like the reality.

Our intake had been told which trains to catch and a truck met us at the station. We were taken along country roads until we arrived at the camp. Coming in through the gates we saw lots of neatly positioned huts surrounding a large open square of Tarmac, this was the *Parade Square* and we were told never to take short cuts across it.

After our driver had signed us in at the guardhouse, we were shown the way to the QM stores to collect our uniforms. There was even a rolled up length of material called a *housewife*. On opening this we found it contained varying shades of cotton, sewing needles, a thimble, some safety pins and some small scissors, so that we could keep our uniforms mended when they needed it. We were asked our sizes and issued with clothes that would surely never fit. Skirts and Battledresses were too long or too tight; hats were miles too big and, loaded down with kit bags and cases, we all looked a sorry bunch.

Our first stop, after we had been shown to our barracks by the sergeant who was going to be in charge of us, was to the Cookhouse for a very welcome meal. We had to get used to eating with strange metal cutlery and drinking from an enamel mug, even now I can remember the strange taste of that first cup of tea, but we were so hungry that it didn't matter, I actually enjoyed the meal. Everyone sat really quiet, looking around at the smartly dressed soldiers on the other tables who, in turn, were looking at us with slight smiles on their faces, as if to say "poor things, they don't know what they have let themselves in for".

That night, after lights were put out and we had all stopped talking excitingly, I jumped up to search in my locker for my *Owbridges*, saying, "Oh. I forgot to take my medicine". The others laughed and asked what it really was, someone even said it was a secret supply of alcohol. We all had a good laugh about it and I kept it up for quite a few nights. Later, thinking over everything that had happened to me, I was very pleased with my life, the girls were friendly and so were the officers.

The following day was taken up by visits to the tailor for alterations to our uniforms and someone showed us how to style our berets by soaking them in water before putting them on our heads and shaping them to our liking. After this they were left on the radiator to dry. I think this was frowned upon really but they did look nice, up at the front for our cap badge and flattened down at the sides.

We were then given a medical examination and 2 injections in each arm. Even though our arms became red and swollen at the tops, we were told to polish our bed spaces (half the width of floor between the beds, extending to halfway across the passageway down the middle of the room) to keep the bloods flowing. When we went into the busy main street of Guildford the next day, we had to turn the tops of our bodies sideways to avoid getting touched on our arms.

We learned to march correctly and were given a test to see whether or not our chosen career path was right for us. My friend Audrey chose to work in the Cookhouse and when we parted to go to our differing training camps, I never ever saw her again.

After a short period at the *Drivers & Clerks Training Centre* in Salisbury – where I passed exams in *Education, Clerical Typing* and *Admin*, I was posted to the WRAC *School for Instruction* at Hindhead in Surrey in the Officer Cadet Training Wing. This was very interesting because as well as the general office work, we 'stood in' as soldiers in need of discipline, in order for the Officer Cadets to gain experience of commanding people. I really enjoyed my time there, I had a job, which I loved and lots of company after leaving work. My best friend was a girl named Maureen (little Mo) who worked with me. We had the same sense of humour and went everywhere together.

I was still smoking then and we both found it hard to make our wages last the full week. The day before payday was the worst. We were both craving for a cigarette and came up with a brilliant idea. The staff sergeant in charge of our office, Staff Howie, an Irish lady who was very nice to all of us, used to only smoke half of her cigarette and stand the rest in her ashtray, which had 9 compartments. Maureen and I would arrive early on a Wednesday morning, before the cleaners, and take the tobacco out of about 3 or 4 of these. After stripping the paper from the back of the silver foil, lining the cigarette packets, we would put in the tobacco and make it into a gigantic cigarette, which was then stuck with office glue! It tasted foul but it did the trick. Every time our cravings got the better of us, we would light this thing up, feel sick and declare ourselves smoke free for the rest of our lives – until the next time. This routine lasted us till we were paid our wages the next day.

All this time, Joe and I were writing to each other and because our writing was almost identical, the girls in our barrack room swore blind I was writing to myself. My birthday is the day before Valentines Day and everyone had to eat their words when a big parcel arrived from Joe. It contained amongst other things, a tiny birthday cake and also 2 cards. To send that to myself would have been taking things a bit too far I think.

Every time my Annual Leave was due, I would send Joe a telegram and he would meet me at *Paragon Station* in Hull (He kept these and we still have 2 of those telegrams now). As the train approached the platform, I would see his head towering above everyone else's and my stomach would turn over. We would go to the little café opposite the entrance to the station on Anlaby Road to catch up with everything that had happened to us. On that first evening Joe would take me back to *New Inn* where we first met.

Once, when I came home, my life changed forever. My Dad tried to persuade us to go with him to Home on Spalding Moor with his band. (I used to sing with them sometimes). Dad said he would go with us to *New Inn* the next night. I must have been very wilful because I flatly refused; being my first night home, I wanted to go to *New Inn* as usual. Anyway, we went and whilst Joe was on the stage, I just happened to look round for my Mam. I saw her standing very close to a man who was sitting down. I didn't think anything about this, because she was always flirting with people when Dad was there. I turned my attention to listening to Joe when suddenly Mam was in front of me looking very worried. "What's the matter," she said. "There's nothing in it. We're only friends". I was shocked. If she hadn't said anything, the incident would have just passed off. I was so upset that when Joe had finished his turn, he took me outside to calm down. He was as surprised as I was, all I could think about was what was going to happen to our family. I found out later that this man (she called him Jess) had been coming to our house for quite a while and helping Mam with the housework when Dad was at work.

On the way to Granny Dixon's house the following day, Dad told me why he had let this go on. It was because he was trying to keep the family together. I knew my parents had had lots of rows but I never thought they would ever part. I was really upset and I felt I hated this man who had broken our family up.

As Joe and I became closer, I found out that he didn't have a very good opinion of women. He thought that they couldn't be faithful to anyone and would stray if they got the chance. I used to tell him this was not always the case, but I don't think he believed me.

My first experience of Joe's jealousy was when we were out at *Half Way Hotel* on Spring Bank West one night, Joe was on the drums and I was just enjoying listening to the music when a soldier came and sat by me. He was asking me where I had been posted to, and we talked about the different experiences we had had. Joe took a break and told me he was just going to the toilet. After waiting about 5 minutes for him to come back I went to look for him. He had totally disappeared. Going out of the pub I saw him at the bus stop across the road and when I got up to him, he said he thought I wanted to be with the soldier instead of him. He soon calmed down though and took me home. I felt angry with him for not trusting me, although I didn't tell him because I liked him a lot and didn't want him to finish with me again.

I had been back in camp for a while, when there was excited talk about postings to stations abroad. Looking on the posters that had been put up, telling all the details about the weather, the way of life of the people who lived there and working routines we would follow, I liked the look of the *Far East* and although

The Adventure Begins

I felt a little apprehensive about being so far away from home, something seemed to 'push me' on to putting in a request for a transfer there. When my posting came through, I felt very excited and looked forward to this new experience. As I didn't have any leave due at that time, I decided to break the news to everyone by letter.

My family all said they were pleased for me, but telling Joe was the problem. I told him what I thought at the time was a little white lie. I said it was a posting and I couldn't say I wouldn't go. Although I wrote to Joe many times, he never replied to my letters. Once again I was devastated; well, one part of me was, but another just couldn't wait for this new adventure to start.

Christmas leave came round and despite not hearing from him, I sent Joe the usual telegram. When the train pulled in at *Paragon Station*, the platform was empty and I felt very sad. I knew Joe liked me a lot and I wasn't going to give him up easily. I went straight to his house in Stanley Street and his mother asked me in. She was angry with me though, asking what I had done to her son to make him lose interest in Christmas and everything. She told me that he had been enquiring about renting houses and getting married, but all of a sudden he didn't want to know. She also told me he had started taking another girl out. This shocked me but I still waited for Joe to come home from work. When he did, he was very 'off hand' to me, although he did let his mother persuade him to take me out – one last time – to talk. I didn't eat much tea that day, wondering what would happen.

We went to *Gardener's Arms* on Cottingham Road and into the little room at the back. We sat by ourselves, neither of us feeling like entertaining that night. We had a nice time, still enjoying each others company, but Joe said that I couldn't really love him if I had chosen to go to another country (He didn't believe I had been posted either). He told me about the other girl and when I asked if she had made a difference to his feelings for me, he just said "it has to her", with no further explanation.

Joe walked me home and stayed for supper as usual. On the doorstep later I was reminded of the other times he had 'packed me up'. Neither of us wanted to say goodnight (or goodbye) and we were outside for a good couple of hours again. In later years, I've often thought that although I didn't realize it at the time, this was the start of a very different journey for me, (the scenic route) which would alter my life forever.

I remember being thoroughly miserable all through Christmas, even though everyone tried their best to make it happy. I was relieved when my leave was up and it was time to go back to camp; to be with my friends and to all the hustle and bustle of my job. Saying goodbye to the friends I had made at *Hindhead* was hard. There were 5 of us going to Singapore though, so I wasn't alone.

There were lots of preparations to keep my mind occupied. We were to go to the *Holding & Drafting Company* in Kingston, Surrey in February, so I looked forward to that. My birthday wasn't the same though, no letter or parcel from Joe. No Valentines card for the next day either. I felt sad because I couldn't just meet him from work to make up and couldn't bear to think of him living his life without me being a part of it.

At Kingston, apart from the staff, everyone was either coming or going. The buzz of excitement took hold of us all. We had to have injections again and were issued with our tropical kit. I liked the dresses, there were different shades of beige but mine was a really pale colour.

One night when my friend and I went down to the local pub, we met two soldiers who were also going abroad, to different places though, and we spent a nice evening with them. As we walked back to barracks, one of the boys called back to Eddie who was walking with me. He called him Shep. I couldn't believe my ears, I thought my friend had told this boy about Joe and that they were 'taking the mickey' out of me and I felt sick. Eddie hadn't told me that his surname was Shepherd – Shep to his friends. He was really apologetic for the mistake and I soon bucked up. We saw Eddie and his mate a good few times but although he asked me to write to him, I never did – he wasn't Joe.

On the last week in February we set out for Southampton to embark on *The Empire Fowie*, which would take me on to my biggest life-changing adventure so far.

CHAPTER FOUR

Stepping out of the Comfort Zone

I WAS AMAZED AT THE SIZE OF THE SHIP. It seemed to tower above us all and I had to pluck up all my courage to walk up the gangplank. The ship was full of servicemen and 12 women going out to the Far East. There were 5 of us WRAC girls going to Singapore or to *Kuala Lumpur*, and when we saw 7 WRAF girls, we decided that we were not going to let the Army down. None of us were going to be seasick. We all believed it was a case of 'mind over matter' – and it worked.

Every morning we counted less and less of their number and felt pretty pleased with ourselves (of course, they could have just decided that breakfast wasn't for them but we didn't think of that). It was pointed out to us that we were not on holiday, so we all had our jobs to do. I was to work in the ship's office for a few hours a day. I don't know what work the lads did, but they always seemed to be lying around on the deck. My new friends and I enjoyed our time at sea, although for me – a non swimmer, it was sometimes a bit daunting with no land in sight.

Stepping out of the Comfort Zone

Someone organised a talent competition and it was won by a group of men, playing guitars and singing. Everyone enjoyed their new type of music. I won 2nd prize, singing 'See the Pyramids along the Nile', and won 7 shillings and 6 pence, which was a lot of money in those days. My friends and I were able to enjoy a couple of drinks in the bar that night.

Native soldiers with rifles, boarded the ship at *Port Said* and stayed until we had cleared the *Suez Canal*. That was a little frightening at first, especially as I had never seen armed men before, but we were told they were protecting us from any terrorists who may sneak aboard so I felt a lot easier.

We went ashore for the day in Colombo, Ceylon and were surprised to see the women carrying building materials on their heads whilst the men just seemed to laze around. As we past Gibraltar, we heard some disturbing news. The *Empire Windrush* – which was a sister ship to ours (the *Fowie*) – had sunk on its way home and the passengers had had to be transferred to another ship. At least nobody had been hurt. It made me think of how vulnerable I was, however, with not being able to swim.

We arrived in Singapore on the 1st April 1954. I had been posted to *Tanglin Army Barracks* just outside the centre of the city. It was a very friendly place and I enjoyed my time there. We were taken by truck each morning to our different work places. I had been assigned to GHQ FARELF, (headquarters of the Far East Landing Forces) and my job was to type confidential reports on trials, which were being carried out, on men and materials in jungle conditions. We were working in a sort of 'hut on stilts', whose walls only reached halfway up, to form windows – It was far too hot for glass.

As well as the Major who was in charge, two other soldiers performed different duties in the office. After work, we would go to the *Union Jack Club*, in the City Centre where the service men and women congregated. My friends liked to swim in the pool there and one night they persuaded me to go in as well. Talking to a soldier (Dennis), I found out that he also lived in Hull. Dennis encouraged me to try to swim, whilst he held me under my chin. I was getting on great until I realized he had taken his hand away. My courage deserted me and I stood up shaking. I suddenly remembered what it was like when I missed the edge whilst learning to swim with school and I had to get out of the water. That was the last time I went in the pool.

I had been in Singapore about ten days when my friend asked me if I wanted to join her on a double blind date with two sailors. I thought it wasn't doing me any good crying for Joe anymore, so I said I would and we met them in our NAAFI. I had my eye on a tall dark haired boy named Stephen John Nicholas and as the four of us walked, I dropped back to walk with him. John told me his ship was the HMS Cossack, which had docked in the harbour. He had a lovely west country accent and told me that he lived in Gloucester. I started to like him, even on that first meeting.

We went out almost every night after that to the *Union Jack Club* and sometimes to the *Seven Storey Nightclub* with our friends, where we could have a drink and dance. It was strange having to get used to the island people, who were constantly staring at us. Once when John bent down to fasten my sandal, we were actually tightly surrounded – It was a bit scary really. On the buses the local people turned right round in their seats to stare at us as well.

After about ten days, John asked me if I would marry him. I was really taken aback. I told him we did not know each other and that he had to ask me again in a month's time! The more I thought about it the more I liked the idea. I couldn't believe someone actually wanted to marry ME. A few days later I couldn't contain myself any longer and told him to ask me again. This time I said I would.

We had to face opposition from John's Mum and even his naval friends — who told me he wasn't the marrying kind. His Mum told me later that it hadn't seemed long since he had written telling her he wanted to marry a *Eurasian* girl.

I was only 20 so I had to have my parents' permission. I don't think they were very pleased either, especially my Dad, because when the consent form first came back from home, it had been signed by Mam and her 'friend' Jess. I replied angrily telling them I would not accept this. The next one came back signed by Mam and my eldest sister. I wondered why Dad hadn't signed it. I never, ever found out whether Dad didn't want to, or whether he hadn't even been asked.

John had taken exception to the conditions given by the Army Chaplain, and he told him we would not be marrying in the church. John took me to a tailor's shop where I had a dress made and fitted for me. Having always bought my clothes ready made I felt like a queen being actually measured and choosing the material. I chose white seersucker material and the dress had a halter neck and a full skirt.

We were married in the *Supreme Register Office* in Singapore on the 10th July 1954. After a meal with four of our friends, John and I set off to spend a week in a hotel in Changi. As I sat in the car waiting for him to finish talking to his friends, I suddenly had a strange feeling in the pit of my stomach. I had married a stranger and this was for the rest of my life. That feeling soon left me though and I looked forward to arriving at the hotel.

I don't think they had many European visitors, because the ablutions were very primitive. The toilet consisted of footmarks straddling a hole in the floor and there was a tall round wooden structure, which may have been a shower – I never ventured in to see what it was. We were relieved to see that our room had a nice big sink.

The glassless windows had big wooden shutters on the outside, which kept the noise out but made us swelter in the heat. We had two choices; if we were to stay cool, we had to listen to people chattering as they played *Marjong* all through the night or we could quietly melt with the shutters closed. There was a beautiful beach, however, and we spent a lot of our time there.

On the last day of our holiday, John was called back to his ship early in the morning. We arranged that I should leave later and meet him back at Tanglin when he came off duty. I really was unnerved standing in a relatively empty (unknown to me) place waiting, for what seemed like hours for a bus to take me back to camp. I wished that I had gone with John early that morning.

The first time I became aware that something wasn't quite right with me was about six weeks after we were married. As I walked to the 'cookhouse' one morning the smell turned me nauseous and feeling so ill I just had to go back to my bed and lie down. I remembered those times when listening to *King Solomon's Mines* on the wireless. I felt the fear all over again, so much so that I couldn't eat. After a few times of this happening, the duty sergeant took me to the *British Military Hospital*.

Within a few days I was pleased to be fit again and able to resume my duties. The doctor had asked me about my wedding ring, but when I told him that I had been married for six weeks, he had just looked at me and nodded his head. I never received any explanation of my mysterious 'illness', and I didn't think I could ask!

I still couldn't eat in the camp, although I enjoyed skinless

Stepping out of the Comfort Zone

square sausage and chips in a café in the city centre when we went out for the evenings. I cannot remember now, but I think I must have eaten something during the day when I was at work.

John and I enjoyed our time together, but I was rather perturbed when, after telling me that he was to be sent home, John started talking about going back to England on his own. He was due to return in the September and although he wanted me to follow him later (because of issues he had to resolve), I wouldn't let him go without me. I couldn't bear the thought of being left in Singapore and wondered if he really wanted to break up with me. It was a relief when he said I could go with him and he explained why he had wanted to go on his own. As we walked up the gangplank on to the ship the smell of cooking really made me feel sick. At mealtimes I would try to eat, but I just couldn't swallow the food even though I was terribly hungry. This time I didn't run back to my cabin though and stayed at the table. I was really upset and frightened by then. I couldn't understand what was happening to me, would I ever be able to eat again?

There were servicemen and their wives at our table and each day they showed their concern for me when I just sat, upset, without eating. Because John had to be on duty, he couldn't sit with me at mealtimes, but the other wives told him of their concern.

One morning about 4 days later, we were on the deck and John bought me a little packet of cheese and biscuits, which I quickly put away. Gradually sneaking my hand into my pocket, I somehow managed to open the packets, taking tiny pieces at a time, I sucked on them. Imagine my surprise when my hand went into an empty pocket – I was elated. Later that day, when we went in for afternoon tea, I ate a full scone. At dinner everyone on our table cheered because I was actually eating. It wasn't long before my rather large appetite had returned and they were saving extra food for me, I felt normal again. We had some really good laughs on the rest of the journey.

We arrived back in England in October and I had to report to the *Holding & Drafting Co* again. The time couldn't go quick enough for me to complete my 'free on marriage' documentation. I think the rules were that I had to stay at the camp for a few days before I was allowed home. I couldn't wait to get back to Hull with my new husband.

Although I had only been gone for 8 months, coming back home a married lady, seemed strange. Everyone in the family was happy to see us and for a while we were content. John had disembarkation leave due and for a while life settled down, although I still had arguments about meals with Mam and she wasn't very happy with us because John would not go out drinking with her. Dad and the rest of the family got on well with John though, we used to spend time at Granny Abram's house when Jean came home from work.

The aeroplane carrying our marriage certificate to the *Naval Pay Office* in Tamar, Malaya had been shot down. I couldn't receive my marriage allowance, therefore we could not give Mam any board money. Although she said it was alright, I know it must have been a struggle for her to keep two extra people. Mam was still going out with Jess although he did not come to our house (maybe because I was there).
One night she came home very drunk and her hand was bleeding. She told us she had cut it falling on the bombed buildings in Melbourne Street. John washed and bandaged it for her and she went to bed. The next day she couldn't remember anything about the night before except that her watch was missing. This led to a massive argument, with Mam wanting to know who had bandaged her hand. When she found out that it was John,

she was very insulting and started accusing him of stealing the watch from her wrist.

In desperation, because by then I was totally fed up with this, I shouted at her "It was me. I took your bloody watch and I am keeping it." Mam was standing in the doorway when I said this and John and I were sitting on the settee. I think he was also fed up of us shouting across him, because he put his hand out backward and smacked me right across my face. I was shocked. No one had ever 'lashed out' in temper at me before. I didn't know whether to cry or be angry. Mam just said, "Oh it was you was it? Well I'm getting the police".

John was very apologetic for hitting me, but said we couldn't stay there any longer. He left that afternoon to hitch hike to Gloucester, to ask his Mum if we could stay with her. I was pleased about that and hoped she would say we could.

The next day there was a knock at the door and two police officers stood there. They had come to investigate the missing watch. I don't think they made much sense of what Mam and I had told them because they left and we didn't hear from them again. Luckily my naval marriage allowance had come through by then and we gave Mam the money we owed her and set off for Gloucester.

A couple of weeks later my sister wrote telling me that Mam had her watch back. Jess had taken it off her wrist when she fell, but Mam never told me this and never apologised to John or me.

Arriving in Gloucester I was struck by the way all the houses in Bowley Road had gardens with privet hedges around them. They were not cramped together like they were in Edgecumbe Street, the streets were wider also. Of course, I realized later that there were different districts and styles of house in every town.

John's Mum and his young brother Norman were very nice to me. She said she would like me to call her Mum, like the rest of her family, which I was happy to do. There was also an elder sister, Jean and brother Roy in their family, who had already left home. Mum asked me what had made the big bruise down my cheek and when I told her I had bumped into a turnstile at the station she wasn't surprised. She said that she used to bump into them as well when John's Dad was alive.

I started working, filling in timesheets at *Gloucester Aircraft Factory* and settled down again. John took me out to meet his friends and sometimes we would go to the cinema. Too soon, his leave was up and he had to go back to his ship. It was usually about 2.00AM when he set off and it became a pattern for me to go to bed before he went, so that he knew I would be settled down for the night. I was glad that I wouldn't have to stay up talking after he had gone because I was always upset. He would be away for three months before coming home again for two weeks.

When his leave was due, John would often arrive back without telling me exactly when he would be home. It was lovely being awakened to the sound of stones, hitting my bedroom window. I would look down into the garden and he would be there, we would spend the whole time visiting his friends and walking together.

Near the end of November a letter came from home telling me that my Uncle Bob had been found drowned in Barmston Drain. I was sad not to be with everyone; knowing how much we all loved Uncle Bob and I was really homesick.

One day, I was feeling a little under the weather and mum took me to the doctors, who then sent me to the hospital. I found out that I was four and a half months pregnant, we were all very pleased about this, especially Mum. She had one grandson who, because of a split in a relationship, she never saw. It was good to think John and I were going to give her another grandchild.

After Christmas I decided I wanted to come back to Hull to have my baby. I missed my family very much. My sister Brenda and her husband Terry said I could stay with them at their house in Witty Street on Hessle Road. This was really kind, because they already had two children in a tiny house with only two bedrooms. It was good being back in Hull again and I soon fell into a routine, looking forward to the baby and gathering my 'layette'.

Suspecting that there were two babies, I had an anti natal appointment at *Western General* for an X-ray. (There weren't any scans in those days). The Radiologist, Mr Jones recognized me from my nursing days and he let me sit outside the room to wait for the results there and then. He told me that the last time he had seen me I was the *Fairy Queen* (in the pantomime) and now I looked more like a *Fairy Elephant!* He confirmed that I was expecting twins. He said he wanted to take a further picture 'to see if there was a third baby hiding behind the other two.' He always had had a great sense of humour, luckily this was not the case and I was given the date of May 27th for the babies birth.

I couldn't believe it. Brenda had told me to ask if there were two babies because I was such a big size, but I thought it was just natural. Working the time back, I realized that when my eating trouble started in Singapore, it must have been because I had been caught pregnant, I don't remember wondering how we would cope; I just knew I would have to manage. I enjoyed living with Bren, Terry and their children. Terry and Linda although, living with John's Mum, had made me wary of being 'in the way' in someone else's house.

When John was home on leave, it was very cramped and one day, he was making a model aeroplane in the living room, whilst I was combing my hair near the fireplace mirror. Without thinking, I stepped back – right onto the model. Of course John was very angry with me, and I felt really sorry for not looking where I was standing.

As the time for the babies' birth came nearer, Bren told me that unfortunately there would not be enough room in their little house for my growing family so when I came out of hospital we would have to find somewhere else to live (Brenda told me years later that Terry and she hadn't liked the way John treated me, but I never knew that).

At the beginning of April, I was taken into *Hedon Road Maternity Hospital* for bed-rest in order to allow the babies to grow more. I was due to stay in until my delivery date near to the end of May. I was resigned to the situation and made friends with the other ladies on the long stay ward, although I soon became bored with having to stay in bed all the time.

After about a week, I was experiencing a nagging backache. Listening to the others discussing the 'on duty' midwife, I heard one of them say "woe betides anyone going down tonight, Sister Smith is on". I called back "Don't say that, it will be me. I'll just wait for the visiting to be over and then I'll go" They all laughed and said "it's alright for you; you're here for the duration". Guess what happened? That nagging backache turned out to be 'Back Labour'. After an examination I was wheeled out into a small narrow white room with just one bed in it. In came the dreaded Sister Smith. She said fiercely, "now then, what makes you think you are in labour?" I tearfully answered that I didn't know what was to happen and that I was scared stiff. That lady was kindness itself, taking me through the procedure step by step and also taking my fear away. She told me that they would not do anything without telling me why they were doing it and what effect it would have.

At 4.00AM and 4.05AM on the 12th April 1955 I gave birth to 2 beautiful baby boys who we called Stephen Charles (5LB 4OZ) and Michael Patrick (4LB 6OZ). Stephen and Charles were John and his father's names. My dad had a dream that I had a boy called Michael, and the Patrick was after my best friend Pat in Singapore I wanted the family names to be given, one to each child but John made a mistake when he registered them.

My Granny Abram who lived opposite us in Edgecumbe Street had said we could live with her, so she had made sure everything was ready for when I came out of hospital ten days later. As the twins were six weeks premature Stephen had to stay in an extra week and Michael two more weeks until they weighed 5LB. I really wanted to feed them myself though, so I was given a pump and a bottle in which to express my breast milk whilst they were in hospital. An ambulance would turn up each night to bring me two new sterilised feeding bottles and take away the ones I had filled.

By this time John was working at the dockyard in Grimsby and coming home every night. At about 2.00AM one morning we were sitting up in bed. I was getting stressed because I was not having much luck filling the bottles, when we heard a car coming down the street. A car door slammed and my mother's voice started shouting loudly and singing "Let me go, lover, - hey Jess," over and over again. I felt so ashamed I just burst out crying. Although John tried to make me feel better, I just couldn't. This became a regular occurrence and it also upset my granny. When the babies came home everyone made a fuss of them. At that time they were identical. It was only when they were lying together that you could see that Stephen was slightly bigger than Michael. Not long after that, I started getting worried that the babies were not getting enough food from me so I put them on to the bottle. Granny was frightened that we would feed the same one twice so she tied a piece of ribbon round Michael's wrist, to make sure we didn't. As soon as the babies woke for their night feed, Granny would have a tray ready to bring upstairs. This would contain their bottles and also tea and a snack for me. Then she would feed one baby whilst I fed the other. I don't know how I would have managed without her for the first few months of their lives. Everyone made a fuss of the twins and we were never short of visitors.

One day, as I was nursing Michael and smoking at the same time, some ash fell onto his neck. I quickly brushed it off, not realizing it would be hot, but Granny had seen me. She gave me a hard slap across the face. It taught me a lesson and I never again smoked near the babies again.

One night not long after this, Dad was waiting up when Mam came home after her drinking session and he told her she couldn't act like this. She swore at him and he hit her. Someone must have rung the Hull Daily Mail about this, because a couple of days later there was a report in the paper. The headline read "WIFE CALLS HUSBAND A BLIND B*!#@$"
I don't think that would have pleased her very much and she left home. The twins were about 4 months old when granny started to get worried about anyone knowing we were living with her and she didn't like me to leave the pram in front of the house. I always had to take the boys round into the back yard. She also liked to buy a bottle of *Guinness* every night, which she kept in a jug in the walk-in pantry. Now and again, she would disappear into the kitchen for a drink. I couldn't understand why she needed to do this secretly, but I think she didn't want John to know she liked a little drink.

John was looking for the tin opener one night and happened to look in the pantry. Granny was really angry accusing him of spying on her, she said that we would have to find somewhere else to live. John was angry, he made me get all our things together and leave right then even though granny had not meant us to go that night. John said that no one would let a service man's family be on the streets on a night. That was 'famous last words'. We set off – it was about 8.00PM when we went to the police station. They rang round all the hostels but they were all full up.

The babies and I ended up at *Beverley Road Hospital Workhouse* and John had to stay somewhere else in the town. It was very frightening. The inmates were all in bed by the time we got there. John tried to comfort me and said it would only be for one night. A cot was found for the babies in a long ward and I lay in a bed next to them but I couldn't sleep. Some of the people were shouting out and I was really scared. Next morning the staff helped me with the children whilst the inmates had their breakfast. The room was very clean but really bare. I was relieved when John came for us and took us to my Dads.

We stayed there whilst John went again to Gloucester to see if his Mum would let us go back. She was pleased to see us all. John had been given a week's compassionate leave to settle us in. After this he could only get home for his normal leave.

I was happy with Mum and Norman. We went for long walks round the town and visited lots of places I'd never seen before, she also took us to meet her friends and relatives. Life settled down into a good routine. Mum went to work and I did the cleaning. I was always praised when she came home. One day, however, I started sweeping the living room when she was there and she soon told me I wasn't doing it right, after that she checked everything I did when she came home. Out for a walk one day, I met one of Mum's friends who asked me how I was getting on with her. I told her I liked Mum, but how she disagreed with the way I cleaned. I think I said she was sometimes a bit like an ogre. I wish I hadn't said anything because that lady, being a true friend of Mums, went straight to her and told her what I had said. I got a real *roasting* when she came in that night. From then on I was very careful when I answered anyone's questions.

When she got over my little 'indiscretion' she was very nice to me. When John came home on leave, however, his Mum's attitude towards me changed, she really was a bit of a dragon, and I always felt nervous and clumsy in front of him. I felt as if I could not do anything right. John could not believe me when I said that she was all right with me when he was away. He told me that one of the reasons he had joined the Navy when he was 15 was to get away from her. Mum used to complain to me later that she could 'do nothing with me' when John was home. I suppose I did try to stand up to her a bit with John to support me.

We had been in Gloucester about 14 months when John told me he had been allocated married quarters at the *Wireless Station* in Peaks Lane, New Waltham, near Grimsby. I was so excited. Our own home at last! I couldn't wait to start packing.

The day before we were due to travel John said he had to go back to his ship in Grimsby and although his Mum played up with him he wouldn't change his mind. Early the next morning, I set off with all our belongings and the twin pram and caught the train to Sheffield, where I changed stations for Grimsby. I stayed in the luggage compartment with the boys in their pram to keep an eye on our belongings. This was the only way I could handle everybody. John met us off the train, we were tired but really happy. We had to wait in Grimsby town for a couple of hours because the house still wasn't ready but eventually we were all taken to Peaks Lane.

The 17 houses were all in a row, standing well back and safely fenced off from the road. The wireless station, behind the houses was also fenced off. Ours was the end house with a garden on three sides. At the other end of the row, the officer in charge of the station – Mr Tibble – lived with his family. We received a very friendly welcome.

Our house had three bedrooms, two living rooms, a kitchen and bathroom. It was very well equipped and fully furnished. There was even a tap on the sink for rainwater collected in a big tank above the kitchen, I was *over the moon*.

We settled down right away, now we wouldn't get in anyone's way. We would stay here until John was given another posting. No one would be able to ask us to leave, provided we followed the Naval Rules regarding married quarters. The only thing that upset me, was trying to cope with everything at once. I found it difficult to manage to get the boys washed and dressed, finish the housework and cook a midday meal by 12.30PM as I was expected to do. When John came home for dinner he would tell me off, saying that his mother brought the three of them up by herself when his father was killed in the second world war and if she could do it, why couldn't I?

One day about five or six months after we arrived, John came home whilst I was cleaning. He asked me what I was doing it for. He said it was 'too little, too late' and that when he could get me somewhere else to live, he was leaving me. I still remember how my legs buckled and I felt sick. I opened the door to go out to the shop, I didn't really want anything but I felt I couldn't stay there. John called me back to talk about it, but I just said "what is there to talk about? You seem to have already made up your mind".

Later on he told me he didn't want to be married anymore. He said that he wanted me, but not the responsibilities that went with me. When I asked him why he had brought us to Grimsby, he said that he could not leave me with his mother. I didn't know what to do, I had nowhere to go. I wished I had tried harder to manage everything, I just hoped that he would change his mind. John also told me that he had started going out with a girl who worked in *Doigs shipyard office*, named Mary. He met her when I was in Gloucester. He showed me a photograph of her and said "actually she looks like you." She also had a son of about six years. Now that he had told me about her, John fell into a routine of taking her out openly for about three nights each fortnight, (round his payday). On these nights I couldn't bring myself to talk to him but I used to wait up afterwards to try to get him to talk to me. I used to see her car parked near our house, before he came in. The rest of the time, he seemed to be happy being with me and was just as loving as he was when we were first married.

When John was out one night, curiosity got the better of me and I searched his pockets for anything that would tell me more about her. There was a letter from this woman, It seemed that her parents had been told that the twins and I were living on the wireless station, so they had made up a story that John was no longer living with us. He was supposed to have been drafted down south. His letters to her were sent via a friend of his who was down there.

In the letter, Mary said that she had told her parents that I didn't want John, adding `well it's true, isn't it? The real shock I received, though, was to read her say "don't forget, I am your wife, even though I'm not Mrs. Nicholas." I had looked for proof and here it was in black and white. I just felt so devastated I didn't know what to do. I daren't let John know that I had read the letter so I just kept it to myself.

Early one Saturday morning I looked in my shopping bag that was beneath the coat hooks in the hall and saw a big remote controlled car. I wondered if John had bought it for the boys for Christmas but I didn't want him to know I had seen it. John was pressing his trousers in the living room and I needed the bag to take to the shops. When I asked him to empty it, he told me to do it. "But it has your things in it" I said, thinking he had forgotten the car was there. He put the iron down and walked towards me. The next minute he had punched me in the mouth and I was banging into the kitchen door. He came over, with a wet cloth for my face and led me upstairs telling me to lie down for a while and saying how sorry he was. A short while later, when I had stopped crying, I suddenly had a strange feeling and went downstairs into the kitchen. John was standing next to the cooker which had all of the taps turned on. I simply walked over to the window, opened it fully, turned the taps off and walked back upstairs. When I came down again, he showed me some scratches on his wrists where he said he had tried to kill himself. He swore he would never do anything like that again – for the second time. I later found out that everyone on the station had known about John and Mary for ages. Their relationship had been going on for well over a year, but he told me he had had to accept the married quarters, which he had requested when he had first come to Grimsby.

When John had hit me, my teeth had been loosened so Mrs Tibble went with me to the dentist in Cleethorpes. He said that because all my back teeth were rotten as well, I would need them all out. I was happy about this but at the same time I was frightened to death of the procedure, apart from the fact that I didn't want to be 'gummy'. The dentist made me feel better by telling me he would take my back teeth out first and then later give me a general anaesthetic to take out the front ones out and replace them all.

Not long after that, John was to be posted to Malta, but when I said how pleased I was, he told me we couldn't go with him. He was drafted down south to await his new posting. Mr Tibble said that the boys and I would be able to stay on the station until he came back and found us somewhere else to live. That was a big relief to me.

John's mum had been writing to ask me what was going on, and up to then I hadn't told her. Realizing how naïve and silly I had been, I told her everything I knew about the affair, including Mary's address. Mum told me she wasn't surprised, evidently John's father had had numerous affairs and Mum had received beatings for confronting some of the other women. She told me she had thought John was getting tired of married life before he brought us to Grimsby, because he had started shutting himself away for hours making his model aeroplanes.

One evening a couple of weeks later, I was just relaxing by the fire when the door burst open and John came in very angrily. He made me sit down for about an hour without talking and then told me to go to our neighbour Jim next door and ask if he would give me an early call, but I hadn't to tell Jim that he was there (John was waiting to go to Malta and had 'jumped ship'. He wanted to get back before he was missed). Of course Jim and his wife Mabel could see how upset I was and I told them John was at home, in case anything happened to me. I daren't let Jim confront John as he wanted to, but I promised I would knock on the wall if I needed him.

I knew that Mary had replied to Mum's letter saying "my 'friendship' with your son finished a long time ago" I didn't know that Mary had then told John about it. He was furious with me and said Mary might even lose the custody of her son over this. We passed a very strange, strained night, eventually going to bed without conversation or contact.

Another time, John arrived home on embarkation leave, bringing one of his mates with him. After tea, they both got washed and changed and went out. The next morning whilst John was still in bed, this man told me how very sorry he was about the situation. He had been led to believe he was going to make a 'foursome' with John and me. He could see how happy we were and he was shocked when he found out that I wasn't going to be there. Before he left, he said he felt awful accepting my hospitality and helping to deceive me at the same time

A few days later we had an invitation to go to the dance in the recreation hut, John would not go but insisted that I go. I was with Mr and Mrs Tibble all night, dancing with their daughters. I had the money for two drinks and Mr Tibble bought me one. When I came home the lights were out and John was already in bed. I thought he was joking when he started to smell my breath, asking who had been buying me drinks and who I had been dancing with. I playfully tapped his chest saying 'stop it' and the next minute I was being punched and kicked out of bed. My arm was badly bruised and I was hurting all over.

It was a relief when John's leave was up and he had to report back to his ship. John had been telling me he wanted me to get a separation now that he was no longer living with me, even though, after making enquiries, I was told that I couldn't do that because it was his work that had taken him away. Sometimes he would write me long loving letters and I would be thrilled to bits. After replying in the same vein, however, I would receive a rather nasty letter saying he hadn't changed his mind.

Life settled down happily for the boys and me. They were running all over the place now and always 'escaping' from my garden. Jim, Mabel and I would chase them back so we could see how they had managed to get out. As fast as we cut off one escape route they would find another. Everyone on the station loved them though and we all got on really well. They were never in any danger because the gate to the road was always locked. My friend Joan would come in to be with me when she wasn't at work and we would dance to the records, sometimes we would go to the recreation hut with the twins and play table tennis or dance to *Elvis* singing his rock and roll songs.

About 10 months after John had gone, one of the other sailors on the station, Don, started talking to the boys and being friendly with me. I asked him in for a cup of tea before he went on duty. He knew all about Mary and we would talk for ages about my hopes and fears for the future. Eventually, even though I didn't love him, one thing led to another and this relationship went too far. Don said he would give me driving lessons and one day, when we were just about to go on the second one, John turned up out of the blue. His tour of Malta was over. He told me to still go but I didn't (I was rather scared of what he would do or say when I got back). I picked the boys up from the baby sitters house and we all went home. John had arranged with his Mum that the boys and I would go back to live with her because he now had to find us alternative accommodation, although he would not be coming with us. The marriage was over.

The journey back to Gloucester was easier than the last time. The boys didn't need their pram anymore, so we were able to travel in comfort in a carriage. Although John's Mum wanted us to stay for good, I wasn't comfortable with the situation. I didn't think it fair because John wouldn't be able to come home whilst I was there. I was sad leaving the family for the last time, we were all upset. Mum was losing her grandchildren and they were losing their grandmother and other relatives, but I just couldn't see any other course of action.

My mam was now living in St Barnabus Terrace in Walcott Street with Jess, who was working at the aircraft factory in Abingdon at the time. She told me we could come to stay with her. My Granny Dixon, great aunts and Dad's cousins lived in Ireland Terrace, Walcott Street, so we would be able to spend a lot of time with them too. It is a good thing that we don't know what is round the corner. I'm sure many of us wouldn't want to go if we did. I didn't realize just what I was letting myself in for with this next phase of my life.

CHAPTER FIVE

Out of the Frying Pan?

LIFE WITH MAM WAS ALL RIGHT for the first few months. I got a job in the office of a laundry on Hessle Road and my elder sister, Brenda had arranged for the boys to go to the nursery school near Witty Street where she lived. My niece was also at the school so she was able to keep an eye on them. A friend of mine from Walcott Street would take them to nursery when she took her own children to school and mam would bring them home. My contentment didn't last long, however. Answering a knock at the door one evening, I was handed a warrant to appear in court. John had found out about Don and was suing me for divorce. When this man had gone, Mam gleefully put on her coat and rushed out, saying she couldn't wait to tell Brenda this news. I felt very ashamed, not only about what had happened with Don, but the fact that people on the wireless station must have been talking about me.

I was very scared of having to go to court but Bren was great. She took me there in a taxi. John wasn't there at first and then he came. I had to be given water and a chair. He stood up and told the whole court that he didn't want me. As I couldn't say the same thing, they adjourned the hearing so that we could try to work it out, I knew that John wouldn't change his mind though.

Shortly after that, I received a letter from Mr Doubleday, the *Clerk to the Magistrates*, asking me to go to see him but I rang him up explaining that I dare not go. He asked me about John's relationship with Mary and why I hadn't told the court about it. He said I could cross petition but I told him I dared not go against what John wanted (He had told me he wanted a divorce, long before he went to Malta).

I didn't have to go back to court again and I don't know what, if anything, Mr Doubleday said to John, or who had told Mr Doubleday about Mary because I had never mentioned her. I just received the papers through the post. Although I was not awarded any money for myself, I was awarded £1.00 per week for each of the boys.

The shame of this stayed with me for a very long time. Whenever I took the boys out I would sit turning my wedding ring round on my finger, thinking that everyone knew that my husband didn't want me. I felt that I must draw attention to the fact that at least I had been married.

Life seemed to settle down again for a while but when I came home at dinnertime one day, the curtains were closed and Michael was standing in the living room, still in his pyjamas. Mam was still in bed in the front room and Stephen was asleep at the bottom of her bed. I was very angry over this and knew the situation couldn't go on much longer. Coming home from work a few evenings later however, I found the boys alone again in the living room and they told me nanna was in the front bedroom with a man. When I knocked on the door she came out, drunk and very angry. A man followed her out and invited me to make a foursome that night with a friend of his. I certainly told him where to go. Mam said to him "don't take notice of her – she's nobody". I found out later that they had gone to pick the boys up from nursery, in that state. I felt really disgusted by the way she was carrying on and stopped her picking the boys up. I made arrangements for a friend I had met at the nursery school to do that for me.

By this time I had started feeling ill but I still managed to go to work and make things as nice as I could for the boys. Mam would come home at all hours of the morning drunk. I would hear her down the passage at the side of the house, once she even brought someone inside. She would spend a lot of her nights at a house in the next street, which had a very bad reputation.

One night, after being out, Mam started shouting at the bottom of the stairs, "Come on, we've got to get away from here, we can't stay, he's coming home" (meaning Jess). I realized she was frightened someone would tell Jess what she had been doing. I told her to go to bed and sort it out in the morning. The next day she told me to look for somewhere else to live because Jess wouldn't want us there. I looked for days and couldn't find anywhere decent, all I found were dirty smelly houses made into flats. I felt really sorry for the girls who had to live with their children, cramped up in these conditions. I became more and more depressed, all I wanted was for my Mam to put her arms around me and tell me that we were going to be alright, but I knew that just wouldn't happen.

Coming home from flat hunting one day, I found that Jess was home. After I told Mam about the awful places I had seen he asked me why I was looking for flats. I told him that Mam said I had to go and he said "It's my house; you can stay here as long as you want to". I was very relieved about that, and it made me feel a lot better. A few nights later, the boys were staying the night with my friend and I went out for a drink with Bren, her husband Terry, Jess and Mam. Later, after going our separate ways, Jess and Mam started arguing as usual. I hung back, so no one would know I was with them, and I saw him hitting and pushing her all the way home. It still carried on when I went to bed. I could hear furniture being knocked over and mam crying.

Not long after that, Jess went back to Abingdon. I was brought home from work a couple of times and went to bed, burying my head under the covers. I felt so scared and just wanted to hide away from this nightmare world I had landed myself in. Mam started saying "He (meaning John) doesn't want the bairns and you can't look after them on your own, get them put away". I was appalled the first time she said it and just decided I would ignore her when she said it again.

A couple of weeks later I came home from work and there was a visitor. It was Miss Roe from *Newland Orphan Homes* on Cottingham Road. Mam had called her to ask her to 'take the boys off me'. She started telling Miss Roe about how I was too ill to look after them. I, of course denied this, saying that it was her who upset me. I was raising my voice because I was angry with her, Mam just said quietly "see what I mean?" After talking to me for a while, Miss Roe turned to go and asked me to take her out to her car. She put her arms on my shoulders and said "Don't worry Marjorie; I've met people like your Mam before. I can see you are in a very stressful situation. We will not take the boys out of your care but if you'll let us, we will look after them for you until you get yourself better. You can take them back whenever you want to." I felt my whole body sag when she said this. I knew I couldn't go on the way things were. Here was someone who really wanted to help us get back to a 'normal' life. Even though I could not bear to hand the boys over into someone else's care myself when the time came, Miss Roe said I had to do this, because she wanted to put my mind at ease by showing me round and meeting their new housemother Miss Salvage.

Mam tried to be really nice to all of us after that, but I just felt I couldn't talk to her civilly for some time. She kept saying it was all for the best and that I could start living again. I think she thought I would be happy the boys were going away and that I would be able to go out with her and share her way of life, but I knew I would never do that.

It took about 2 weeks to organize. The boys had to have medical checkups and the paperwork had to be filled in. I tried to be happy, but there was a leaden feeling in the pit of my stomach. It was awful, knowing I couldn't do anything about the situation.

On the day they were expected at the homes, I found it really hard. On the bus the boys were happily chattering about everything they saw, they loved bus rides. Of course at only three years old they didn't understand what was happening.

Miss Salvage (Aunt Sally) was a very nice, friendly lady. She met us at the door and made us very welcome. Her house was just like a large family house. It was very comfortably furnished and decorated. There were plenty of toys and play areas for the children – I think there was room for about 8 children but I can't really remember after all this time. I do remember that the kitchen had a big table and chairs in the middle of it and a large *Aga* range. My boys were the youngest there at that time and the only set of twins in the home. I was very pleased that I had seen where they were to live and I felt better about it although leaving them was the hardest thing I had ever done in my life.

On my way back down Newland Avenue to Dad's house, I felt really empty inside. I remember thinking that no one in the world needed me now. Dad had said I could come home, this

Out of the Frying Pan?

time only leaving if I wanted to, and not because someone asked me to. I was really happy with this and decided to put all my bad memories behind me. I never went back to Mam's house again.

I was able to bring the boys home every weekend from Friday tea time till Sunday night and I would have them for all the school holidays, so it wasn't quite as bad as I thought at first. I told them that Auntie Sally was looking after them until I saved up for a house. We used to talk about this a lot, I couldn't see Stephen and Michael for 3 weeks to enable them to settle down, and the time really dragged. I was a bit shocked when I did see them because they were in the *Sick Bay*. There was an epidemic of Measles and the boys had caught it, they also had new clothes on and it upset me because, for the first time in their lives they were wearing clothes that I had not bought them. They had settled down very well though, and everyone made a fuss of them. When important visitors came, they were always introduced to Stephen and Michael.

I wrote to John at his mother's house telling him what had happened to the boys and me. I was shocked to receive a nasty letter back saying if he (John) had known about it; he would have taken them to Gloucester – not to live with him, but to put them in some sort of home nearer to his family! His mother had told him, though, that in her opinion, 'if he were to do this, then I would probably go right off the rails and end up on the streets!' I couldn't believe this. He had told me in Grimsby that he didn't want the responsibility of the children, he didn't even know how to talk to them and yet now he had contemplated depriving them of my love as well.

I changed my job and started working at a fancy goods shop, *T Cross* in Anlaby Road. It was very interesting, I liked checking all the new stock and looking at all the different items.

Crossing by the City Hall for the bus one morning I suddenly felt so ill, I thought I was going to die. I was shaking all over, I couldn't breathe, I felt sick and dizzy, I couldn't swallow and my legs wanted to collapse. I managed to get to a fruit shop under the City Hall and ask to sit down. They rang a taxi for me to take me back home. I couldn't understand what was happening to me, I had never felt so ill in my life before. As I neared home the feelings subsided. My Dad was at work when I arrived but my sister was at home. After telling her about it and having a cup of tea, I went to lie down on my bed thinking I must have caught some mysterious illness.

Every day I would attempt to go, but as I reached the town again the symptoms would return and journey seemed so terrifying, I would give up and take a taxi back home. In our bedroom we had a curtained off alcove which we used as a hanging wardrobe and when Dad came home for his dinner, I would hide in there, too ashamed of myself to tell him about it.

When I eventually did, Dad persuaded me to send for the doctor, who couldn't give me an explanation for these feelings and just gave me tranquillisers to calm me down. I thought that I must be going mad and that scared me even more. I had always been an outgoing, keen to try most things kind of person, even going to the other side of the world, and yet now, here I was, frightened of being outside the house. I had to give up work and sign on for sick pay because I was so frightened when I went into the town, although I was able to pick the boys up on a Friday. This was the only time in the week that I felt better, but as I couldn't bear to give them back on the Sunday night, one of my friends would take them for me.

Later on, after taking the tranquillisers for a while, I was able to work again, this time in the office of a wood yard, *Glixten Doors*. I made friends with the lady (Eve) who ran the canteen.

Out of the Frying Pan? 117

We found that we had something in common. My Dad used to play the drums at a dance hall in Abbey Street where Eve's late husband was the MC. She recognized him from the photo I took in to show her. I told dad about her and as there was a function coming up at the *Blind Institute* he asked me to invite Eve to go along with him, which she did and they enjoyed the night. She told me later that they hadn't really liked each other at first, but as they went out more, they knew they wanted to be together. Eve and I used to laugh a lot in the canteen and she would say how funny it would be if she married my Dad and became my stepmother. I would say that if Joe and I met again and got back together he would be her son-in-law.

This turned out to be very prophetic, because one day my youngest sister had been with Mam to the *Aerodrome* at Brough where they saw Joe, who was then working for the *Hull Corporation Telephones*. Mam told him about me being back in Hull with twins and that I was divorced. Joe said "Tell her to come to Botanic (on Spring Bank) and I'll take her out". Although Mam didn't give me the message, my sister did and I hurriedly wrote a letter to Joe telling him that I'd love to see him but I daren't go to Botanic.

As the next day was Good Friday, I was on tenterhooks not knowing if there would be a postal delivery on that morning, and whether or not Joe would come.
As I dressed and combed my hair on the evening, I was shaking with nerves and excitement wondering if he would turn up. At 7.00PM on the dot there was a knock at the door. My heart did a summersault as I saw Joe standing there. We had a lovely evening, telling each other what had happened to us in the 5 years we had been apart. I told him all about John and Mary and even Don and how John had got a divorce. Joe told me about the girl he had started seeing when I wrote telling him I was

going abroad, her name was Mavis. They had later got engaged but she had 'gone off' with her neighbour. Mavis didn't like Joe entertaining either, this was a strange coincidence because once when John and I were in one of the clubs in Hull, someone asked me to get up and give a song. John said to me "if you get up on that stage, I am leaving".

Joe went with me to meet Stephen and Michael and they took to him as if they had known him all their lives. Joe also thought the boys were great. We went together to bring them home on a Friday night and Joe would take them back on Sundays. Joe told me later that he was shocked to see the difference in me and thought he would have to 'take me in hand' otherwise I would not last long the way I was. I was in a vicious circle really. I could not eat If I knew I would have to go out, because I thought that I would be sick and choke myself – although my Granny Dixon had told me that probably I felt sick because I wasn't eating.

Dad and Eve had decided to get married and as Eve wanted to bring her daughter to our house, he said he was sorry but I would again have to go. This worried me, the bad times seemed to be starting again. When I told Joe however, he said that he was going to take me home to his house. His mother and father were happy about this. I would have Joe's bedroom and he would sleep in one of the attics. His sister and her family would have the other one and the front bedroom.

Joe's Mum (Ida Mary) and I used to have 'afternoon tea' together in the front room every day. She would put one of her best tablecloths on the small table in the window, and I would go just round the corner for a cake to have with our tea whilst we had a chat.

One day she said to me, "I don't know, I take you into my house, you get your feet under my table and you make a play for my son". She searched her handbag and brought out a photo and said to me "this is the girl I wanted him to marry". I was so surprised, it was me in my green army uniform. I tried to tell her this but I don't think she was convinced. She also brought out my green woollen gloves that I had left 5 years before. She had kept them all that time, but didn't recognize me because I had altered so much. Ida Mary was terminally ill and her memory often played tricks on her.

I tried to go to work again on a few occasions but when Joe's Mum saw the state I was in she told me to go back to bed. She said she would look after me. I couldn't believe her kindness, she was treating me like her own daughter. I had always called her Mum and I was glad. Talking to Joe one night, we decided I should leave work and sign on for Sickness Benefit again.

One night when we were all in bed, I heard Mum shout "Come on, out of there, I'll have none of this hanky panky in my house". Only when Joe and I appeared from different bedrooms was she satisfied that we weren't sleeping together (despite what her daughter had told her). We knew her illness was affecting her mind more than we realized. Not long after that Joe's sister decided she needed the room in the attic that Joe was using. This meant that he would have to come down to his own room and there would be no room for me. His Mum said she was sorry but 'Bloods thicker than water' and you'll have to go. Joe was very angry with this and said to his mum, "If Madge is going then I'm going with her".

The landlord of the Botanic pub had a flat to let in Louis Street and arranged for us to move in there. We told him and his wife that we were having the boys for their 6 weeks holiday and they were fine about that. The flat had one big room and one smaller room. The landlady showed us round and suggested we could have the bigger room for living and the smaller room for sleeping. We looked at each other because we had both thought of having a bed in each room, anyway, we decided that her way was best. We cooked our meals in a pan and steamer on a gas ring and used the fire to boil the kettle or fry food. Washing up was done in the bathroom sink and clothes were washed in the bath. We were allowed to go into the middle room downstairs to light the fire on the range in order to get hot water. This felt great and we were really happy to have a place to ourselves at last.

One day during the school holidays, I was hanging out our washing in the garden with the boys and talking to the neighbour across the fence. I saw Michael go up to stroke the landlord's Alsatian dog, which was tied up next to the french windows. I saw him put his arms round the dog and before I could do anything, I heard him scream. The dog had turned its head and bit Michael at the corner of his mouth. I managed to get him away whilst the neighbour called an ambulance and we took him to hospital, where he had stitches in his mouth. That evening, before Joe came home, I was 'summoned' downstairs to see the landlord. His wife took the boys into the kitchen whilst he motioned me into the sitting room and pointed to one of the settees. He asked me what I was doing in the garden and really told me off for being in there. He said he didn't have a dog licence and could get into big trouble. I felt like a child, being sat down and told off. When Joe came home he saw I was upset and he went downstairs angrily to tell the landlord what he thought of him. After this the downstairs was kept locked, we could not get hot water or go into the garden to dry our clothes.

Joe's Dad, Granddad Pop, used to come for me in an afternoon and take me across Spring Bank into Stanley Street to see his Mum. Every time we went to see Joe's Mum she begged us to come back, she said we could even share a bedroom. She also used to ask me to go into hospital to get better. In the September, after a traumatic 'dash' to York to see her other daughters, Grace

Out of the Frying Pan?

and Anne she died. Even though I was scared, I decided that I would do as she had wanted and go for treatment.

When we arrived back at the flat one-day, Mrs Vessy our neighbour told us that a man had been looking for me. From her description I knew it must have been John (I found out later that Dad had given him my address). As John had once told me that if I ever went with anyone else, he would kill me, I was really frightened but Joe made me feel better because he told me he was there to protect me.

On the day I was packing to go into hospital, Mam and my sister came to see me. I thought she was gloating. I remembered what she always told me when I was a child – that I was daft and she was going to have me put away. I felt it was really happening. It 'scared me stiff', but I knew it was my only chance to get well again. Joe took me in a taxi to *Delapole Hospital* in Willerby where we were shown into a doctor's office in a long bungalow and I was given a physical examination. I was terrified, not knowing what treatment they were going to give me, and what the other patients would be like. After waiting with me for a little while, Joe had to leave. He told me later that if I had cried he would have taken me home again. The lady Psychiatrist, Dr Powell was really nice. I found out that I only weighed seven stone three instead of my usual ten stone. She told me that I was to be given an injection of *Moderate Insulin* every day, to improve my appetite and make me eat properly.

The bungalow was divided by a long corridor, which was blocked off in the middle. Men stayed on one side and women on the other. I was taken to one of the 4-bed wards leading off this. There was also a big sitting room, a games room and about 3 or 4 smaller wards, as well as a kitchen, bathrooms, toilets and doctors rooms. At the end of the corridor, near to the doctors' room, there were about four single rooms with barred windows. The bungalow was surrounded with grass and I was told it was the best ward in the hospital. The patients were mostly very friendly. Part of the cure was to see people in a lot worse than you being admitted and to see them gradually recover.

Just as I was settling in that first night, a nurse came and said to me "Your husband is here to see you." I told her that Joe wasn't my husband, but that we were going to get married when my divorce became finalized. The nurse replied, "Oh, but he told me he was Mr Nicholas". The thought of seeing John again brought the same feeling of dread, rising up from my stomach, my head felt dizzy and I just wanted to curl up under the covers in my bed and hide away. I was also worried what Joe would say if he knew that I had seen and spoken to John. Seeing my reaction the nurse told me not to upset myself because I did not have to see him. John told the nurse that he did care what happened to me because I had been his wife.

The next morning, Miss Roe from *Newland Homes* rang to say that John had arrived there and was asking to take Stephen and Michael out for the day. She needed my permission for this to happen. I told her about the letter that John had written, talking about putting the boys in an orphanage in Gloucester, and telling her of my fears that he would not bring them back if he took them out. Miss Roe told me not to worry. She would tell him he could only take them into the grounds. That was the last contact John ever made with any of us.

When everyone had gone to breakfast, I was taken to a side room, given an injection of insulin and left to read or sleep. After half an hour, a nurse brought in a glass of glucose and orange juice. By this time I couldn't see to read. My eyes were blurry and I was shaking all over. The drink took this feeling off however, and I felt like a queen when I was asked to order anything I wanted for breakfast, which was then brought to me in bed. I had this treatment every day whilst I was in the hospital. I even got to like the taste of the glucose and orange juice, which had really put me off at first.

Some of the patients had to have *electric treatment*. They were put into beds side by side in a room. They were all given medication to dry their mouths and later the beds were taken one by one into another room, the sound of the treatment was awful. I used to talk to the patients for as long as I could before they went in but they all had to lie in a darkened ward for a few hours afterwards and suffered really bad headaches. I think this treatment was to make them forget what had made them ill.

I settled down into the routine of the hospital, even enjoying the companionship of the other patients. It was a great relief not to have to battle with myself every time I had to go out. On one occasion, however, we all had to go over to the main building to listen to a concert and even that was traumatic for me. Joe used to bring the boys to see me on a weekend, which really bucked me up, and they were a hit with the other patients also.

When I had been in for nearly four weeks Joe came in smiling. He was rattling some keys, which he put into my hand. His friend Alan, had managed to rent a house at 10 Montrose Terrace, Stanley Street, but he'd found out that his furniture was too big so he couldn't take it. Joe went to see Lakin the landlord, and after two or three journeys and some serious grovelling, he was given the tenancy. We were both over the moon, it was only a very small 'two up and two down' house, down a terrace near Joe's Dads house, but it sounded like a palace to me. Joe drew me a sketch of what it was like and I wanted to go home with him there and then, but I had to wait until the Saturday morning when I was due for a weekend's leave.

Joe came for me in a taxi and we first went to his Dad's house where his sister Eva made me thick, buttered toast and strong sweet tea. These were the things I had missed in hospital, tea never tasted like the real thing there. A little later Joe led the way out of his back yard, across some waste ground, where a house had been pulled down, and into a back passage, which took us to OUR house. Alan had helped him clean and wallpaper the living room. He had put a settee and coffee table in and even his television. The bedroom was also furnished, we sat in silence for what seemed ages, just being happy to be together in our own place for the first time in our lives. Eva later brought us cooked Sunday dinners, which meant we could stay by ourselves instead of rejoining the family.

The house had a tiny back yard containing a toilet and a coal-bunker. The back door opened onto the tiniest kitchen and a door to the right led into another small room, which was the living area. At the other end of this, a door opened into a room at the front of the house. On the right between these two, a closed in narrow staircase led up to two small bedrooms, one at each side.

On the Sunday night, when I was supposed to go back to the hospital, I rang the ward and asked permission to stay out longer. I was given an appointment to see Dr Powell on the Tuesday morning. I told her about the house and that there was such a lot of occupational therapy there. She said she was pleased with my progress – I had gained a stone whilst there but I was still fearful about going out. Dr Powell looked at me for what seemed ages and then said, "So, you want me to 'kick you out' do you?" She said that, because as I now had Joe and our own house she would let me go, but she also said that if I had still been moving from place to place all the time, she wouldn't have let me.

When I got home I rang Miss Roe from Newland and told her what had happened. I told her we wanted the boys back and she was very happy to let us take them that weekend. Luckily, Joe had enough furniture to fill the house, so we didn't have to worry about that. When Joe had been engaged to Mavis, he had bought a good lot of furniture, which, because he was still paying for it, he kept. The living room was only big enough for 1 settee and 1 chair so the dining suite and the other furniture had to be stored in the front room.

As we brought the boys in and they were exploring, Michael said to me "Is this our 'saving house'?" (When I first took them to Newland, I told them that as soon as I could save up for a house I would bring them home for good). We told them it was and they realized that they were never going back to Aunt Sally's anymore. The nightmare of being on-edge because I was living in someone else's house was over forever. This was to be the start of a new and infinitely better life for all of us.

One night we were reminiscing about Joe's Mum thinking we were sleeping together, we laughed and Joe said his Dad still had an old fashioned attitude. Joe said he wouldn't let him stay overnight in our house whilst he was working on it.

He used to come for him at 9.30pm on the dot, saying "Come on lad, you have work to go to tomorrow and I want to lock up". Sure enough, for the first week after I came home, Pop appeared in the doorway saying the same thing; Joe was 31 then. We tried to think up ways of telling him that we wanted to be together, but chickened out. In the end though, Joe had to say that I was frightened to stay on my own. Although he grumbled about us not being married, Pop never came for Joe again.

We had a lovely Christmas. A big box of toys was delivered for the boys from Newland. My *Decree Nisi* had been granted in the November and I felt really safe and happy for the first time for years. We bought a gas cooker and Joe asked a friend of his (another Alan) if he would fix it in for us. I could hear them laughing together. It seemed to me that it had been years since I had heard that, and I realized how much I had missed out on FUN. As Alan was testing the cooker, there was a shout from the kitchen. The pressure must have been too high and Alan's beret had caught fire. It was not serious and they couldn't do anything for laughing.

Our tiny back kitchen was just an empty room. The water tap was next to the back door in the small yard. Joe and his mates found a deep white sink and a small wooden table on the rubbish tip whilst they were working in Hessle. He cut the table legs down and made a hole in it's top to fit the sink drain; a length of water pipe was found which enabled the outside tap to be brought through a hole in the wall to stand over the sink. The only thing they couldn't get hold of was waste pipe. Not to be deterred, Joe cut a bicycle inner tube and attached it to the sink drain. The other end was fed through another hole at the bottom of the wall and secured by wire to stop it falling back into the kitchen. This worked well until someone (mainly me) would forget about its construction and just tip a full bowl of water straight into the sink. The weight of the water brought the end of the inner tube back through the hole and into the kitchen where it flapped around as if it was alive, flooding the tiny space – I spent quite a lot of my time mopping up water!

A door high in the wall over the sink turned out to be a cupboard, which sat over the coal-bunker in the back yard. Once this had been scrubbed and painted white, it made a good pantry although everything had to be well covered. In the corner between the sink and the cooker, Joe had fitted another small table, which gave me a bit of workspace, there wasn't even enough room for 2 people to stand in the kitchen at the same time – but we had great fun trying.

To give us a table in the living room, Joe found an oblong

piece of wood, which he attached to the stair wall. Fixing two legs onto this, we were able to use it for meals or when we needed it, and fold it down at other times. Another *improvement* he made was to take up two flagstones from under the window in the yard and make a tiny garden to grow flowers. Joe and I made arrangements to get married on March 7 1960. Before that, we had to take the boys to see the headmistress of *Wawne Street School*, on Spring Bank, were they were due to start attending after the Easter holidays. I asked her if they could take Joe's surname of Shepherd, as we didn't want them to have a different name to us. She agreed and filled in all the necessary forms.

Stephen and Michael settled down well at school, after all they were used to mixing with lots of children and they soon made friends. It was only a couple of streets away and I made friends with other mothers going there. I was pleased that, after the initial journey, I was able to take and collect them without any worry.

One day Joe came home from work and told me that, on hearing of our impending wedding, his foreman had told him he must be stupid for 'taking on someone else's kids'. Although Joe said that he didn't think that way, I wished he hadn't told me. The feeling, that I was lucky to have him and that I should be grateful that he 'took us on' stayed with me for many, many years. Joe's job was, at that time not well paid. Now, instead of only having himself to keep, he had four of us and my only contribution was the eight shillings a week Family Allowance I received for the boys. Although John was supposed to pay £1 each for the children, more often than not, when we went to the *Court Collecting Office*, nothing had been paid in.

Our wedding day arrived. Joe went to the Registry Office with his friend Alan, on the bus, stopping at the pubs along the way for courage and I took the boys in a taxi. A girl I had met in the hospital, Doris, had lent me a black and white check suit to get married in and my next door neighbour, Pauline, had offered to stay back to set out the small buffet we had organised at home. There were only a few of our families and friends at the ceremony and when Joe repeated his name, Joseph Charles Arthur, everyone burst out laughing and had to be quietened by the registrar. It was a very enjoyable day for all of us. Dad told Joe that he knew I'd be alright now that I had him to look after me. When we came downstairs the next morning, the remainder of the wedding cake had turned into a shell of marzipan and icing. A trail of cake crumbs led upstairs and into the boys' bunk beds. They had certainly not wanted the party to end.

Joe could not understand my illness and thought I did not like people noticing me. He would say "No one will look at you; who do you think would want to look at you?" I couldn't explain that it was nothing to do with anyone else. The fear was inside me.

On a weekend Joe would go out for a drink with his mates. When he came back he would start telling me off for being so weak, even though the next day he would apologize and say "Give me as much back as I give you", "You know I would never lift a finger to hurt you". I could never answer him back though; I was too afraid of getting a 'back-hander'.

There was one thing I did that I am really ashamed about. A few months later, Doris wrote to me asking for her suit back, but because I really liked it, I had worn the skirt a lot. Consequently, constant washing made it a paler colour than the jacket. I thought that if I washed the top as well, the suit would end up the same colour. I tried to press the jacket but couldn't get it to look right. Anyway, I ended up sending the suit back as it was, with a note of apology. It was a terrible way to repay a very kind gesture from a friend and I still feel really bad about it after all these years.

Out of the Frying Pan?

In the August time I found out that I was pregnant. We were all really happy about this. Apart from the initial sickness, for which I took medication, I felt physically better than I had done in years. This lasted right through my pregnancy.

The baby was due to be born at home in the middle of April, but in spite of many false alarms he wasn't born until May 1st 1961. The midwives were really good, they had brought their bags twice, staying the night and then packing them up saying "he just isn't ready yet". We were getting really worried now. After a third night, the midwife was relieved by a new nurse. This lady told me that if I would "drink this liquid" (I can't remember what it was now), she guaranteed the baby would be here within an hour, which he was. Gary David, arrived weighing 9LB. The midwife, Ann who later became a very good friend of ours, had to apply grease to his body instead of bathing him, because, being 14 days overdue his body had stopped producing the natural grease protecting babies and his skin was cracked where he had been curled up. I used to lie watching him for hours. He never cried, only looked round the room with big blue eyes, he seemed to be taking in everything around him. On his third day we told Ann that we were really worried about him, he seemed to look black. As Ann was greasing his skin, she gently pricked him with his nappy pin and saw no reaction; (she told us this later, of course). After confirmation from the doctor that something was radically wrong, Gary David was taken to *Western General Hospital* (now HRI) on Anlaby Road.

My health deteriorated again. The depression and fears had all come crowding back in and I felt trapped by my feelings, again thinking I was going mad. Joe and other members of the family went to see Gary David regularly and even though I couldn't get there, I made myself go to the nearby phone box and I rang the hospital every day. The nursing staff were wonderful and would talk to me openly about his condition. I would try to make them tell me there was some hope. I would question everything they said to me and couldn't bear to think that he wouldn't get better. One day when Gary David had been in hospital about six weeks I had had what I thought was a positive report. The boys were at school and Joe had persuaded me to have some fish and chips for my dinner. Suddenly the door burst open and Pop came in crying. The hospital had rung the nearby shop and the lady who owned it couldn't face us. She went to Pop's house and asked him to tell us. Evidently, because Gary David couldn't digest his food, he was being fed on glucose, and as he grew, this wasn't enough and he had had two heart attacks before he died. We were asked if we would allow a post mortem on Gary David because it was very difficult to operate successfully on babies of his age. We didn't have to think about this. Here was a way for us to see a reason for his short life; by making something positive out of a very negative situation.

Pop and Joe decided that his Mum's grave would be opened so that Gary David could be laid at her feet. I was feeling so stressed and ill by then that I could not face going to the funeral. We didn't get the full report of what they found. My doctor said some of his gastric juices were missing so he couldn't digest his food. This was the same time as the babies affected by *Thalidomide* were being born. To my way of thinking, maybe the morning sickness pills I took were not enough to affect Gary David's limbs but they could have been the reason for the Gastric Juices being missing. I have never talked about this to any of the doctors so I have never had my suspicions confirmed or denied, I just felt cold inside. My arms were empty and nothing that was said to me made me feel better.

By then I had been prescribed *Largactil* tablets for severe depression and it was only Stephen and Michael who gave me something to cling on to. I dare not be alone in the house and quite often I would ask Michael to stay at home with me (Stephen enjoyed learning at school and didn't want to stay away). All the time I wished I was pregnant again and every month that I wasn't I felt sick with disappointment. Joe used to tell me that we should be happy to be a family with our two boys, but I couldn't get over the feeling that I had let him down. I wanted to give him children as well. I couldn't watch television programmes with babies taking part and passing prams in the street made me turn away and rush home again.

A few months later, I found out that I was pregnant again. I couldn't wait to start wearing my maternity smocks (I think I thought it would only be true then). I was given vitamin and iron tablets and also milk tokens. Only then did we start making plans again. The happiness was only short lived, however; because when I went for my six months check up, the doctor said I should be bigger than I was by then. He gave me two tablets to take, saying that if I was pregnant they would not hurt the baby, but if I wasn't they would start my periods again. I was really upset when I found out that I wasn't really carrying a baby after all. This had been a 'phantom pregnancy', nature's way of giving you a rest from all the stress of not conceiving.

Joe had carried on going out with his friends on Thursday, Friday and Saturday nights and Sunday dinner times as he had always done. Often he brought them back for supper on a Saturday. I liked to meet them as they all had very quirky senses of humour. A year or so later, however, it started getting too much. If there wasn't much food in the house, Joe would start on the meal that I had planned for the Sunday. The next day, when he had sobered up and I told him we had nothing left he was upset with himself. He even went round to one of his friends' houses one week, to 'borrow' a meal. I was pleased that he realized that this could not go on, he stopped inviting them round and even cut down on the times he went out. One of them though, wouldn't take the hint and began calling after he came from the pub, when we were in bed. Joe went down to talk to him once or twice and then had to tell him in no uncertain terms not to come again. Another time, Joe had just been paid his holiday money, when a workmate, Stan, went to talk to him. He told him that he owed a sum of money and he was going to be taken to prison if he didn't pay the court bailiff. Joe brought the man to our house and he told the story to me. We both decided that we couldn't let this happen whilst we had the extra money. The man said he could get it back to us in two weeks time when we would have needed it ourselves. As the time went on the man didn't come back with the money and Joe had to go back to work early to get the housekeeping money we needed. This person dodged Joe all the time from then on until one day Joe cornered him and told him the money was not worth losing a friend over, so we had both decided to write the debt off to experience.

All this time I had been struggling with the fear of being outside, often having more bad days than good ones. I found an article about a condition called *Agoraphobia*. The symptoms were the ones that plagued me. I wrote to a lady in Lincolnshire, telling her about myself and in turn she sent me a monthly newsletter called 'The Open Door'. A doctor, Claire Weekes, wrote a long article in it, about the condition, every month. She was an Australian GP who started specialising in nerves when lots of her patients came to her, suffering from nervous illness. Dr Weekes soon had first hand experience herself, after a traumatic time trying to get back to work too quickly following a serious operation. Dr Weekes says that when the first panic, usually brought on by a very stressful situation, strikes, the symptoms are so traumatic and devastating, that long after the cause has

Out of the Frying Pan?

faded away, patients are still frightened of the fear that comes with the panic. It is this 'fear of the symptoms of fear' that she treats. I bought one of her books, 'Self Help for your Nerves' and I cried with relief to realize that this is a genuine illness and that I was not going mad after all. Many other people were also experiencing the same thing. Having this new information gave me renewed willpower. I was determined to fight to get myself better. Armed with this new insight, and following Dr Week's advice, I started to be able to go short distances from home by myself. I felt really proud and I thought that all my troubles were over at last, although there was still a limit to how far I could travel. Joe didn't like me reading the books, however. He said that I should talk to him about how I was feeling. I couldn't make him see, that he couldn't understand the illness any more than I could.

I hadn't seen my mother since the day I was going into hospital, but it didn't worry me too much because I couldn't forget her attitude towards the boys. One day Mam came round to see me. It was a surprise but I wondered why she had come. Whilst we were having a cup of tea she made it clear that she didn't think much of the house that we were living in. I told her that at least I had a permanent home and I was happily married to Joe. I said that I had more than she had, because she was only living with Jess and if he asked her to leave she would then have nowhere to go. I know that was nasty but I felt angry with her, we had an argument and I'm afraid I almost pushed her out of the back door. I remember the twins had just come home from school and wanted to know why their Granny had left so quickly.

About this time, Stephen and Michael had a medical at school and I was asked to take them to see another doctor. He explained to me that Michael was thin for his age and needed 'a bit of building up'. The doctor said that Michael was just not quite up to the physical standard for his age and recommended that he should start attending the *Open Air School* on Cottingham Road. Stephen would be able to go with him so that the twins would not have to be parted. He assured me that it was nothing for me to worry about, but the boys would both benefit from the fresh air. The School bus picked them up at the top of Stanley Street each morning and dropped them off there at night. A helper saw them across the road.

I started working afternoons in the office at *Kenningtons Laundry* in De Gray Street on Newland Avenue to help out with money. Joe's sister Eva picked the boys up and took them home until Joe collected them after work at 4.30PM. I was able to get a bus at the top of the street and there wasn't much walking at the other end. As I had prepared tea before I went to work, Joe had only to put it in the oven.

One afternoon before Christmas I could see the fog closing in, as it got darker. I started to feel a bit stressed by this and hoped it would clear. At five o clock someone walked with me to the bus stop. After standing there for quite a while, we were told that the buses had stopped running. I was getting panicky now, as I realized I dared not walk home to Spring Bank. I decided the only thing for me to do was to go to Dads in Edgecumbe Street. After having a cup of tea with him and my stepmother, Dad said he would walk me home. I begged him to call at *Dunhams Taxis* in Grafton Street, but Mrs Dunham said she wouldn't let her husband drive in that fog, which was quite understandable really. There was nothing for it but to hang on to Dad's arm and go forward. Even though 'you couldn't see a hand in front of you' I felt really safe. Dad, being blind, was very confident and with his words of comfort to me as we walked, we made it to Stanley Street safely. Jo had been worried about me, thinking I would be cowering in some alleyway somewhere. By the time we'd had a cup of tea, the fog had lifted and Dad was able to get the bus back home. Joe had kept my cooked meal warm and I was very grateful. I hadn't realized how hungry I was. I did feel proud of myself though for thinking out what I should do instead of having a full-blown panic.

A couple of months later I saw an advert asking for an Office Manager at *Blind Institute*. After talking it over with Joe, we decided I should apply for it. The money was really good. I didn't tell Dad, however, until I had been accepted for the post.

At my interview with the Manager, Mr Platt, and because there were no questions about being related to any of the staff, I didn't say who I was. I wanted to get this job on my own merit. Anyway I was successful and told Dad. He was very surprised that I had gone for it but he was pleased. He used to meet me off the bus near *Monica Picture House* and we would walk down Alexandra Road, onto Beverley Road and into work together. Dad was always full of very good advice and I always felt safe with him. I remember when it was really cold and I shivered as we walked, Dad said to me "Put your head up, don't shiver, and just pretend it's a nice warm day". I know that sounded silly, but I tried it and it worked. I still do this today, thinking that Dad is walking by my side.

I had been there a few days when Mr Platt asked me into his office. He had found out who I was and said that if he'd known when he interviewed me, I wouldn't have been given the job. He said that after all, Dad and him were, sort of, on opposite sides (Dad was the area representative of the RNIB at that time) but he was pleased with my work. I assured him that Dad and I never discussed work and he was fine after that.

I was really happy working there. At home, we were able to afford little extras and I felt very content with my life.

The following April I started having heartburn again (which had always been a sign of pregnancy for me). This time we dare not plan ahead too much even though we were really happy. I left work in the August, this time however, I was getting tired rather quickly and check-ups revealed high blood pressure so I had to rest as much as I could. Dr Marsden said I could give birth at home, even though there was a suspicion of my carrying twins again, but it was never looked in to.

I had been smoking for 15 years and I always thought it helped me to calm down. I had tried many times to stop, but never successfully. Once I thought that if I bought seven packets I could ration myself out to a packet a day. There was a high cupboard on top of three drawers in the alcove of my living room. I threw the cigarettes as high as I could into the cupboard, feeling positive that I could control my cravings. I smoked the first packet quickly, thinking that I could practice going without for the rest of the first day, that was a complete failure. Halfway through the week they had all gone. I had found them by climbing up on to the drawers – then, being tall, I could easily reach to the back of the top shelf. Another time I asked my friend Pauline, next door to keep them for me and not to give me more than one packet a day, no matter how hard I pleaded with her. After a couple of days she couldn't bear my begging for them and gave me the lot back!

I had stopped for about a year once, but when Joe was given a treadle sewing machine and had mended it, I said "give me a cigarette to celebrate" There I was again, hooked as bad as ever. On my sister's visits, I used to wonder what she did with her hands all the time, when she wasn't constantly raising them to her mouth to smoke. I had been having bad bouts of bronchitis and each winter they were getting progressively worse. I had a constant bad taste in my mouth and couldn't smoke without having a cup of tea to take the taste away. When I inhaled the smoke I felt as if my chest was on fire. About two months before my baby was born I felt I couldn't stand it any longer, on a visit to the doctor, he told me that if I stopped smoking I would never get a bad chest again. I took this to mean that he had given me a new lease of life and I decided there and then that I would never smoke again.

In a couple of weeks the medication I had been given for the bronchitis had made my chest a lot better and the cravings started to come back. I only had to remind myself of the taste and the burning to put me off any thoughts of lighting up again though. I have never had the slightest inclination to smoke from that day to this, Joe used to say to me sometimes "Come on, let your hair down it's Christmas, have a cigarette". As a heavy smoker himself, he never understood that if I had even one I would be hooked just as bad as I used to be.

There was a patch of damp on the ceiling in the corner of our bedroom and whilst I was pregnant it started changing its shape. It looked like the face of a baby girl, with blonde hair cut into a fringe at the front. This made me feel good; maybe this was telling me that I would have a beautiful baby girl. Then I noticed another smaller, darker patch underneath and to the side of the face, this took on the shape of a little skull. Everyone who came had a look at it said the same thing. I didn't realize till later how prophetic this was.

Shortly before I was due to give birth, my legs were so swollen I looked like the *Michelin Man* who sat on top of a van advertising tyres. I couldn't bear to lie down in bed so I slept in a chair with my feet up. At 4.00AM on 13th November 1964 Caroline was born weighing 4LB 1OZ. Joe had bought a pair of toy walkie talkies and Dr Marsden rang downstairs so that I could be the first to tell him of her safe arrival. Then the doctor spoke to Joe and told him that there was another baby as well. This baby didn't want to be born, so Dr Marsden had to literally pull him out. All through the pregnancy I had suffered with a nasty pain on my right side so I thought that maybe it had something to do with it. I felt as if all my stuffing had been pulled out when Christopher emerged weighing 3LB 13OZ. After Stephen, Michael and Gary David had been born, I had immediately sat up, eager to see my visitors, but this time I just felt dreadful. Someone gave me a mirror and all I saw was too big black patches for my eyes in a chalk white face – I looked like a Panda.

Caroline had taken quite a lot of the oxygen the nurses had brought and there wasn't very much left for Christopher. The babies were quickly taken to the *Hedon Road Maternity Hospital*, but Christopher's breathing never got established and he only lived three days. I only remember seeing Caroline and couldn't kiss either of the babies for fear they would be infected with my cold, but ever since then I have felt really guilty. I felt as if I had abandoned him.

Another strange thing happened. Among the many congratulation cards we had been given, were two almost identical ones, except that one of the babies had on a blue beret and the other one a pink one. A few days later I noticed that the pink card was missing. No one had touched it. I thought later that maybe we had to keep the boy card because we couldn't keep the baby. We were all very sad about losing Christopher, but at the same time relieved that Caroline was alright. I felt I just couldn't bear the pain of thinking too deeply. She stayed in hospital for three weeks until she reached 5LB. She was so tiny that I dressed her in dolls cardigans, one of which she still has today. As she grew, I just lived for the times when she was awake so that I could tend to her and play with her. When she was asleep I just sat and watched her.

The living room floor was so cold and had a feeling of damp, so when Caroline started to sit up, we bought her a big wooden playpen which had a strong floor. This was the size of her 'little world' when she started walking also.

Christmas times had always been a bit of a worry to us. We weren't able to save money during the year so Joe bought wood and used it to make *Rocking Horses*, *Garages*, *Forts* and *Dolls Bungalows* to sell and for the toys for the three children. They were really good. I would to do the decorating in the houses. One year it was actually Christmas Eve day when we finished the last house and were able to rush out at the last minute and buy things for ours family. Joe always made the best of anything he put his mind to. He had an allotment at the back of *Botanic Crossings*, growing vegetables and flowers, and he made the shed really comfortable for us by putting in chairs and a wooden table. With a kettle and a teapot, it felt as if we were on holiday. There was also a big greenhouse where he grew tomatoes and cucumbers. In the summer I used to pack up our dinner and we'd stay there all day. It was like being in the country to us. As we walked back home it felt as if we had really been away for the day. Once or twice on a bad day, I would stop at the railway crossings and not dare to go any further. I thought the crossings would close and stop me ever getting back home. My heart started racing and I felt as if I couldn't get my breath properly. My legs seemed paralysed and wouldn't move forward. Joe and the boys would go on alone whilst I went back with Caroline. When this happened, the journey back was terrible. I thought I was miles away from home and would never be able to get there. I also felt so guilty that I had let myself and the family down – again.

We had been in Stanley Street for about six years when we received a letter one day telling us that our houses were going to be 'compulsory purchased'. This was the best news we had heard in years. We were given a choice of areas and chose Bricknell Avenue, although we were warned that there was a very long waiting list for this area. Joe used to take us in his car to see the building of Orchard Park behind North Hull Estate. He didn't really like the way they just used concrete instead of bricks. Shutters were put into place and concrete was poured into them to make the walls. It was a nice open area though with lots of grass. We looked into some of the finished houses and they looked quite spacious inside, still his mind was made up – We would wait for Bricknell Avenue.

It was whilst we lived in Stanley Street that I met up again with Barbara, who lived in a terrace at the top of the street. She had also lived in *Lansdowne House* the same time as I did when I was nursing at *Western General*. Her sister Pat was my friend when we were at *Sidmouth Street School*. Stephen and Michael used to play with Barbara's sons John and Anthony.

One day the boys were going to West Park and were walking down Walton Street. Stephen decided to cross the road to get some sweets. He didn't look where he was going and ran into a moped. Although he wasn't hurt, the driver took his name and address and called the police.

Our boys were in the tin bath in front of the fire, when there was a loud knock at the door. Joe answered it and had a few words with the policeman who stood there. It seems he had called to see if they were alright and it had been decided that he should come in to give them a bit of a 'frightener' hoping to make Stephen more careful crossing the road. Michael as well as Stephen stood up and they were both literally shaking (without their boots) as the policeman gave them both a talking to. Stephen soon forgot however, because not long after this, Michael came running in to tell us that Stephen had been knocked down by a motorbike opposite our back passage in Norwood Street. This time, running across the street, he had just clipped the back wheel of the bike and had landed with his chin on the kerb. That night he couldn't sleep for the pain so I settled him into an easy chair by the fire and stayed up all night with him. He couldn't even eat comfortably for quite a while after this.

The boys both enjoyed going to the Sunday school at the top of the street and collecting stickers for good attendance. They were also in the *Cub Scouts*. One weekend, the scouts were taking the boys to a camp across the River Hull. As the ferry was pulling away, Michael shouted to us "What if we forget what you look like?" "Can we have a picture of you"? We laughed as we reassured them that they wouldn't forget us in two days and we would be waiting for them when they returned. Because the boys were at *Open Air School* they were taken for a two-week holiday every year, sometimes it was *Hornsea Convalescent Home* and sometimes, one at Bridlington. In March 1966, Stephen and Michael were at Bridlington. There were only two occupied houses left in the terrace. We were battling against mice and black-clocks, which still kept coming back despite all Joe's efforts. Caroline only had the size of the playpen to move around in and we were both getting really fed up. Joe decided that we couldn't wait in these conditions any longer, so he asked me to ring the council and tell them we would go to Orchard Park. It would be good for the boys to come home to clean air for a change.

 We spent the next couple of days packing our few belongings and excitedly talking about what life would be like in a brand new, much bigger house. That same week the letter offering us a house in Feldane dropped through our letterbox. On the night before we were due to move from Stanley Street and knowing that the houses were due to be demolished, Joe and his friends had taken off any wood they could find and burned it to keep warm. I woke up the next morning to find doors, shelves and other things missing. I remember that, because the house was now so open, I had been a bit scared, although Joe reminded me that we would be gone in a couple of hours. It was a Saturday so he wouldn't have to leave me to go to work.

When I looked back at my time in Stanley Street, I felt mixed emotions. For so much of the time I felt as if I was in a black void. It had been great at first, to have a house of our own, but so much had happened in those six short years that I just couldn't wait for that period of my life to be over.

Top Left - Me aged 5, EVACUATED in Scarborough (1940)
Top Right - Mum & Dad - just married (1928)
Above - Newly married with my friend Pat (left) in Singapore (1954)

ABOVE - Mum (with necklace) & Dad (far left) having a drink with friends (1940). RIGHT - Joe at the microphone during happier times (1954).

HOUSEWIVE'S . . .

may we call on you to bring you FRESH DAILY

Local Market Garden Grown

SALADS, FRUIT *and* VEGETABLES

★ AT PRICES TO SUIT YOUR PURSE

So please look out when your **Mobile Market Garden store's** *about.*

PROPRIETOR'S :-
A. SHEPHERD
and
J. SCHOOLER

IDEAL PRINTERS LTD. OF HULL.

Flyer to promote the families new Fruit & Veg Van business (1978)

Top - The family on holiday at Butlins (1978)
Above - Me living in the `now` (2007)

CHAPTER SIX

A Brand New Start

Knowing that the new estates were filling up, the dairies were in competition with each other to make sure of getting our custom. They were offering to take people to view the houses and also supplying a box full of cleaning materials. This was very welcome. We had arranged that when we received the letter allocating us the house, I should go with Joe's sister Eva in the daytime and Joe would go with his mate Alan after work in the evening, which we did.

We turned off the main Hall Road at the *Arctic Ranger* public house and found that the road swept round into a half-moon shape. The Danes were in alphabetical order starting at Axdane at one end and finishing at Limedane where we had come in.
As we turned into Feldane we saw that the houses went in rows of four or five, behind each other. There were open fields at each end of the Dane. The house we had been given was no. 57 and was known as a 'big three', as opposed to a 'small three' or 'four' bedroomed house. It was halfway down on the left hand side

of the Dane, and last but one in a block of four houses — all big threes except the one nearest to the road, which was a four.

Through the front door a square hall led into a good-sized kitchen on the left, a cloakroom/toilet on the right and a big living room opposite the front door. The window almost filled the end wall and looked onto a decent sized garden. A door to the left took you into a 'dinette' (which was as big as our living room in Stanley Street). A passage way led back into the kitchen, which was fully fitted with wall as well as floor cupboards. It even had an electric cooker and lots of sockets. The whole floor, apart from the kitchen was tiled and had under floor electric heating. Wide, open plan stairs went up in the middle of the two rooms and led onto three good-sized bedrooms and a bathroom.

Eva and I both liked the house, but because they lived on the front of Stanley Street at No.7, they had to wait a while longer for their allocation. Caroline was now eighteen months old and she toddled to her hearts content, enjoying hearing her feet clumping on the bare wooden staircase and bedrooms. She had never had such freedom. Joe and Alan also gave their approval to the house and we couldn't wait to move in, which we did on April 10th 1966.

Going outside to the end of our block, we discovered it led into a concrete square of ground adjoining the block of houses in Gildane and making a safe pedestrian passageway from one end of the Dane to the other. My friend Barbara, (Barbara next door), her husband Johnnie and sons John and Anthony, were already in the end house next to ours and we met Joan, her husband Bert and sons, Michael, Paul and Phillip, who were our neighbours (on my other side). The house at the road end of the block was still empty. We were all very excited at the brand new houses in a completely new estate which we had been given and all became very good friends. Joan, Barbara and I used to go

A Brand New Start

exploring to see what the difference was between the sizes of the houses. We would look through the empty windows and count the floor tiles. We agreed that ours was the best-proportioned house of them all – of course!

We were to find out that it wasn't such a good idea for the estate to be so open. Not long after we moved in, Caroline disappeared from the garden. Even though she had only been gone for a few minutes, she was nowhere to be seen. We looked all over for her, calling her name, I kept imagining I heard her crying in other gardens but a few minutes later, a lady came into view carrying her, telling me she had been looking for us at the same time. I'm glad really that this danger was brought to our attention early on, and from then we were always doubly careful with security. Bert learned that we couldn't keep anything on our kitchen window ledges if the windows were open. He had taken his watch off to wash his hands, putting it on the ledge and then walked away forgetting it for a few minutes, but when he went for it, it had gone. As the windows were on a swivel, it was easy for someone to put their hand in and take anything – they could then run through the blocks and be long gone before anyone would even know things were missing. Another day Joe had his coat taken through the cloakroom window, which didn't swivel. Anyway, we told everyone we could, to make sure that these things did not happen again.

When it came time for Stephen and Michael to come home, Joe borrowed a car and went to Bridlington to fetch them. They were also happy to be in the new house. Stephen had been transferred from *Open Air School* to *Sir Thomas Stratton* on Spring Bank, so it was easy to get him changed again to *Sir Leo Schultz*, another brand new school that was not far from the top of the Feldane. I wrote to the Head Teacher at Open Air School telling him about our move and asking if Michael could also attend

'Schultz', which he readily agreed to.

Everything was working out well and we all loved our new home. The icing on the cake was being told of the impending birth of our next baby in the October. Joe was very good at drawing, so having a house with pure white walls was like a dream come true for him. In the boys' bedroom, he painted the whole of one wall with the 'Mad Hatters Tea Party' from *Alice in Wonderland*. A large picture of *Humpty Dumpty* filled the opposite wall, surrounded by smaller pictures of *Ba-Ba Black sheep* and *The Cow Jumping over the Moon*. He painted two walls in the bathroom with a seascape in black and white and which included dolphins jumping out of the water and a big yellow sun in the corner. On the back wall of the first landing he painted an iron balcony looking out onto a beautiful Mediterranean sea with tiny boats on the water. Everyone who saw it was very complimentary.

Caroline's' friend Katie, who lived in the block in front of us, was given a puppy which she used to bring with her when she came to play. Caroline was frightened of this little dog and if she went to the door to find Katie and the dog there, she would run back into the dinette and climb up on the sideboard to get away from it. Joe decided that the way to help her get over her fear was for us to buy a puppy also. After talking it over, we decided on a Lassie type collie, which would be good with the children and we sent away to a farm in Wales and gave them our order. The puppy arrived at *Paragon Station* in a strong cardboard box and Stephen and Michael went to collect it. On their return Joe opened the lid and stood the box on its side but didn't take the puppy out. Caroline saw the little dog who sat cowering and shaking in the corner and after a minute or two she slowly crept towards it and picked it out. After giving it a drink and some food, Joe told her that she must let it rest for a while to get over the trauma of its long journey. It wasn't long before the little dog started exploring its new surroundings. Caroline was delighted and from then on they were inseparable. A family conference decided on the name – Lassie – not very thought provoking but it suited the latest member of the family.

Lassie grew into a beautiful looking dog with a long beige and white coat. She was a mirror image of *Lassie* the famous 'film star'. When we used to take her on the field or on the 'green hill' she would run with all her coat flailing out behind her and I thought no dog had ever looked more beautiful.

A couple of months later, Dorothy and her family moved into the house at the end of the block. We all used to meet in different houses for morning coffee. Someone would provide the drinks and I would make scones, which were eaten hot with lashings of butter. Then we'd all go back and clean our houses, It was a great laugh. Dorothy, because she had only just been given her house, would come in saying "I know somewhere you haven't dusted". Naturally Joan, Barbara and I had already found these places, including the tops of doors and the top of the wooden swivel window frames.

Gary John was born on 21st October 1966 and we were all delighted. I was secretly very pleased that I had given Joe a son after losing the first two. We chose his name because we had liked it from the start, but gave him the John after Joe's Dad and my Granddad. 15 months later, on our eighth wedding anniversary, 7th March 1968, we were given the best anniversary present we had ever had. Our second daughter Diane was born. She was different in colouring from Caroline, Gary and Michael, who were all blonde with blue eyes. Diane was the image of her Dad. Joe was thrilled to bits. Joan said she looked like an Indian Papoose. I had been a bit wary of the birth because Gary had stopped helping in his delivery and I had to do all the work without any desire to push. I was pleasantly surprised however, when Diane arrived with no trouble whatsoever. She was a quiet baby. I often had to wake her up for her feeds.

Whilst we were all still happy with our new arrival, we were suddenly given a rude awakening. Gary had always been a very energetic toddler, he seemed to need only a few hours sleep. In the night if the slightest noise woke him, he would scream for ages. Joe would try to pacify him but he would be rigid in his arms. I used to take him downstairs so that Joe could get his sleep, to be fit for work the next day.

One evening, when he was about 20 months old, we were just enjoying the peace and quiet after a hectic day when Gary walked into the living room. Joe and I were sitting on the settee and Gary just walked over to chair in the corner of the room and sat, quietly watching the television. We looked at each other in amazement – this wasn't the toddler we knew. We decided not to say anything in case it 'broke the spell' and he would start screaming again.

The next morning at six o-clock, I woke up and went downstairs as usual. Diane was still asleep but Gary walked into the kitchen, whimpering. He didn't seem to want to be put down, although he wasn't crying. I carried him on my hip whilst I prepared the breakfast and made sandwiches for Joe's dinner. Gary started being a little sick, but instead of this making him feel better, he seemed to get quieter. When Joe came down I showed him how the baby was. He brought Diane's cot downstairs and I put Gary into it, placing the still sleeping baby into her pram. Gary hated to be 'fenced in', in the cot and normally he would have climbed straight out again but this time he did not murmur. Joe and I were really worried by now, knowing that something must be radically wrong. I went outside to see if I could find someone who had a telephone and was up at that time in the morning. Luckily, Sid, a man who worked at *Blind Institute* was coming down the Dane. He knew about First Aid and came in to see the baby. Straight away, he brought his walkie-talkie into the house and I was able to ring our doctor. After telling the receptionist – Pauline – Gary's symptoms she said she would ring the doctor at home because he had not come into the surgery yet. The doctor rang for an ambulance without even seeing the baby. He had realized how serious his condition was. By 9.00AM Gary was in *Castle Hill Hospital*. He had had all the tests, and treatment for Meningitis had been started.

Joe went with him and stayed most of the day, whilst I looked after the other children. On the evening, a friend took me to the hospital. Normally I wouldn't have been allowed in the room but, although I didn't realize the reason for it, the nurse let me sit, holding Gary's hand for hours. I was willing him to get better but at the time there was no reaction. The next day the nurse told me they hadn't expected him to last the night and that's why they had let me be with him. As Gary started to recover we could only stand outside and look through the window. He didn't seem to know how to use his fork and spoon anymore, his food kept dropping from his fork when was only half way to his mouth and we were worried that he wouldn't get enough to eat and drink. He was always drinking when he was well and his favourite was orange juice (Looking back on this now, however, I realize that perhaps it was the Tartrazine in the orange juice that made him hyperactive).

A friend of ours knew a nurse on his ward and asking after Gary, she was told that he was thought of as a miracle. All his later tests had shown negative and he was allowed home after four weeks treatment, being left without any after-effects of the illness. It was thought he might have picked up the infection by eating soil out of the garden. The doctor said he could have eaten a shovel full without any ill effect, but it would take just one tiny piece infected with the bacteria to have caused all this trouble.

We had bought Gary a *Triang* baby bike and when I brought him home, he had forgotten how to ride it. He also had to learn to walk and recognise everyone again but it didn't take long before he was back to his normal self – without the hyperactivity and the screaming, which was a relief.

Later that year, Joe was sent, by the *Telephone Department* to Otley to learn how to use some new equipment. He had always been really careful over safety in the house and as well as telling us repeatedly to make sure everything was switched off when we went to bed, he put the words 'IS ALL SAFE?' across the wooden rail on the first landing, so that we would remember.

Things started changing on the estate. Danepark School was finished; a public house had been built opposite to the top of Gildane on Hall Road, and a block of shops at the front of Dibsdane was completed. The shops made life a lot easier for me as I was able to go to the *Post Office, Grocers, Greengrocers, Butchers* and the *Fish Shop* myself without any panics, as they were only about two minutes from our house. This small amount of freedom made me feel almost 'normal' again.

The vans stopped coming round now their custom had dwindled, except one known by the children as the 'goodie van'. This also sold a selection of groceries and vegetables.

Joe and some of his friends started a committee at the new pub, *The Rampant Horse* (known as Ramp) and for many years they raised money to take the children from the Danes on outings and to have Christmas Parties. They would have *Easter Bonnet Parades, Quiz Nights,* and *Sports Days* on the field opposite Feldane and *Pram Races* round Dane Park Road as well as other entertainments to raise funds.

Stephen and Michael both settled down at *Sir Leo Schultz*

School and we were pleased that they were near home. One thing we didn't like, however, was the way the pupils were able to call the teachers by their christian names. They seemed to have 'moved the ceiling' and lost some of the respect from the pupils. After school, the boys had joined the choir at *St Michaels* and also the *Naval Cadets*.

One day, when he was about three and a half years old, Gary was playing on the front step when I called him in for his dinner. To my horror, he was nowhere to be seen. Children were coming home from school, cutting through our block to get to the other danes and I sent Stephen and Michael on their bikes to look for him. I started searching, keeping the other two safely by my side as well. My heart was in my mouth and I was just thinking of calling the police when I saw a lady with some children and a pushchair coming down the walkway. She shouted, asking me if I'd lost a little boy. I just cried with relief. Evidently a boy had passed our house on his way home to Isledane and had taken Gary with him, leaving him stranded in the middle of the dane. This lady had found him, realized what must have happened and had taken him into her house until it was time to take her own children back to school. I never let any of them play out at the front again. Joe bought swings and roundabouts, which he put up in the back garden and all the children (including their friends) played there when we weren't with them.

The stress of nearly losing Gary had made me anxious again. Going out was again difficult for me. If I had needed to go to the van on an evening and it was more than 1 block away, I could not make the journey and had to ask Stephen or Michael to go for me. When it came time for Caroline to start school, Barbara next door took her. Although it was only across the road and through one of the blocks on the opposite side the thought of the journey terrified me. I would follow as far as I dare and stand, (feeling really afraid of moving further away from home, yet guilty because I couldn't), till Barbara came back. Once home again, I was determined not to give in to these feelings next time. It was always like this. Without the pressure of having to go anywhere, I would feel really brave and determined to conquer the feelings the next time. Yet, later on I would just crumble with the fear. I carried on leaving the house just after them every day and each time they went, I followed a bit further, until one day I was actually standing at the school gates. As I stood, a lady came down the path towards me. She told me she was Miss Richards, the Head Teacher. She said she had seen me getting gradually closer and wanted me to walk down the path with her to look through the classroom window. She said Caroline would be very happy to see me.

My heart was in my mouth as she took my arm and we started walking what seemed to me miles to the classroom. It was worth it though to see Caroline's face as she smiled and waved to me. Walking back to the gate, I thanked Miss Richards and told her how surprised I was that it wasn't as far as I had thought. From then on, I was able to go with Caroline every day and I even started following the van when I needed anything. I was over the moon with myself. My comfort zone had increased tremendously, and I gradually increased it further, thanks to the help of Dr Weekes and her books on *Agoraphobia* and *Nervous Illness*. The strange thing was that my perception of distance seemed to have altered. Before, I had looked at streets and houses, thinking they were miles away but now I could see how close they really were.

Joe's Dad, and his sister Eva and her family were now living at no.33 and Pop would come to our house almost every day. He was very unhappy and spoke of leaving, although he did not know where to go. He had not taken kindly to leaving Stanley Street and could not settle in their new house. With seven people in our house already, we could not even offer to take him in. I used to see him sat on a seat outside the shops in Dibsdane sometimes and would bring him home for a meal. He was 80 years old and wasn't able to care properly for himself. Joe brought the doctor in to see him and he was taken to *Beverley Road Hospital*. Before he went, Pop said, "I won't be coming out of here son". Although Joe tried to pacify him, he told me when he came home that he was worried about his Dad. Even though the doctors could not find anything wrong with Pop, he died about eight days after he went in. We think he had willed himself to die because he could not get used to living in the new house in an entirely new area. Joe was inconsolable and blamed everyone for not being able to care for Pop properly. On the day of the funeral, Joe was, naturally even more upset. I tried to help him by telling him that it was not his Dad he would be burying, because Pop had already gone on to his new life. I also told him that he had gone through the worst thing he had to face, when he was first told of his dad's death. I think that had made him strong enough to face the day. I stayed at home with the children, instead of going to the funeral.

Caroline had always enjoyed rough games and loved nothing more than to play football. Joan's son Phillip, who was a little older than her used to play in the square with her all the time. He wouldn't let the other boys be nasty to her, but he used to try to show her he was stronger than her, by fighting with her himself. A year or so later, even the older boys used to call for her to play football with them. They all wanted her on their team.

One year we bought her a big celluloid doll that was called Simon to get her interested in 'girls' toys. She was happy with it at first but it wasn't long before she had pulled its head off and was kicking it round the garden like a football. I really enjoyed looking after the little ones, Caroline, Gary and Diane.

They were all very pleasant, happy children. I spent most of my time reading to and playing games with them. I would watch the children's programs on the television with them, explaining what was happening, joining in the play and singing the songs with them. I would be so engrossed that the time would just fly past and I would have to rush to get the tea on before Joe came home. I felt I was creating my own childhood over again.

Before mealtimes I would sit all three of them on the cupboard top, I suppose mainly because I could keep an eye on them all, that way. I would wash three faces, six hands and six legs. We made this into a game and we all thoroughly enjoyed it. Tea was an important time for us; all sitting together round the table, talking about what had happened during the day. After tea would be bath time, followed by a 'calming down' period when we would read with the younger ones or play quiet games with them before bedtime, this was another ritual. I would sing lullabies and quiet songs to them until they were asleep and it would sometimes take about an hour before I was able to get away. They would keep asking for them over and over again. I loved singing to them though, so I didn't mind.

On a Sunday, after bath and hair washing time, they looked forward to sitting on the floor in front of me whilst I dried their hair with a towel. Caroline had long blonde hair and Diane's was the same length but dark, like her Dad's. I don't know who enjoyed this most. They remember all these rituals today.

A new shopping centre had been built near *St Michaels Church* between Ellerburn Avenue and Orchard Park Road. As well as others, there was a *Grandways, Chemist, Skeletons, Butchers, Post Office, A2Z, Freezer Shop,* and a *Hairdresser*. Later, from our back window we saw the three blocks of Mildane Flats being built at the bottom of Gildane. The complete walls were lifted into position on each floor by a big crane. Whenever we had a spare minute we would watch their progress.

It was always had a strong desire of mine to return to nursing, so when a position came up for a Nursing Auxiliary on the 5PM till 9PM shift at *Hull Royal Infirmary*, I applied for and got the post. Joe was able to look after the children. I met one of the Nursing Sisters whom I had known when I was training and she was pleased to see me. She said that the rigid conditions in the 1950's had lost them many good nurses.

Back home, the girls were fascinated by the little paper caps that were part of the uniform by then and Diane would ask me to bring one home for her. Instead of throwing them away, I brought two of the caps home and both the girls loved wearing them round the house. I think that is why they decided to join the SJAB when they were older.

After school, when the children were playing in the square outside our house and it was time for them to come in, I would take Lassie with me to the door and say to her "Round them up Lassie". This caused them to laugh and run round. Lassie would somehow get them all together near a wall and stand with her nose on one of them and her tail guarding the other. This was a ritual they all looked forward to.

Stephen and Michael left school, Stephen was a very good artist and got a job at *Brough Aircraft Factory* with a view to going into the Drawing Office and Michael started an apprenticeship as a Painter and Decorator.

One Saturday afternoon in 1970, my niece had come to help me with preparations for Gary's fourth birthday party and I was baking pastries, when there was a knock at the door. A couple stood there, who told me that their 15yr old niece, a girl Stephen was friendly with, had run away from home and they thought he had gone with her. I just couldn't believe this and told her he wouldn't do anything without telling us first. He had never been out of town before and wouldn't know where to go. This lady told me that her niece was used to travelling the country and had been in trouble many times before. She was living with her aunt and uncle as a last resort. If she misbehaved again, she would get a custodial sentence.

When Joe came home, he was very angry. We both hoped that Stephen would walk in at teatime and prove them wrong, but this didn't happen. We still had to have the birthday party because we didn't want the other children to know how worried we were — but my usually mouth-watering pastries were like rocks. It was a good job that there were lots of other goodies for the little ones to eat. Later that evening a police detective came to see us. He had been looking at the drawings done by both the youngsters and said that to his mind they were drug induced. This was a great shock to Joe and me. The detective told us that up to now, there wasn't a drug problem in Hull. He said all we could do was to wait for Stephen to contact us.

I asked him what trouble Stephen would be in if they had been sleeping together and was told that because of what was known about the girl, no action would be taken on that score. I just couldn't take all this in. The following Wednesday, we had a phone call from Stephen, he was very upset and told us that his friend had accepted a lift from a lorry driver who would not take him. He had no idea where he was. Joe told him to find a police station and wait there. Joe rang our station and was told to take the money for Stephen's train fare to them, after which Stephen was put on the next train home. He had had a big shock and after a good telling off, a hot bath and a good meal, he told us he would never go off like that again. An officer from the *Drug Squad* came to see us and told Stephen and Michael the risks of all the different drugs. We were really upset that Stephen had been experimenting with them and Joe was devastated. He couldn't help blaming himself, thinking that Stephen was rebelling against him because he wasn't his birth father.

We spoke to teachers at the school and our doctors about this. It made us feel a little better to be told that 'drug culture' affected people from all walks of life. We were told that young people don't think of other peoples reactions, the only reason they take drugs is to get 'kicks'. They never think of what it may do to people around them.

I rang Stephen's manager at Brough and told him what had happened. He was very nice and said he was pleased with Stephens work and he could start back the next day. Only a short time after that, however, he disappeared again. This time he was brought back home a few days later, wrapped in plastic bags. He had been sleeping in a wooded area on our estate near the 'Green Hill'. Unfortunately, this time he had lost his job.

This started a pattern of Stephen staying away for days and being brought back. I had been so worried about all this that I had had to take time off work and thought it better that I stayed at home, so I gave my notice in at the hospital. That was the end of my nursing career.

In 1971, when the boys were 16yrs old, Joe's sister Grace and brother in law, (also Joe) came to stay with us for a few days. That evening the boys went out as usual, after being told not to knock at the door later than 11.00PM, because they wouldn't be allowed in. It was important that Grace and Joe were not disturbed. With the children all settled in bed we had a very enjoyable evening and went to bed happily. We were awakened about 1.00AM by shouting and a loud knocking at the door. It was Michael. Stephen had bullied him into knocking us up because he didn't want to get into trouble himself. He had even punched

Michael to 'persuade' him to take the flak. The noise woke our guests and we all ended up downstairs. Grace was terrified and made her Joe promise to take her home as soon as possible.

After sending Michael to bed, Joe was furious and told me that Stephen had just gone too far this time and couldn't live with us any longer. When he eventually came home, (after spending the rest of the night at the top of the flats) I had to tell Stephen that he would have to find somewhere else to live if he wanted to keep on with his present lifestyle. This hurt me more than anything I had ever done, but I knew the situation couldn't go on. When Stephen had been drawing one day, a month or so earlier, Gary had been playing with his cars on the floor and came a bit too close to Stephen, who had put out his foot to push the little one out of his way. Of course, he was told off for this at the time, but we worried about what he would have done if we hadn't been in the room.

Stephen came to see us now and again. I was pleased to see him because I didn't want to lose contact with him altogether. He was my son and although I hated the things he had done, I still loved him very much. Once when he came, he told us that he was going to be taken to court for selling drugs. Joe didn't go with him this time however, because he said he couldn't condone this behaviour. Stephen was sent to a detention centre in Lincolnshire for six months. He promised us later that he never wanted to repeat that experience and we hoped it would have changed his outlook on life. I'm pleased to say that he has always kept his promise.

Things settled down again, and with a friend looking after the children after school, I was able to take another part time job, this time in a *Plumber's* office on Newland Avenue. I enjoyed the work, being responsible for all the various clerical duties that had to be done. This was the kind of challenge I liked, doing the same thing all day long had never appealed to me.

In 1973 when I was 39yrs old, I thought I was experiencing the change of life. Imagine my shock when I discovered I was pregnant, once again. We both loved children but not at my age, I would have been nearly 40 when the baby arrived. My initial reaction was fear. I didn't know whether I could go through another birth. I was working in a job that I loved and Diane was now at school. I thought I had finished with nappies and sleepless nights. I never told anyone the way I had felt though. Joe and the children were thrilled with the news. It didn't take me long to get over my panicky feelings though and we all started making plans for the new baby. This time, because of my age, I had to be booked in at *Hedon Road Hospital*. When I told Miss Richards the head teacher about my pregnancy, she said "If this baby is like your others, you'll have nothing to worry about! This made me feel proud, but I thought "you haven't seen them arguing together at home". Joe told me that we can't expect them to be on their best behaviour all the time, we must be thankful they know how to act when they're out.

Around the July time, Michael came home one day with a girl I had never seen before. She told me he was leaving home to live with her. We were all upset about this but we knew that at 18yrs, he could make his own decisions. He told us later that he had also been experimenting with drugs for as long as Stephen had. This was a complete surprise to us, because he had never shown any sign of this at home.

My sister rang one morning out of the blue and told me that Stephen was at her house, telling her he wanted to go into hospital to come off the drugs. I asked her if she would ring the surgery for him to make an appointment to see the doctor. Soon after that, Pauline the Receptionist rang me, asking if we would let Stephen come home for a while, because he couldn't be admitted to hospital without an address. Of course we agreed at once, we were happy to think that that he wanted to get his life sorted out. Whilst Stephen was on his way home, Joe prepared a good hot bath and a cooked breakfast for him. We hoped he would feel a little bit better when he had had these. After his bath, Stephen sat down to eat his meal. We had to keep encouraging him to eat though, because he just kept turning round to his Dad, crying and saying, "I'm sorry Dad".

Later in the day, Joe took Stephen to *Delapole Hospital* and stayed with him whilst he was assessed by the Psychiatrist, who asked him, among other questions "What do you think about the fact that you are in danger of killing yourself". Stephen replied that it would just be another experience. Joe was very upset by this answer and said, "It'll be your last experience. You mustn't think like that". When he came out of hospital we let him stay at home, to hopefully give him a new start. It didn't last long however, I think maybe he had grown used to living away from home and he left a couple of weeks later. Michael's girlfriend didn't stay with him for very long either. We found out that he was still experimenting with drugs.

I left work in the September. My boss tried to persuade me to go back after, saying I could take the baby with me. But of course, I wouldn't hear of it. Every time I went for a check up at Hedon Road, I was kept in for a few days due to high blood pressure. The last time I went, they decided to keep me in until my delivery date.

The baby had been due around Christmas but the 'powers that be' in Hedon Road, decided that the wards had to be empty by then and they started a programme of inductions. Our baby, whom we called David, after our first-born and George, which was my Dad's name, was born in the early hours of 16th December 1973. In those days the delivery room was out of bounds to anyone except the staff but just when I was so tired I wanted to give up, a familiar figure poked her head round the door and came to my side, encouraging me. It was my friend Ann, the midwife who had delivered Gary David. I was so pleased to see her that she seemed to give me a new 'spurt of energy' and it wasn't long before David made his appearance.

He had so much fat round his face that his eyes seemed to be all puffed up. When the family saw him, they were delighted and we all said he would be like the beer that Joe used to brew – it always improved with age, they were right. After a couple of weeks the swellings had gone down and David was a lovely baby with blonde hair and blue eyes, but the image of his Dad. When he knew the birth was imminent, Joe had let the children stay up. The nurse had promised to ring him when the baby arrived. They spent their time the following evening, making banners, saying things like 'Welcome little Stranger, It's a Boy, and Well Done Mum' etc. in coloured bubble writing. These were hung round the room when we arrived home the next day (David still has these mementos).

Joe had told the children that they could go with him that afternoon to pick us up, so it was a lovely surprise for them when they came home at dinner time and found us already there. Diane told us that when she had asked for the afternoon off, her teacher had given her a cuddle and told the class how wonderful it was to bring a new life into the world. Once again, we had lots of visitors, all welcoming the new arrival. I felt really fit and better than I had done in ages.

Caroline was a great help to me. I used to take her with me for support when I went shopping after school. I used to buy my groceries for the week so that I didn't have to go every day, always writing a list before hand so we could both learn where things were, to make it easier. By the time she was about twelve,

Caroline would help me collect the groceries and we would get home faster. I was always on edge when I had to go anywhere and my mouth would be so dry that I would never be able to speak on the outward journey. Although she enjoyed going out with me, she couldn't understand why I couldn't join in with her excited chatter, and once she told me she might as well be going out with the dog (We've laughed about this on several occasions over the years). On the days when my nerves let me down, I would go as far as I could, maybe up to Isledane, before fear wouldn't let my legs move any further and Caroline would take the list and the trolley from me and do the shopping by herself. When she returned we would go home together, this time both of us would be chatting away, (it is strange, but always on any return journey I would feel so good that I could have stayed outside for hours) but I would breathe a sigh of relief that another 'ordeal' was over and I wouldn't get into trouble for not doing the shopping. It worried me, however, about how Caroline would feel, having all that responsibility, but she told me it made her feel grown up. As well as the trauma of the journey, I couldn't bear the thought of being 'trapped' in the shops when there were queues of other customers.

All this time, Lassie had been acting a bit strange. She wasn't eating much or wanting to go out. She would just lie down, disinterested in everything and everyone. I feel really ashamed of it now, but I grew rather impatient with her, thinking that she was just being lazy, and trying to move her out of my way. We soon realized that something was radically wrong with her and called in the Vet. He said that Lassie had contracted a disease in her womb and would have to have a hysterectomy straight away, although he did not hold out much hope for her because the infection had spread through her blood. Joe put a cover in the back of his car and followed the vet to his surgery. We had to wait until the next day before there was any news of how she was. We were told that she hadn't regained consciousness after the operation.

We were all devastated by this news. She had been one of the family, she was only seven years old. None of us ever wanted to own another dog. Evidently Lassie must have picked up the infection from another dog at some time. The Vet said that this was an unfortunate liability with pedigree dogs.

Caroline always enjoyed being out, playing on the field at the bottom of Feldane or going for walks with her friend Julie and others whenever she could, she still loved playing football At school she was good at her lessons and liked playing Rounders as well as other sports, whereas Diane loved dolls and dressing up. It was nothing to see her run upstairs four or five times in the day and come down with different clothes on. She loved experimenting with make up and hairdressing, so we decided to buy her a Girls World doll whose face could be made up and whose hair could be styled.

Christmas time was a bit of a trial for us, due to the fact that we had to hide the toys in all different places to keep them away from prying eyes. This particular year, I thought I had searched everywhere when we came to wrapping them on Christmas Eve, but it was on 6th January that I found a carrier bag under my bed, which turned out to contain Diane's Girls World. I have never lived that down. Diane always says that she believed in Father Christmas until one year when she was about eleven, she heard me trying to get a doll's pram down the stairs, bumping it down each one.

Gary was quieter than the girls; he liked playing with Action Man toys and each year we added more of the men and their equipment; including the tank, the helicopter and the climbing frame. His interest vanished though when David bit the fingers off them all and they could no longer grip onto the ropes. Gary also loved anything to do with Nature and Science so we bought him books on these subjects and a microscope with which he investigated life in the garden and in the water butt. He also had an interest in making model planes, which he hung from the ceiling in his bedroom. As well as being in the under 11s football team, Gary enjoyed taking part in plays, learning the violin and being in the school choir. Because he loved school and learning, we had no trouble getting him to do his homework, after which, and on the weekends, he would go out on his bicycle with his friends.

One day, my Aunt Jean rang to tell me that Mam had had a stroke. I told her that I wasn't bothered. I hadn't seen her for many years, since I first moved to Stanley Street. As I sat on the settee with Joe that night, he picked up on my feelings and told me to phone her. He reminded me that whatever has happened, she was still my mother. When Jess answered the telephone I told him how, at first I thought I didn't care, but I knew that really I did. Jess said that whatever a person does in this life, they will have to answer for it themselves. I went round to see Mam and from then we became closer than we had been all our lives.

David was just one year old when I found I was pregnant again. I was devastated, although after the initial shock of it, Joe was once again pleased. He loved children, as did I, but all I could imagine was history repeating itself, giving us three babies in just over three years. This thought wouldn't go away and was making me feel really ill again, mentally as well as physically. I told Joe that I couldn't go through with it and although he was angry with me, that didn't make me change my mind. When a psychiatrist (who was needed to give his opinion on my mental health) visited me, Joe stayed in the garden. The doctor told me that it was most important for me to be able to look after the children I already had, so he authorised the termination. It was to be a hysterotomy (as in a caesarean) and sterilization, which, I was told, would cut down the risk of infection. This was carried out at the *Princess Royal Hospital* on Salthouse Road in Hull. It was the first time I had been in hospital for an operation since I had had my tonsils out. All kinds of fears came into my mind. What if I didn't go off to sleep properly? What if I didn't wake up? I was taken into a ward full of expectant mothers who were experiencing difficulties and I felt really bad about the reason I was in. The nursing staff were very kind to me and even though I had told the patients the reason for my operation as well, no one showed any ill feeling towards me. The night before, I said my prayers, asking for the doctors to find no complications and when I woke in the night, afterwards; I thought, now that the surgeons had done their work, it was up to me to get myself moving again. Joe brought the children to see me during the 11 days I was in, but in those days, they couldn't come into the ward and had to look through the window. It felt very strange, to see them so near and not be able to give them a cuddle. Later, when it was time for me to be discharged, David wouldn't even look at me on the way home. It made me feel sad but I realized that he couldn't understand why I had left him. It didn't take long, however, before he forgave me in his own way, and things returned to normal. I felt very relieved that my childbearing days were over though.

    Joe had never liked housework. He was of the 'old school' who classed it as 'women's work'. He used to say that he was the breadwinner, not the housewife. Years earlier, whilst I was in bed after giving birth to Diane, a day trip from Ramp had been organised for the children and their parents. Joe had volunteered to organise the food so, because I couldn't go downstairs and do it, everything (including a couple of helpers) was brought into my bedroom, so I could still do my share. Another time he brought a bowl of water and a bag of potatoes up for me to peel for the tea. I used to tell him he was born 100 years too late. He should have been alive when I would have had to call him Mr Shepherd! We have both had many a good laugh around this idea. This time, however, he boasted that all the work had been done and he even said that the housekeeping money had lasted the whole week, saying that he didn't know why mine usually ran out the day before payday.

Coming home I soon got to the bottom of these boasts – Joe said he didn't know that the rent, insurance and other payments had to come out of this money so they hadn't been paid. I don't know where he thought it came from though. Showing me round the immaculate downstairs, I was really impressed until I went into the bedrooms and as well as unmade beds; I found a gigantic pile of clothes that needed to be ironed. "Oh yes" he said – "but I don't like ironing". Whilst I was in hospital, he had told me that the washing machine had leaked all over the kitchen floor and it had taken him ages to mop up the water before calling the plumber. I couldn't help laughing until my stomach ached. I just thought 'welcome to a woman's world Joe.' I found out later that Shirley, the wife of Joe's friend Stan had been round helping him and that she had also helped with the shopping. They had all gone to Stan's house for tea sometimes also.

To help me recover from my operation, Joe arranged for Caroline, Gary and Diane to spend two weeks at his sister Anne's house in York and he took them there. I enjoyed the evening, having less to do and being able to relax earlier than usual. The next day, however, I just kept wandering into the tidy rooms, looking at the made up beds and thinking that it didn't seem right. In the end, Joe told me that he had taken them to give me a break, but if I was just going to miss them every minute, he would bring them straight home. I decided that I would just relax and enjoy some quality time with David and Joe whilst I could.

The children liked going to York; Caroline and Gary and Diane went together once again later. Diane, who had made friends with her cousins, also went a few times by herself. Now and again, I would go with Joe to Ramp, sometimes with family and other times with friends. I always became nervous when it came near to closing time though. I didn't like being near people who had had too much to drink and might start fighting. What I enjoyed most of all though, was when Joe brought me two small *Pony's* (a British sherry) and a *Babycham*; together they were my favourite drink. I had never liked the taste of beer. When the children were all safely in bed, we would relax together and laugh all evening. It reminded me of our courting days and I would fall in love with him all over again.

We always gave the children birthday parties, Diane and David on their own and Gary and Caroline together as their birthdays were only three weeks apart. Their party was held exactly between the two dates. On all the occasions, they were allowed to invite two friends each (I thought 12 children were enough to cope with). Joe had made a mini 'stage' which lived in the back of the shed when it wasn't in use. As well as the usual games, everyone was invited to take a turn doing their party piece, and the one who was the best would get a little prize – then, so that no one felt left out, a smaller prize was given to everyone who entered. There were usually the same people there every time so it was good to be able to see the way the children blossomed as time went on.

I used to fancy myself as a wonderful cake decorator. The only thing was, the finished article never ever turned out as I had hoped it would. This didn't deter me though, and I would try different style cakes every time. The unveiling was always the same, whether it was a Christmas or a birthday cake. When everyone was gathered round, I would walk in with my 'offering' (which had been hidden from sight before) and theatrically take of the covering. After the first time I had done this, when everyone didn't know how to act to save my feelings, I made the whole ceremony into a huge joke. We all looked forward to this unveiling and it caused real merriment all round. On Diane's seventh birthday, I attempted an Apple House Cake. Slices of apple made the tiles on the roof and marsh mallows formed the windows. It wasn't too bad though, but it didn't hold its shape for long. My brother came and took photographs of that party so we do still have a record of my 'masterpiece'.

I used to enjoy going across to the school helping to sort the items for a jumble sale or other event when they were raising funds. On Sports Days I would help on the refreshment stall. I had felt very safe going to the school since Miss Richards had taken me down the path to see Caroline in her class. A few years later I sat with children who needed a bit more practice with their reading. The only time of year I was a bit uncomfortable with was the summer. Joe always bought a cheap old banger car, saying that if it lasted us through the year we would have had our money's worth out of it. I knew he would always want us to take the children out for days, which was only natural, but the thought of being out all day terrified me but I would 'make' myself go most of the time. As the time came nearer, I would go into cold sweats at the thought of being away from home, I wouldn't be able to sleep either. I did not let Joe know how I felt though, because he didn't understand and would get angry with me. There was one time I remember vividly. I was having a few bad days but I had made the food and prepared everything we needed, determined to conquer my feelings. When I sat in the car I just froze, and all the old feelings washed over me again. I just wanted to run up to bed and pull the covers over my head. I really panicked, telling Joe I couldn't go. He told me to take David and stay at home. The rest of the day was really dreadful, I cried with guilt and sadness because I hadn't been brave enough to go with them and join in their fun and trembled with fear at the thought of the 'telling off' I would get when Joe and the children came home. He still couldn't understand the illness, he thought any kind of illness was weakness and that it was not to be given in to. When they arrived home though I didn't get the reception I expected although the atmosphere was a little frosty at first. Caroline handed me a white heart shaped stone that they had found on the beach. On one side was written 'heart of stone' (I wondered if that was the way Joe felt about me) and on the other side it said 'we love you, to mummy – Gary, Diane and Caroline'. I treasure that stone very much and I wouldn't part with it for the world. The three older children were doing well at junior school by now and they all achieved high marks in their academic work and loved all sports.

I had been bugging Joe to give me driving lessons for ages, thinking I would feel better if I was in charge of my journeys, and after being taught how to 'drive a chair' and answer questions from the Highway Code, he took me to a quiet lane a couple of times and let me practice driving. I really enjoyed this and thought that if I passed my test I would be able to go to lots of places on my own. It would be the answer to my problems. Although Joe was pleased with my progress, the lessons only lasted a short time however because there was soon to be another dramatic event for us to cope with.

Joe had been given a sort of promotion at work. As an experiment, his boss, Mr Knights had formed about eight of the 'wiremen' into 'two man gangs" who had been trained to fit phones into peoples' houses, as well as wiring them up from the telegraph poles. This saved a lot of time, for the customer as well as the men, because installing telephones before that, entailed visits from two different departments. This experiment was a great success and as far as I know, it still works today.

One day, at the end of 1975, Joe started having trouble with his eyes. He couldn't see anything clearly. Working in and out of the traffic, he had to be alert to many dangers, so it must have been very scary not to be able to see properly. By the evening he couldn't even see the numbers on the buses and had developed double vision. He even needed to hold on to his partner's shoulder to cross the road.

Going to see the optician the next day, he was told he would have to see the doctor. He then, referred Joe to a specialist, who, in turn, diagnosed cataracts in both eyes. This man explained to Joe that there were two types of cataracts. One came on slowly and was age related and the other was usually the result of an earlier accident to the eyes or it was stress related. The specialist said he didn't like to see anyone as young as Joe (he was only 47 yrs) having this condition and he was given a date for his first operation the following June.

Over the next couple of months Joe's sight deteriorated rapidly. He told me it was like looking at things through a white curtain. All he could make out were splodges of colours, not even proper shapes. It really upset him that he couldn't see our faces clearly anymore. He also said it was like seeing everybody gradually disappearing in front of him. I had to be with him all the time, It scared him to be by himself.

By the January I couldn't bear to see him like this any longer, so I wrote to his specialist explaining how things were and how upset we all were because of his suffering. The result of this was that his appointment was put forward to the beginning of March, which made it a bit better.

The time came for the operation on the first one of Joe's eyes, and we were all on edge. Joe had never been in hospital before and didn't know what to expect. I could tell he was rather anxious about the whole experience. The three older children and I spoke together about what we could do to help their Dad. They had taken RE at school and I told them about my knowledge and belief that if two or three people were gathered together in Jesus' name, He would be with them, answering their prayers, so we all decided that we would ask for His help. We sat quietly on the stairs and said a prayer. This made us feel better and we were certain that their Dad would be all right. I busied myself in the house whilst Joe was away. My Aunt Jean had given me a carpet, big enough for the dinette and the stairs so I cut it to size and fitted it, it was the first time we had ever had a carpet that covered the whole room, not just in the middle.

Stephen had moved back home to make sure we were all OK whilst Joe was away and had painted the stairs and landing the day before; so it would all look nice and fresh for when Joe came home. Through work he had joined *The Health Scheme* (although that wasn't its name at that time), which meant he would get a certain amount of money for each night he was in hospital. He was so pleased with the way the dinette and the stairs looked that he spent the extra money on a fitted carpet for the living room. It was supposed to be red but when it was down it looked more like a bright orange colour and every time I vacuumed it, it rucked up in the middle. I used to walk through the rooms feeling really 'posh' to have carpet everywhere. There had even been enough left over to fit the hall and the bathroom.

The operation was a success and Joe was discharged from the hospital with a list of what he could and couldn't do. This included keeping away from smoky atmospheres and not to look down etc (I thought, at least it would keep him away from Ramp for a while, although he couldn't stop smoking). He was given spectacles with a really thick lens to compensate for the one that had been removed. Now that the hospital visits were over, life settled down again and although it seemed to be difficult for him to get used to the heaviness of the glasses, which gave him stress headaches, he was very pleased to have some sight back.

Joe always made sure that there were lots of things going on at home for the children. He would say "Let them bring their friends here, so we can see that they are alright". He believed in the saying 'Out of sight, out of mind'.

For Christmas that year, we had bought David a drum kit, Gary a guitar, and Caroline a small electric organ. With Diane singing on the microphone they had a field day entertaining us and anyone else who came in. We were talking about holidays one day, and the fact that we had never had one, when Joe decided that we should be able to afford a week in a chalet bungalow if we went after the season in September. Looking through the *Hull Daily Mail*, we found one in Skipsea, which sounded ideal. This brought on the same reaction in me as usual, but I knew I couldn't disappoint the children – or even show the slightest hint to Joe of how I was feeling. Whenever I knew that I had to face something that terrified me, I wasn't able to sleep. I would lie in bed and often the same thing would happen. I would get the feeling that my head had swollen as big as the pillow and my mouth was really tiny. I remembered to ask God for help and I would say the 23rd Psalm (The Lord is My Shepherd) in frantic desperation. It was amazing how this would work, by the time I reached the end, my fears would have gone and I would fall to sleep. Every time this happened though, I was always a little worried whether it would work again. Now, I even felt confident enough to make the journey.

I knew Skipsea wasn't far away and that it was only a small place, so I would soon be safe inside again. As we were going to 'live' there for a week, it seemed as safe as home to me and I would still have a nearby base to come back to when we went out. Joe's sister (Auntie Ann) had come to stay with us for a while, so we took her, as well as Caroline's friend Trisha. The chalet looked really nice and it had a narrow glass roofed extension at one side. Caroline and Trisha chose to sleep in there. What we didn't know, however, was that the glass roof leaked and when it rained in the night, the girls got drenched. We had to squeeze up to get everyone into the chalet. The weather was quite nice for the first few days and the children enjoyed playing on the beach, which was only down a few steps, a few yards from the front door. David had never seen sand before and he was delighted with it. Joe made the sand into the shape of a car and David would have sat in it for hours if he could have. I would make sandwiches so we didn't even have to go back for dinner. I felt really safe and happy there.

We did have one catastrophe though. Caroline was playing at jumping off the breakwaters when her toenail was pierced by a piece of wood. I even felt brave enough to take her to *Bridlington Hospital*. Luckily there was a stop just across the road, for the bus which also stopped outside the hospital. It didn't take them long to take the splinter out and as well as praising Caroline for being so brave, I felt really proud of myself for taking her on my own.

The weather changed. It was freezing cold in the chalet, we bought coal from the camp shop and Auntie Ann made it her task to find driftwood and fallen branches every day so that we could have a fire. The steps down to the beach were taken away and notices were put up warning everyone to stay off the sands. We used to watch the waves splashing high onto the roadway in front of the chalet. The amusements were still open though, so we would take the children there and pass the rest of the time playing all sorts of indoor games. Joe was really good at making up different things to do. That holiday is still talked about today; it causes laughter when we remember it though we decided that we would never go away at the end of the season again.

David had always loved cars and would sit in a big box pretending to drive it. Joe even drew a dashboard and made gear sticks and a steering wheel to make it seem more real. One day Joe came home with an old tin Ford type car he had rescued from the Hessle tip. He painted it up and the bairn just loved it. It didn't last long however, because its edges were sharp and we thought it was dangerous. We then bought David a red pedal car with big eyes painted on the front (It was called the 'funny-eyes' car), and he would ride up and down our back garden path for ages. When he was too big for this, Joe found an old bus steering wheel to which he attached half a broom handle. David just loved this, especially when someone gave him a bus driver's hat. He even had a roll of tickets to hand out to us as we sat on chairs, which acted as bus seats behind the driver. He also loved playing with hats and when one of Joe's friends brought him a white hard hat, he was in his element.

Gary had always liked to help younger children and when he was 11yrs old he saw an invitation for people to join the *Police Force*, which he cut out and sent in. We were surprised when he received a letter from the Chief Constable thanking him for his interest and inviting him to apply again when he was older. He still has that letter.

Joe had a really good imagination. He loved making up stories for the children and roping everyone in to act out some play or other. Every Christmas, he would organise all of us, getting us to learn the lines for different characters, to put on the play, A *Christmas Carol*. He even made us masks out of lino. After the first few years, instead of looking forward to this, we would groan inwardly. It was always the same play. Joe used to say that Christmas wouldn't be Christmas without Scrooge and the Ghosts.

When David was three and a half, the nursery school at Dane Park was finished and he was one of the first children to go. I used to think that he looked too big for the nursery, because like the rest of the family, he was tall for his age. When later he started the junior school though, my opinion was changed completely. I stood watching him walk down the path, thinking, he's too small to be going to 'big' school.   David had inherited Joe's artistic talent and when he was only four years old he copied a picture of 'The Perishers' almost perfectly. We were all very proud of him. David also liked watching snooker on the television, and said he would like to learn to play. We bought him a small snooker table for Christmas and were fascinated at the way he could pot the balls every time. David liked dressing up so Michael gave him a waistcoat, which I took in to fit and we bought him a striped shirt and a bow tie to complete the outfit. He would let his Dad grease back his hair so he looked more grown up.

In the middle of the following year, Joe's second operation was carried out and after he had recuperated, he went back to work, relieved that he didn't have to go back to the hospital anymore. This time he was told that because of lack of insurance cover, he couldn't work outside, so he was given a job cleaning the stores with a long handled brush and shovel. He hated doing this and when, after a short time, he was offered the opportunity to leave work due to ill health. We talked it over and decided that he should. We were both happy to be in this situation. There would be a lump sum of three thousand pounds and a pension, which would be augmented by *Invalidity Benefit* after a six-month period on sick pay, so we wouldn't be any worse off financially.

In March 1978 at the age of only 50yrs Joe left 'Telephones' for the last time. I didn't realize then, but this was to start the absolute worse period of my life.

CHAPTER SEVEN

A Dramatic Change

THE 'LUMP SUM' CHEQUE WAS DELIVERED and Joe went to the bank to withdraw it – taking it all. He laid all the bundles out on our bed and we all sat looking at this money. It was more than we had ever seen in our lives. After a family conference about what to spend it on, it was decided the first thing we would do was to buy a full new set of clothes for each of us and then spend two weeks at *Butlins Holiday Camp* in Filey, so I booked for all of us, including Stephen and Michael to go in the beginning of June.

The day we were going into town for the clothes I had a really severe panic attack. After a sleepless night and an 'I can do it/I daren't do it' time, which I kept to myself, I told Joe that I had a bad stomach and couldn't go. This was true in a way. After many trips to the toilet the pains in my stomach were really bad. I knew it was nerves that were causing this, but I didn't have the courage to go out with this happening. Joe was furious and went off with the children. I was beside myself, pacing up and down, telling myself off for being so weak, but not daring to go after them. Luckily Stephen happened to come just then and I told him. He was great and told me he would take me if I wanted to go. Telling myself that the feeling and pain would go off as soon as I started out, we went to catch the bus — and I DID feel better! Luckily we caught up with Joe and although he didn't talk to me at first, he was pleased that I had made the effort. As I walked the panics came thick and fast at first, but remembering Dr Weeks saying "let the feelings wash over you and see them subside", I did that and even though they came again a couple of times more, they became weaker each time until they stopped altogether. When we got home with all our shopping I realized that I didn't get shoes and Joe very nicely offered to go back himself to get me some!

Over the past years, I had found it difficult to manage the bills and I fell into the trap of getting credit and loans. I used to cash in the insurance policies every couple of years to help me to pay the debts off, but I always shared the money with Joe. The weekly food shopping and the rent was always my first priority however, so the payments to the creditors would be erratic to say the least. This meant renewing the loans to make them up. I used to get nasty letters from the creditors and was even issued with court summonses. At least then, I was able to pay the debt at a reduced amount each week. This situation worried me greatly, but there was nothing I could do about it at that time. Joe wouldn't let me go to work, saying that my priority was to stay and look after him.

Joe was not interested in the money side of running the house. He used to hand his wages to me; taking back some for pocket money, and the rest was to be used for housekeeping, which he always said was my responsibility. Now and again, however, when he could see that something was getting me down and he would get me to tell him how I was (or was not) managing. This always led to a big row, ending with Joe helping me to sort things out, and with me promising to talk things over before I bought anything else. He said I had to ask myself three things... "Do we need it? Can we afford it? Is it worth it?"

With some of his retirement money, he paid all the overdue installments on the debts and that took the worry away from me again for a while. If anything needed replacing and I asked him if I could buy it, he would say "What's the matter with the one we have already? I'll mend it". I changed my approach, and instead I would ask him to have a look at whatever it was, for me. I knew that he would take the thing apart and not be able to put it together again, so I had achieved my goal because he would then tell me it was beyond repair and I would have to get another one.

If Joe decided that he wanted to buy something for the house, he would look in the catalogue and ask me if we could afford the payments. If I said we could not, there would again be a big row, with him accusing me of getting hidden debts that he didn't know about. He even threatened to take over the housekeeping – but he never did. I used to absolutely dread these confrontations. In the end I just went along with what he wanted and tried to juggle a bit better. I got to such a stage that I wished I could go to sleep on a Thursday night, pay day, and wake up on a Saturday morning when all the 'callers' had been, so I could still have a bit of money left in my purse.

One of the hundreds of happier memories I have was when one day, Michael took David to see ET and he was so taken up with it that Joe decided he would make him one. He drew a pattern and cut it out of some orange felt and I stitched it together. It really did look life like and David still has it now. This gave me the idea to make other soft toys, which I could sell to help the finances. I started buying the patterns and the material, and became really good at it. There were *Teddy Bears, Pandas,* and *Dogs with bones in their mouths, Early Birds, Robins, Kitten nightdress cases,* as well as three feet tall *Bugs Bunnies* and *Sylvesters* along with oversized *Tweety Pies.* Joe always made the eyes for the toys; giving them *Disney*-like expressions.

One day some little girls came to the door asking if we would take in this blue Persian cat, whom its owner no longer wanted. Of course we did, and a couple of weeks later we discovered that 'Mitzie' (the name we had given the cat), was pregnant — maybe this is why she wasn't wanted. We didn't mind though. We loved her already. We asked Auntie Ann if she would like to come to *house and cat sit* for a couple of weeks whilst we all went to Butlins and she readily agreed.

The day of our departure arrived; the mini bus turned up and we set off (with everything but the kitchen sink). Again I was extremely nervous but, of course, I could not show it — everyone was excitedly chatting so no one noticed. Once we had booked in and had found our chalet, I felt better and busied myself with getting everyone allocated to their various beds and stocking the kitchen. After I had been down to the different attractions I felt more comfortable and was able to move about the camp easily.

Joe and the twins found the pub and settled themselves there. That turned out to be our meeting place to decide what we were going to do each day. The men took the three elder children and always went before David and me, I would tidy up and make sandwiches for our dinner and prepare a hot meal for the teatime. I was pleased that I could stay back till midday because getting up in the morning was the worst time for me. I always felt stressed. Later in the day, however, I would feel better.

There was one club, *The Beachcomber,* where a Hawaiian theme was carried right round the room. A river ran through the centre, over which a wicker bridge carried everyone across to the bar. At one side, a three dimensional set, depicted a scene which changed, from a lovely beach view with palm trees and birds singing, through to absolute silence, followed by a darkening sky and a thunderstorm with rain falling into a sort of pond in the centre front. After this came the erupting of an enormous papier-mâché volcano — before going back to the peaceful scene again.

We all enjoyed that and went there on about three or four evenings. During our stay we also watched the children dancing and visited the cinema along with other activities. Crossing the site was a chair lift leading to a *Big Wheel* right on the cliff edge. Stephen and Michael tried this out and sometimes took the elder children with them. Joe had taken them shopping by himself one day and came back with a present for me. It was a thin metal bracelet with a piece of heart shaped metal on the front. Engraved on it were the words "Joe loves Margery". I was pleased — even though my name had been spelt wrong. These words were from a man who would never tell me he loved me. He used to say that when he met me the second time, he just felt sorry for me. Looking into the bag of presents later however, I found a thick identity bracelet — which made mine look very cheap and nasty — which he told me was for his friend Joe. I felt very hurt, angry and jealous over this, but he had had a drink and I didn't want to cause a row, so I never told him.

Joe had never made a secret of the fact that he hated women — often me as well, when he was drunk. Now, it seemed to me that here was the proof of how far down I was in his estimation, yet to this day, I still treasure that bracelet and I wouldn't be without it for the world.

After the first week, Joe and I decided that two weeks away from home was really too long. David, who had been a bit 'wowwy' for a couple of days, suddenly developed Chickenpox, and before I could offer to take him home, Joe said that he would take him. Ordering a taxi and leaving us with some money, he was away. I must admit that, although I didn't like the fact that Joe wasn't with us, I was rather relieved that because Caroline, Gary and Diane were older, I would be able to relax. When I didn't feel like going out, Stephen and Michael went places with them. We spoke to Joe and David every night and as our money had run out after a few days, we all wanted to go home. We were relieved when we found out that the Minibus driver could come for us a day early.

Arriving home, it was good to see that David was almost well and that Mitzie had had her kittens. When she recovered from this Joe took her to the vet and had her spayed. A little while later she went out at night and didn't come back. I worried that a gang who were operating at that time had stolen her, but maybe the most likely explanation was that the girls who had brought her to us, had taken her back.

David started 'big school' and really enjoyed it. In his first year, someone from the *Lapidary Society* went to talk to the children at Dane Park and other schools. They set them a competition to see who could draw the best picture of the precious stones to be found on the seashore and in the caves. David was one of the winners and we were invited to go to the *Guildhall* to see the children collect their prizes, we were able to see the pictures of all the entrants and there was also a buffet set out for us. I had never been inside the *Guildhall Public Rooms* before and it was lovely to see how ornate everything was. It was a really proud day for us and all the other parents.

Although Caroline had enjoyed her time at Dane Park Primary and Junior Schools she didn't settle down at Newland High at all. We had asked for her to go to Sir Henry Cooper, which was a new school in Thorpe Park Road, where most of her friends were going, but for some reason this request was denied.

A Dramatic Change

She didn't make as much progress academically as we would have liked, but she still enjoyed sports, especially throwing the Javelin and Table Tennis, but football was still her first choice. All the children except David had been in the Choir at *St Michaels* on Orchard Park Road for quite a while. They all looked very angelic in their uniforms and had started attending weddings and other celebrations and they were very proud of being paid for their attendance.

Diane enjoyed playing *Hockey*, *Netball* and *Racing* and was very good at *Gymnastics*. Joe had taken the girls to a church hall on 37th Avenue, to learn *Tap* and *Ballet Dancing*, the year before, but it was not Caroline's thing and she stopped going. Along with her friend Julie, the girls also joined the *St John Ambulance Brigade* as I had done, and they enjoyed meeting with other divisions in Doncaster for a special parade. That didn't last too long for Caroline though because didn't like wearing the *old style* uniform, which she had been given. When a team of Irish Dancers was formed at Dane Park, Diane joined and did well. The team each won a medal and danced at the *City Hall*, *Holy Name Church* and *Catherine Ellis Retirement Home* on Ellerburn Avenue opposite the Shopping Centre.

Joe discussed what he could turn his hand to next, with his friend Joe from Ramp. They both came up with the idea that we could buy a van and they would start a round selling *Fresh Fruit & Vegetables* door to door. They did all the preliminary work necessary, including testing the market and trying to find the best supplier to meet their demands. I suggested voluntarily registering for VAT even though we wouldn't earn enough, because we would be able to claim back the tax on the van and other fixtures and fittings that would be needed. Of course, I offered to do the job of bookkeeper and was immediately taken on. Caroline used to help me with these, she was very good with figures also.

In July 1978 the van was bought, and 'Shep and Joe's Mobile Shop – Fresh Fruit and Veg delivered daily to your door' was printed on the sides. Flyers were printed and taken out round the Danes and the Thorpes, which were to be the areas covered. The two Joe's used the lounge of the pub as their office so that they could cash up each day whilst quenching their thirsts. Around September, they decided that there wasn't enough money in the business to keep two families, even though they did three rounds per day, so by mutual consent, we carried on on our own and I went out with Joe every day. It was a great feeling; talking to the customers and hearing them say how fresh the goods were.

Early each morning, Michael would drive me to Humber Street to collect the fresh produce and when we came back Gary and Diane would weigh out some of the potatoes into 5lb bags and Caroline and I would wash out the van. When I had made sure everyone had had breakfast and taken David to school, we continued the rounds, with me serving the customers and delivering orders. I always felt safe in the van. I had brought a drink with me (in case my throat went dry, as it sometimes would) and I knew Joe would take me straight home if it was necessary. Caroline took over from me when I couldn't go. If there were any heavy items, Joe would carry them to the houses. To help out he also bunched up the flowers from our garden and Diane took them round to sell them (She told me a long time later that she hated it).

Towards Christmas, Joe bought stocking filler toys which people paid for weekly, but the success of the whole venture was short lived. A lorry driver's strike just before then had made things difficult for us, and when we had a heavy downfall of snow, which turned to ice, the white glare affected Joe's eyes making it impossible for him to drive anymore. He also had

A Dramatic Change

trouble carrying the four stone bags of potatoes to the houses without slipping. The children and I had a door step sell to clear our remaining stock. Our hall was turned into a shop and it wasn't long before most of it was cleared.

When it came near to the time for us to start back after Christmas and the weather had improved, we again had a family conference. The children told us they did not like me being out all the time and having someone baby sitting now and again. Caroline said it reminded her of when I had been in hospital and Stan's wife Shirley had helped to run the house, especially organising the shopping. She told us how grown up she felt when she and I were doing the shopping together or she went by herself, and she did not like someone else taking my place. Michael wasn't living at home and therefore couldn't commit to all the driving, so we agreed to call it a day, I think everyone breathed a sigh of relief. Looking back, I just seemed to be out all the time, cooking the meals and telling the children we wouldn't be long. This was the first and only year that I didn't have all the preparations for Christmas organised. I had felt like a machine, instead of a mother and I didn't like it one bit.

One thing we had arranged for Christmas however, was a five-foot snooker table, which Joe said was for all the family. David had to stand on a chair to use the cue, but he still managed to learn the game and would nearly always win the matches he played.

Someone down Isledane was selling an old piano, so Joe bought it for us. I was thrilled to have it and enjoyed playing. The children, however, didn't share my enthusiasm. This was disappointing to Joe who hoped that one of them would want to learn to play. When Dad and my stepmother Eve, came out with us, they would always come back to supper and Eve would play whilst we all sang. Sometimes when we were on our own,

Joe would ask me to sing for him and it gave me a great feeling to still be able to hit the high notes as I used to. He would say to me "You've still got it lass" and I would feel I was 'special' to him.

Now that everything was back to normal, we all settled down again. Joe sadly resigned himself to the fact that he would never be able to work again and he turned all his energies into the garden – and of course, meeting his friends at the pub, which was happening now on a more regular basis. Joe loved his garden and spent a lot of his time there. We had three small Apple trees in the side garden and a Pear and a Plum tree at the far corners of the big one. The shed at the bottom of the garden was adorned with a *Climbing Rose* (named Schoolgirl), on the right side, intermingling with *Clematis*, (Barbara Jackman) on the left.

At first I didn't like gardening, so I was given the job of weeding the beds. I became fascinated with the tiny roots and progressed from pulling out weeds to actually planting flowers as well. We also had a greenhouse in which we grew tomatoes, cucumbers and one year, even melons. As Joe was a heavy smoker and nicotine would kill the plants, I grew to enjoy the planting and pinching out of the tomatoes. He was very methodical and all his seeds and planting conformed to the information in the *Readers Digest book of Gardening*. I enjoyed working with him in the garden, but although he wanted me outside with him all the time, he *drew the line* at helping me with the housework. In the winter, he would plan out what he would grow the following year, with all the relevant times of sewing, planting, lifting etc. As well as flowers, Joe grew vegetables and one year he decided to grow potatoes. He even bought the bags, which would stand on upturned boxes to store the potatoes in the shed when they were ready, unfortunately that year, there was a drought and a hosepipe ban. When the time came to lift the crop, there were only enough potatoes to half fill an old pillowcase, instead of

A Dramatic Change

there being about 8 bags, to see us through the winter. This was a great disappointment to both of us – but we did eventually see the funny side of it and it caused a laugh as he told his friends.

Stephen moved in with his girl friend Audrey. They had met the previous year whilst he was painting a mural for her next-door neighbour. When Audrey's husband had sadly died, Stephen had supported her through her tragic time. Audrey had two children left at home, Arthur, who had left school and Hannah who was then eight years old. Caroline started taking her lunch to their house instead of eating it at school and, along with her friends Julie and Andrea; Diane sometimes went to see them after school too. Audrey was a very friendly lady and we all got on well together.

On our 20th wedding anniversary Joe and I had both decided to celebrate at home. When the children were all safely in bed, we toasted each other, laughing and talking over different events in our lives. As we talked about what we may be doing in our next 20 years, I suddenly had an awful feeling in my stomach, and I cried. Although I told Joe that it was because I was so happy, I know now that this was an *inner knowing* that we didn't have as long as that left together.

We started reminiscing about the *entertaining* period in our lives and how the experiences we had had since, had taken us away from that path. Joe asked me if I regretted not singing and asked if I would do so again given the opportunity. I told him I still loved singing and I hoped I would be able to sing again one day, perhaps in the *Old Folks Homes* or *Hospitals* or something. It was the wrong thing to say because Joe was angry with this, he said that we have had our time and that it was the youngsters chance to do their thing now. Of course, I said I was only 46 and that I certainly hadn't had my time. I had no wish to give up on my life yet, luckily his anger passed and we enjoyed the rest of our evening.

I had never seen as much of my family as I would have liked, but I used to go to my youngest sister's house every two weeks to have my hair styled. My other younger sister would sometimes come as well. Dad and Eve would alternate between visiting us and playing host to us every couple of weeks also, but Joe never went with us. I had found out years before that he didn't like visiting anyone. Once or twice at Christmas time, I took the children to family parties at my Mam's house in Earls Court. I also visited my brother, but as he was in the Merchant Navy, I didn't see him so often. On occasions when I was feeling low, Joe would tell me that all my family *looked down on me* and he would tell me that *I was* as good as they were. I knew this wasn't true because we all got on very well with each other. On other occasions I would be feeling confident and happy with myself, especially when we had company and I was talking about the different jobs I had had. Later Joe would say "Who do you think you are? trying to be better than everybody. You're nobody". I never knew how to react when he spoke like this and was always on edge in case I said the wrong thing.

Once, right out of the blue, he said to me "This isn't working". When I asked him what he meant he said "This marriage — what are you going to do about it?" I didn't think I had done anything wrong and didn't know what he wanted me to say. All our married life I had just accepted the way he was with me, because I knew how good he had been to take on my children (as his foreman had told him years before). All the old feelings of insecurity and fear washed over me. I was also scared of him telling me to leave. I couldn't bear the thought of having nowhere to live again, so I would end up saying that I would be different, and I would try harder, although I didn't know how I could. That seemed to pacify him and he would change the subject. These things always happened after he had been out drinking, when he was sober he was so nice and a very caring person.

Joe had been telling his drinking pals Jack and Bob about *The Beachcomber* at Butlins and they all decided to go again the following year, only for a week this time. They were taking their families as well, and we had decided to take Hannah, Audrey's daughter with us, so I was given the job of arranging all the bookings for the 17 people. Joe found a really big bottle and we started saving all our spare change for the children's spending money. It soon mounted up and they were all getting very excited.

The night before the holiday Hannah stayed with us, and Joe emptied all the change from the bottle onto the carpet. Everyone joined in counting and separating the coins into 35 piles; (one each for 5 children for seven days), which were then put into separate bank bags. Joe said that this way there would be no arguing or begging for more when that day's bag was empty – of course it didn't work out when the holiday started. As soon as he had had a drink he gave in, giving them more, but it was a nice thought and doing all the counting and bagging had been fun for the children.

The days fell into a pattern for the grown ups, the men and the children would go down to the centre early and get settled into the pub whilst we women tidied up, visited each others chalet and relaxed. Jack's wife Iris had brought her mother and their daughter Debbie, whilst Bob and his wife Jill were with their children Peter, Nicky, Suzanne and Kathleen. We would take sandwiches and drinks down so we could all eat together but when we women wanted to go round the shops the men didn't like that idea. They went off on their own. They sometimes took

David to the snooker hall to see how he would manage on a full sized table (standing on a chair as usual) and although it wasn't as easy for him; he still managed to win some pennies from the other players.

One day, Joe was annoyed with me for not going down to the centre in the mornings (even though he knew I didn't like the idea of just sitting in a bar), so I agreed to try the chair lift with him and David. I had never been in one before and the thought of being so high up in such a small seat didn't make me feel confident at all. When we all got in, Joe rocked the chair so much that I felt sick and vowed no one would ever get me in it again. I had learned to accept whatever Joe did but Iris and her mother complained bitterly, especially when Jill decided to go with the men instead of supporting us. We started calling the holiday `the Ramp's Outing'. We had the last laugh though, the Hawaiian show in the Oasis bar was broken, so Joe wasn't able to show Jack and Bob what he had been talking about. Iris and her mother said that would be the last time they would go on holiday with them, and I agreed with her.

The following year, I started getting a bit depressed and tired again. The housework and running the family was making me feel ill. This, as well as the strain of the *Agoraphobia* did get me down periodically. I always felt guilty at not being able to manage things like other people did. I didn't want to go back on nerve tablets though, because after years of taking *Librium* and realizing they didn't stop the panics, I had gradually weaned myself off them. I think Joe had recognized that I needed support that time, because he organized everyone to help me, giving me time to myself and I was soon able to take charge again.,

Barbara, next door, once came in when I was scrubbing the kitchen floor and said to me "I wish I could see where I'd been when I wash my floor" (because it never seemed to get dirty). I thought that if she had as many people as I had trampling in over her floor, hers would get dirty as well. She would ask me why I didn't have a routine like she had, doing different jobs on different days and saying that that would keep the house clean all the time. I told her that that wouldn't work in my house, I had to *start from scratch* with the work every morning. The things I did yesterday needed doing again today.

I did try to get the children to help me though. I even made out a roster for them, saying that these things had to be done to earn their pocket money. Once I even put prices on the various jobs, telling them to choose what they wanted to do. This didn't last too long though, because when Joe realized what I was doing, he would say to them "You're not doing her work for her. She is the housewife and it's up to her to do everything". I just felt deflated. I couldn't win!

Now and again on a Saturday morning though, Joe would say to me. "You stay in bed for a while; I'll show you how it's done". I would listen to the bustling around going on downstairs and eventually Joe would bring me up a cup of tea and say "Come and look". On going down, I would find everything sparkling. He had organised the children, not by asking them, but by telling one to clean the brasses, one to polish, one to vacuum and one to clean the kitchen etc. I told them how pleased I was with everything but I couldn't help thinking that I wouldn't have been allowed to do that!

Most days Joe would go out to the pub at 11.00AM till 3.00PM and on some occasions, again at night. At first I didn't mind this because I knew he wasn't used to being in the house all day and he told me he had to be in 'men's company'. He missed being able to have 'serious' conversations! Joe didn't like me talking about getting a part time job to get me out of the house and would say that even though he wasn't working, he was still the breadwinner. To Joe, working was something that had to be tolerated in order to live. He couldn't understand that I actually enjoyed doing the job that I was trained to do and that by forbidding me to do it, he thought he was actually being kind. The highlight of my day was when the children were at home. Joe had always insisted on them bringing their friends home when they were younger, instead of them going out. We hardly ever had tea just by ourselves, there were usually one or two extra guests.

In the winter, Joe insisted that there was always hot soup to warm them up when they came in from school and they always looked forward to that. We played games together and I would teach them songs and we would sing round the house. Joe organised a Snooker championship with the twins and anyone else who wanted to be in it as well. He would set the table up in the living room, which was the biggest room in the house, but we still had to climb over the furniture to get round it. Of course, even though I couldn't play, I joined in. The matches lasted several weeks with someone being knocked out each week. The 'playing roster' was put up on the wall so that everyone knew who was playing against whom. David would put on his snooker outfit and slick his hair back, it was always a great laugh. A lot of the times he would win the title of *Champion of the House* but once it was actually me that got it. Of course that was definitely more by good luck than good management in my case.

Our dining table only fitted 6 people so Joe bought a 5 FT piece of chipboard, which was fitted over it on special occasions and set up in the living room. On Sundays and on special holidays, it was nothing for me to cook for about 12 people and I loved doing it. Since he retired, Joe's workmates often came to see him and they always had a good laugh about everything under the sun. I enjoyed sitting in with them (as well as keeping them supplied with tea). One friend, John, who had been mates with Joe since their teenage years, came more than the others and one day was commenting on our stairs being in between the dinette and the kitchen. After the first landing, the second set of stairs 'turned round on themselves' to end up side by side with first set. They joked about this, with Joe saying that he hoped he didn't die upstairs because they would have to stand him up in his coffin and lift him over the banister. They both had a really good laugh about that (The saying that there is many a true word spoken in jest turned out to be true in this instance).

I had always had difficulty telling any of the children off. I would look at their faces and just would not be able to stop myself from laughing. Through gritted teeth I would say to them that even though I was laughing I was still very angry with them and would send them to their rooms to 'think over' what they had done. It was never long though, before they would come to me and apologize for whatever, and all would be well again.

Caroline left school and started working at *Jackson's* grocery shop on Chanterlands Avenue. She also joined the *Reckitts' Ladies Football Club* and as that was her favourite sport, she really loved it. Diane left Dane Park and went to Sir Henry Cooper School with Gary. She did not like one of the teachers there, he was a real bully to all of the children. He had a big stick in the shape of a matchstick and would threaten the class, telling them that they couldn't report him. He would say "What would the headline in the papers be – teacher hits child with matchstick". Diane always seemed to rub him up the wrong way and he would constantly pick on her. She didn't really enjoy many of the academic lessons, although all the children had been at the top of their classes at Dane Park. She was happiest doing her *Gymnastics* and PE Gary was not too happy at Cooper school either, he felt it was too big and impersonal. Although he did well academically, he had no idea which direction he wanted his life to take.

As she came into her teenage years Diane started being difficult to handle (especially for me). She argued with everyone and wouldn't do anything I told her. If she decided not to go to school she wouldn't hang around outside – she just wouldn't get out of bed! Diane would threaten to leave home as soon as she was 16 and Joe would tell her that he would pack her bags for her. One day he even did this, putting them on the step outside, but she brought them straight back in herself. Sometimes I would try to send her to her room in exasperation, but she would sit on the bottom of the stairs, making herself so heavy that I just couldn't move her.

Joe would say to me "You two don't get on. She hates you and you hate her". I knew this wasn't true, because deep down, she was still my little girl and it hurt me for him to say that.

One day Joe heard me calling Diane up for breakfast and on my third call he went up to her room. I shouted at him not to get angry with her and followed him up stairs. She just pulled the covers over her head, swearing at him as she told him to leave her alone! This made him furious with her because Joe never swore in front of any of us and I had to be really angry to say even a mild swearword. As her Dad pulled the covers off her, Diane darted to the bathroom, Joe broke the lock on the door and hit her with his belt which he had taken from its place on the stair side. This upset all of us, It was the first and last time he had ever hit any of the children. Because he had marked her skin, he wouldn't let Diane go to school for a couple of days.

Joe's drinking was getting worse by now. He started making his own beer and when the twins or his mates came, he would persuade them to drink it with him in the daytime, even if they didn't really want to. I also made some Sherry, which tasted very nice. Not liking the feeling of my head spinning when I lay down – as it would if I had more than two glasses – I always kept within my limitations. After going to the pub at lunchtimes, Joe started being nastier than ever with me and I was pleased when he went back out again on a night, as it gave us all, not only me, a few hours respite. As the time for him to come home came closer though, I couldn't talk and I began to get uptight and had all the feelings of panic again. He had never hit me but the horrible things he said made me 'curl up' inside and feel physically ill.

I would meet him in the hall and give him a kiss and a hug to try to make him be nice to me. It worked for a few minutes and would take me off my guard, but he would ask me questions (I can't remember what, now). If I answered wrongly, he would look at me with such hate in his eyes and I knew nothing would stop the tirade of nastiness that would last until he eventually took himself to bed. I would wait till I thought he was asleep before I went up myself. The next morning he would not remember anything he had said and wondered why I was being quiet with him.

On one of our many nights in together which I loved, Joe told me he thought his life was over. He said "I just want to get a few more years on that lad's (David's) back and that's me finished". I was upset at this and I said again to him that my life wasn't anywhere near over. I said I wanted to be on the top of the tree seeing my family getting bigger beneath me (Looking back, I had only said I not we, and I didn't realize the truth in that statement till later).

Christmas time had always been a very happy time for us. I always made several fruit loaves as well as the cake and would bake 9 dozen jam, lemon and mince pies. I had started cooking the meat the day before, because there didn't seem to be much power in the gas on Christmas Day. When this had been done and the children were all in bed, Joe would stand at the bottom of the stairs ringing a little Indian bell which sounded like sleigh bells and would call up to them "Hurry up and go to sleep, or he won't come" then Joe would help me to wrap the presents and fill the stockings before we went to bed. When Michael, Stephen, Audrey and their family came the next day, we would all have a drink whilst I cooked the dinner. In later years, by the time we started eating, Joe had already had too much and started being sarcastic and nasty to Stephen and Michael as well as me. He would wait until everyone was served and then get up and go to bed (He would often do this on ordinary days as well, preferring to take his demijohn of beer instead of eating). It got so bad that I eventually told him to go out on Christmas Eve instead. I knew that he would get so drunk that it would take three or four days for him to get over it. At least we would all enjoy the rest of the holiday.

When he had been in the garden one day, I noticed some funny coloured bruising on Joe's arms, which he said were from catching himself on the roses. I was a bit anxious about these, especially when they didn't fade; I had seen something like this when I had been nursing and asked him to get them checked out at the doctors. When he said they were nothing to bother anyone with, I just gave up trying to persuade him.

One year, Gary and Caroline were getting bikes for Christmas and Joe asked Diane if she would share a new one with me. She agreed because she didn't really like them anyway and she knew that I really wanted one. This proved to be a lifeline to me though; instead of forcing myself to go to the shops, which made me really anxious, I could now tell myself that I would just ride towards them and could turn back if I needed to, this took the pressure off me and I never once turned back. As well as the shopping, I used to go to my Mam's house in Earls Court and

A Dramatic Change

even to my brother's in Haworth Park on Beverley High Road. I couldn't have felt better if I had been given a fortune.

After Lassie had died I said that I didn't want any more animals as it would be so upsetting if anything happened to them, we had gone through a succession of unwanted pets including a stray dog which had followed Joe home once. After a bath and a couple of journeys back to the pub with him, the dog disappeared. A baby chick in a cardboard box didn't last long either. Another time he brought home a budgie, which he had found in a tree. It had taken him ages to catch it, but when he let it fly in the dinette, not realizing that the living room window was open, it flew straight out again. A boy once brought a really nice Labrador and sold it to Joe for two pounds. We only had it about a week when the same lad came begging for it back. He had stolen it and the owner had told him to get it back. The back shed was once turned into a breeding place for *Roller Canaries*. I liked these though; they had a really beautiful song. They lasted quite a few months but I can't remember what happened to them.

After he had been out one day, Joe asked the children if they would like a dog. Of course, they were delighted. He had seen an advertisement for *Pedigree Springer Spaniels* at Beverley and even though I was protesting loudly, saying I wanted nothing to do with it, he rang up and arranged for two of them to be brought to our house so that we could choose one. When they came, he tried to make me look at them and get me involved in choosing. Eventually he wore me down and I told him which one I thought looked the nicest. We called the dog Scamp and it really was. The children were so excited, even though we tried to calm them down. Scamp would not be told what to do and no one could do anything with him, he raced all over the house after everyone and when we took him for a walk on the field at the bottom of Feldane he always jumped into the drain and smelled really bad. Of course, I complained about it and all Joe said was "You chose him". He made Scamp a big dog kennel at the bottom of the garden and kept him on a long lead during the day. On a night Joe brought him indoors.

One night Joe went out to Ramp as usual and although the girls went to meet him as they had started doing, he was not in the pub. They were told that everyone had gone on to a party, but they didn't know where, so I just had to wait until he came home. At about one o clock in the morning, the phone rang. It was Joe. I couldn't understand him properly, all I could make out was that he was in a phone box and I had to come and get him. He didn't even know where he was. I went with Caroline and Gary up to the phone box at the end of Feldane, but I dare not go out anywhere else looking for him. It was scarier to me, being out in the dark. He could have been anywhere.

I rang a taxi and told the driver about it, asking if he would look into the phone boxes in the area to pick Joe up. About 45 minutes later, there was a loud bang on the front door and when I opened it, Joe just about crawled in, really angry with me for not bringing him home. He wouldn't listen to reason and just kept being nasty with me, but he did let me bathe his hand before going to bed. He told me the next day that he had been at a party in the Thorpe Park Flats and later his friend Joe had brought him to the entrance, thinking that he knew his way home. He had fallen down and lost his glasses, (without which he had no sight at all, only coloured shapes) and had had to feel his way home, sometimes on his hands and knees. He was so angry with me for not coming to find him, that he never ever let me forget it. He even told Jean, one of the barmaids, about it the next time we went to Ramp, thinking that she would tell me off as well. Jean told him that if he was her husband and this had happened, she wouldn't have even let him back into the house!

The pub was becoming more of a home to him than ours was. If he didn't have any pocket money of his own left, he would ask me to give him some. Sometimes it seemed better to give him the money, especially if he had been out at the dinnertime; at least I would get some peace. The next morning, of course, he would not remember anything. I started saying to him "To think, I even gave you the money to go out and you still come back and turn on me. The children had started getting angry with Joe because of the way he treated me when he was drunk, but I used to tell them not to take my side because he ended up turning on them as well. All my married life Joe had been nasty to me over my relationship with Don (the sailor I went out with when I had been married to John), I sometimes thought that that was why he hated me. He stood on the landing one day and put his face close to mine and said quietly "I'm going to give you hell for the rest of your life". I felt trapped and frightened. Talking to the family after any of these episodes, I always made some excuse for his behavior – he was a big strong man and he hated the fact that he would never work again – he was frightened of being blind, and other reasons.

Diane used to say to me "Leave him Mum, I'll come with you". I knew however, that no matter how bad things got, I could never leave because as well as loving the sober Joe, I knew I would not be able to face life with nowhere to live again. Once I even took a taxi to my Dad's house in Edgecumbe Street and told him what had been happening all this time. I had never told any of my family about it before. Eve's first husband had died of cancer, but he also drank heavily and his personality changed towards her, just as Joe's had. In my desperation, I even asked her how long she had had to endure the pain of it before he died (I think I was looking for some non-existent kind of time limit to help me to cope with everything).

I started telling Mam and my sister about it as well. Although I would feel brave enough to think about standing up to him when I was with my family — it was a different situation actually facing Joe during the bad times. It was a great relief however, to be able to get some emotional support from outside and not just from the children.

By now Joe was drinking his home brew before it was ready even after he had been out. I started looking forward to him drinking too much because he would go to bed for hours and I knew that when he woke the next day, he would feel ill and allow me to look after him and for a short while I would have the kind, caring, wonderful man I fell in love with, back.

Joe would often get really bad headaches when the muscles over his eyes would go hard and the tension in his neck was really painful. He still wouldn't get treatment from the doctor though. David used to sit on his Dad's shoulders and massage his head and neck until he felt better. Joe used to say that this was the only way to take the pain off.

On our 24th Wedding Anniversary, we had decided to celebrate at home as usual and after everyone was in bed and we had settled down, Joe brought out an Eternity Ring he had bought for me. It was lovely, and I was pleased because my first one had split with age. We couldn't afford one or even an Engagement Ring when we were first married. Joe told me he would buy me a new Wedding Ring the following year because this had also worn thin.

When Caroline was 19yrs, she met a boy called Chris. He was working for the council installing new windows in our houses and they started going out together. A few months later, she told me that she was pregnant. We were shocked at first but

A Dramatic Change

we both knew that we would stand by her and help as much as we could. The next day, in answer to a question from Joe, Chris told us they both knew what they were going to do about it. He said that it was a mistake and that Caroline would have an abortion. Joe and I were both upset about this and he told me to ring Chris' parents to arrange a meeting with us all to sort it out. His mother was not very nice, saying "This relationship with Chris didn't mean anything and he was finishing with her anyway". She said "In this day and age, these things are just the end of a good night out". They all came to our house to talk about the situation and although Caroline had already told us she wanted to keep the baby, when Chris asked her in front of all of us, she cried and ran into the kitchen. I followed, telling her it was only her decision that mattered. We would stand by her whatever choice she made. With this support, she was able to tell everyone that she wanted to keep the baby. Chris then told her that he didn't want to have anything more to do with her and he and his parents left. Caroline was really upset, but she knew she could rely on her Dad and me.

After all this, Caroline was feeling the strain of everything that had happened so Joe asked Auntie Ann if she could go to stay with her for a couple of weeks and Caroline went off to York. Whilst she was away, a letter came for Caroline. We knew from the handwriting that it was from Chris, and we were very tempted to tear it up but we knew we couldn't. We gave it to her as soon as she came home. After reading it in her room, she came down and showed it to her Dad and me. In it Chris had said he was sorry and that he wanted her to meet him, which she did. He told her he did want to marry her and they set a date for 3rd December 1993. Although we were unhappy about this, Joe said "let them marry to give that baby a name – we'll have her back within a year" (this also turned out to be very prophetic).

Feeling rather down one day, I decided that I had had enough of worrying about debts, so I made a table of the firms that money was owed to, how much, the amount I paid and how long it would take to clear each debt. After this, I worked out an affordable payment for each of them and wrote to the different companies offering to ensure this was paid every week. I'm pleased to say they all agreed. As I finished one account I put that amount onto one of the others to bring it down faster. Every week I would fill in my table so that I could easily see my progress, I felt really pleased with myself for taking a positive decision about this, at least I was taking a bit of power into my own hands.

At that time Gary had been taking an interest in home computing, so for Christmas we bought him a ZX 81, which was just about the first one out. Gary also asked David if he would like to learn to play the guitar, so after being taught some of the basic chords, which he picked up very quickly, David was soon playing pieces on Gary's guitar. Joe and I were very proud when we heard them playing. My brother came down one day with his guitar to show us some pieces that he had learned, he played a Spanish song and David asked if he could have a try at it. We were all amazed at the way he picked up the tune just by listening and watching his fingering. The next day my brother came back, bringing the guitar and his instruction books. He gave them to David, saying, "You could do with this more than me." David was over the moon.

Caroline and Chris were married in the *Registry Office* and we made a really nice buffet for them at home. They were given a house on Preston Road and our life returned to 'normal'. As Chris was working, I went with Caroline for all her pre-natal appointments. Alan, who lived at the end of our block, took us and also waited to take us home. We were all happy to know that everything was going well.

A Dramatic Change

Joe's bouts of drinking and anger were getting progressively worse. He was drinking his homebrew before it had ferment and would growl round the house when his drink had gone. I told the children (bravely) that if he started on my Sherry (which also wasn't ready for drinking) I would pour it down the sink. When I came home from the shops one day, I found that he had taken one of my demijohns up to bed with him. I immediately – but nervously – poured the other one away, as I had promised. Later I was very surprised and relieved when Joe never even mentioned it. Now and again, I would go to Ramp with Joe thinking that if I was with him all evening he wouldn't turn on me. I enjoyed it at first but when people came across to talk to us, he would start looking angrier, accusing me of giving them the eye. No matter how much I told him that I only loved him, and wasn't interested in anyone else, his mood just became blacker and blacker.

Knowing that I couldn't do anything to stop him when he was angry, I had decided to ignore him. I had taken this step a couple of times before, and once I had even gone to sleep in another room. These silences didn't usually last more than a few days though, because he would always make me laugh and that would be the end of my retaliation.

One day Chris came down with Caroline and he was really telling her off. It was something about her not doing the housework or the cooking properly (I cannot remember exactly). Joe was sitting on the settee and Chris was standing behind it. Suddenly I saw Chris put his fist towards Joe, who leapt up and nearly jumped over the settee to get to him. Chris backed off and apologized but made Caroline leave with him there and then. After they had gone, Joe was angry, but then he turned on me, asking if it was true that she didn't know how to do whatever it was – and why hadn't I taught her. He had forgotten that he wouldn't let any of the children do the housework with me. Early in the morning of the 16th March 1984, I received a phone call from Chris telling us that he was with Caroline at *Hedon Road Maternity Hospital*. He wanted me to take his place because he had to go to work. After seeing David off to school, I asked Alan to take me there and I arrived in good time to comfort and support her whilst she was giving birth to my first grandchild, Sarah Helen, who was a beautiful little girl, looking very much like her Dad. Joe didn't like hospitals and wouldn't go, but he sent her a card saying he was proud of her and that she 'wanted a medal as big as a dustbin lid'.

When it came time for Caroline to come home, Alan took me to fetch her to our house until Chris came home from work. Joe had brought down a deep drawer from the bedroom, and it made a very comfy makeshift bed for the baby. I asked Chris if he wanted me to go to their house each day for about a week, to show Caroline how to get into a routine with the baby and he agreed. Alan again took me and I arranged for him to bring me back home at six o clock when Chris came from work. At about half past four Chris came in angrily, saying that he had walked out of the job, I knew Caroline was a bit strained with his attitude and I also felt uncomfortable so I asked if he wanted me to arrange for Alan to pick me up straight away, instead of waiting till six o clock. He just said, sulkily "Do what you want". When I then asked if he would still want me to come every day to help he said "No", so I rang Alan and left, feeling a little sad about things. I told Joe and he was unhappy about this as well because he knew I was looking forward to showing Caroline the ropes, but we knew it wasn't our place to interfere in their marriage.

Caroline used to bring Sarah to our house, walking from Preston Road because even though Chris had known she was

A Dramatic Change

coming, he used to leave her money to buy bread but didn't leave her any bus fares. We always made sure that she didn't have to walk home though.

Joe and I had lots of arguments about the way they were living. Caroline would tell him about it when she went to meet him from Ramp, she was still his little girl and he wanted to protect her. We always came to the same conclusion though, that we were powerless to do anything about it.

Around the middle of May, I suddenly had a dreadful feeling that I was going to die. This scared me, not only for myself but especially when I realized that – because I had always dealt with the family finances as well as the housekeeping – no one would know how to do anything. By the time I had made out lists of instructions, shown the children how to work the washing machine etc. and shown Joe what needed to be paid out each week, (saying that I wanted him to know about the finances as well as me) the feeling of dread had passed and I felt fine again.
A few weeks earlier, looking out of my bedroom window one morning, I had seen the girl who lived behind us, Ann, cleaning her windows. Ann had lost her husband, who was only in his 30s, suddenly, the year before. It was the first time I had seen her for a few months and I felt a deep sadness for her, wondering how she had been able to cope on her own with two young children, I did not know that I was to find out for myself about this before very long. Once more I felt the need to fight the ongoing mental abuse by not talking to Joe; the silence had lasted for two weeks and I was determined I would stand my ground this time. The day before *Father's Day* I grudgingly gave in and we started talking again. Even after trying to get my point across I didn't feel that I had said everything I wanted to say. The next day, the only card Joe got was from Caroline, the others had deliberately

not sent him one. I knew he was hurting but he did not go out and the day passed happily.

On the Monday, Gary had finished his leaving exams in the sixth form and Diane was due to sit her last one the next day. I was still plagued with the thought that I had not told Joe everything that was on my mind. I felt that I just had to clear the air and I told him how unhappy I was because of the way he treated me when he came home. He had never drunk so heavily or been so angry and nasty to me. He couldn't understand this and said that he had only ever tried to protect me, and 'put some guts' in me, and now he knew he had succeeded because I had turned on him. After I told him that he was the only person in the world who ever treated me like that, he promised that he would try to go out only once a week if I would go with him. I was happy with this, although I didn't know how long he could keep it up.

Over the last six months or so he had even turned on me when I had been out with him, especially if anyone had smiled at me during the evening. I always knew what was coming by the stony looks that he kept giving me, despite all my efforts to cheer him up. I did feel as if we had cleared up most of the things I wanted to say and decided to put my feelings behind me and start again. We made a deep meat pie together for tea, Joe always made the filling and I would make the pastry for the crust, which had to be held up by an old teacup. Everyone always enjoyed it. It was his specialty, apart from the Curries. These contained everything I had in the cupboard and were often given to anyone who happened to be visiting on the night they were made. Not even the children and their friends were safe from it. I was told it was much too hot but no one ever did (or was allowed) to refuse it except me. This was always good for making a jovial atmosphere though. After our meat pie tea that night, I sat on

A Dramatic Change

Joe's knee and warily told him that I had to go out for about an hour and a half, saying that Diane would look after him whilst I was away. My Aunt Jean worked at *Lloyds Bank* on Newland Avenue and her sister in law, who did the cleaning with her, had been taken ill. I had arranged to cover for her without asking (I wasn't talking to Joe then, so I made the decision myself). Although he didn't like me going, he agreed that I should. Diane had gone out after making sure her Dad hadn't needed anything. David was drawing a picture of some butterflies for Barbara next door's grandson and Gary was out with his friends. After a really nice evening, we all went to bed happily and Joe turned Diane's light out. Joe and I laughed at silly things for ages. Then, saying he had heartburn, he went downstairs again for some *Gaviscon*. Coming back, he climbed into bed telling me that even though he had also taken some of my 'jungle juice' (this was my name for the *Bicarbonate of Soda* I used to take when I was pregnant) he couldn't get rid of it. He put his arm across me and said "oh, that's better", then we had a private joke and he just started heavily breathing out for what seemed ages. This alarmed me and I shook him, calling his name a couple of times before shouting for Gary to come from his room.

Gary immediately started trying to breathe into his Dad's mouth whilst telling me to ring for an ambulance. He had to tell me again to do it because I was just transfixed. Whilst waiting for the ambulance, thoughts were just racing round in my head. I couldn't take in what was happening. I didn't know what I would do next. I think I knew that no one would be able to save Joe, and part of me hoped that I was right, secretly not wanting him to be revived, wanting to be free from all the mental abuse I had put up with over the years, yet my overriding thought was hoping that help would come very soon.

It wasn't long before the ambulance and our family doctor, Dr Parker, arrived and sent Gary and me downstairs. After an examination, they told us that Joe had suffered a massive heart attack. Because he didn't have any diagnosed illness, Dr Parker said that they would have to perform an autopsy. I told him how I seemed to be slow at sending for help and was also worried whether he could have been saved if I had acted sooner. Dr Parker told me that the attack had been so massive that nothing could have been done for Joe, even if Dr Parker himself had been there when it happened. I asked also if the autopsy would be able to tell if Joe had had any brain disease caused by the drinking, but the doctor said softly that they wouldn't even look for that, only for the cause of death. Knowing how the drink changed Joe, I thought having a brain disease may have been an explanation. The ambulance man told me that because he was already dead, they shouldn't really take Joe away, but, owing to the time (it was about half past two by then) and the fact that there were children in the house; they would take him to the hospital mortuary if I wanted them to. I couldn't think straight and agreed with them, although later I agonised over whether it was the right decision or not.

CHAPTER EIGHT

A Completely Different Life

THE DOCTOR HAD GIVEN ME A TABLET to help me to sleep, but I didn't want to take it and Gary and I didn't go back to bed that night. We drank endless cups of tea and even turning the fire up full didn't stop my uncontrollable shivering. I had heard about people dying of a broken heart soon after their partner had died and the thought frightened me. I didn't want that to happen to me. I knew that now, I had to be mother and father to Gary, Diane and David. Stephen and Michael were settled and Caroline was married now and they weren't dependent on me anymore. I vowed to myself that they wouldn't lose out on any opportunities they would have had if Joe had still been with us.

When I heard Diane go to the bathroom really early in the morning, I went up to her and told her what had happened. Naturally she, like all of us, was inconsolable. Diane remembered her Dad turning her light off and couldn't understand why she hadn't heard me calling Joe's name and then shouting for Gary. She thought, surely she hadn't gone to sleep as quickly as that, and this really upset her — not only then, but also for years to come. Although we had talked about this many times, it was only when I was writing these events that I really understood her problem and was able to clear up the misunderstanding, putting her mind at rest. Her Dad had turned her light off when he first came to bed and not after he had been down again for medicine, just before he died.

David was only 10yrs old by then and we all decided we wouldn't wake him up early to tell him the sad news. When he came downstairs we all tried to comfort him. I had always believed that somehow *life goes on* after we die and we were soon to get a sign that perhaps this was true. We were all sitting together in the dinette, when suddenly an unmistakable 'Joe' smell filled the bathroom and landing. I checked with the children, asking if any of them had an upset stomach but they hadn't. Somehow I knew that this was Dad, feeling as bewildered as we all were over his sudden departure.

I rang my brother, then my Dad, and next my Mam, telling them what had happened. Of course everyone was shocked. No one could believe that his life had ended so suddenly at only 56 years of age. My brother went to give the news to Caroline and Chris, who had, in turn, told Audrey (Stephen had gone into the town on an errand). They all came straight round and we talked about the arrangements that needed to be made. Chris drove Stephen to the hospital, the registrars, the undertakers and *Corporation Telephones*, whom Joe had worked for, and that took a lot of the pressure from me. The Death Certificate told us that Joe had died from *Ischemic Heart Disease* and *Chronic Bronchitis*. We all thought that this could have been partly due to the alcohol and the cigarettes that he had smoked, one after the other.

Whilst Stephen and Chris had been gone, Audrey told me that Michael had gone camping and she didn't know where

A Completely Different Life

he would be. After I had said I would ring the police because they would be able to alert other stations and find him, Audrey told me that he was really in prison. He had been sentenced to two weeks for not paying fines, but had sworn them to secrecy because he did not want to upset us. I rang the padre at the prison who told me he would pass the message on, and said he was sure Michael would be able to attend his Dad's funeral.

That night Gary, Diane and David huddled together with me in my bed, talking, crying and even laughing about the good times with their Dad. David was the only one who didn't cry. At the time I thought he was being really brave. I was very proud of his 'grown up' attitude. He said that however much we cried, nothing could bring his Dad back. I felt so very sad that he had lost his Dad whilst he was so young. I worried that David wouldn't be able to remember much of his young life when he grew up. Joe absolutely doted on David and there was nothing he wouldn't do for him, or any of his other children. After that, we fell into a routine of sitting on my bed, allowing each other to talk and grieve openly. Diane even slept with me for quite a while because she said her own bedroom seemed so empty. First Caroline had gone, and then it was her Dad and she felt that she had to *keep her eye on me* because she was scared that if she slept in her own room I would also 'disappear'.

Joe was taken to *Shepherds Rest Rooms* in Beverley Road, so that people could pay their last respects to him. Gary, Diane and I went to see him on the Sunday morning but said afterwards that we wished we hadn't gone. I had decided that I would arrange for Joe to be cremated. Death was a subject that we never ever discussed, so I didn't know his feelings about it. For myself, I didn't like the idea of standing round an open grave and thought it would be easier for all of us to just stay in the little chapel.

For the next few days I tried to keep things going as normally as I could; somehow getting through the housework and making the meals for everyone. I think someone did the shopping for me, but I can't really remember who it was. Stephen & Audrey and Caroline & Chris came to be with us as often as they could and we were never without visitors, family and friends. Caroline and Chris said I could have Sarah with me for a few days and I was very grateful for this because it stopped me thinking about things too deeply. I do know that when a person receives a great shock, such as this, nature steps in and releases a natural sedative to enable us to carry on. If that didn't happen, people would be dropping dead, whenever they had tragedies in their lives.

The day of the funeral arrived. We all thought that, at 10yrs old, David was too young to join in this very sad time, so he went off to school as usual. Caroline couldn't face the pain of it and stayed at home with my friend Carol to prepare a meal for everyone, although Chris did come to represent his family.

The undertakers had brought the coffin home earlier that morning and put it on the table in the dinette. It really upset me when it was time for Joe to be taken out again for the last time. I didn't want this to be happening. It was just a bad dream that I wanted to wake up from but couldn't. I was aware of people standing by the roadside as the cortege passed, and having to walk past them into the little chapel, but I had no idea who was there, the boys held onto me but I couldn't shake off the desolate feeling in my chest.

Arriving home, I almost fell into the chair and Dad came over to comfort me. Even though everyone was there, I just broke my heart and felt as if I would never stop crying. I just couldn't keep my feelings under control any longer. When everyone except the children had gone, I felt much better – as if a great weight had been lifted from my shoulders. I knew that whatever I did from now on; however many mistakes I made, no one would criticise

A Completely Different Life

or mentally abuse me anymore. I also realized that, even with my nervous illness, I was a far stronger person than Joe had ever been. I knew now, that the shouting, bullying, putting down and controlling, had all been hiding a very insecure, frightened, but still very caring person, which was (without the alcohol) what Joe's true character really was, and this was the man, who I loved and missed so very much.

Looking back, I felt gratitude and great relief to be given the opportunity for Joe and I to talk things over, (after my two weeks of silent retaliation) and that his last two days with us had been spent happily.

In my bedroom there was a built in double cupboard which had a hatch in the ceiling leading to the false roof. It also contained a shelf and clothes hanging bar. We all referred to this as the *white wardrobe*. For some reason, I grew anxious whenever I had to open this door because it mostly contained Joe's clothes and I always felt that I would see him in there. After about 10 days of this worry, I decided that the only thing to do was to pass these clothes on to other people, so I asked Stephen to do this for me, which he did. That night I had a dream that Joe was lying next to me in our bed. He said to me, "All my clothes have gone out of the white wardrobe". After telling him why I had let them go, he replied "But I'm not dead, Madge". We then had a conversation in which he said that he couldn't come downstairs because everyone thought he was dead, but decided he would take someone else's name so everything would be alright. I know this sounds silly, but it is the only way I can relate what Joe said. Somehow, I seemed to understand that this dream was Joe's way of telling me that there really was a life after this one.

Then there was the `pin' mystery — Joe would fasten his tie onto his shirt when he went out to work or anywhere, by putting a tiny gold safety pin at the back of it. I had put this, with other personal items of his into the pretty biscuit tin, (which my Granny Dixon and Great Aunts had given me when I went to Singapore). One day I found that pin on the mantelpiece in the living room. Feeling puzzled, I replaced it. The next day it was on the unit and I put it into the kitchen drawer. Imagine my surprise when next it turned up under the fireside rug. The children told me they had not been moving it and I couldn't understand what was happening so I just put it out of my mind.

Everything started getting back to normal – whatever that was. Gary went to work for my brother, making slot machines and Diane was at college on Sutton Road. I only had David at school now and things were a lot easier. I had kept up with my arrangement to finish the debt off and now I had almost paid everything back, this was a great feeling.

The first couple of times I came home on my bike after the grocery shopping were very emotional. Joe had always been there to help me in with the groceries and make me a cup of tea. I missed that dreadfully. Even when I wasn't talking to him, he would still do the same.

I found that people's reactions were strange also. At the shops one day, a lady asked me to describe all Joe's symptoms before and on the night he died. She said that she wanted to watch her husband in case it happened to him also (I realized later that this is the way I had been with my stepmother Eve, when I was desperately trying to put a limit on the way I had been suffering at that time). Another lady who I only knew by sight, knocked at my door, asking what I was going to do with Joe's greenhouse, and could she have *first refusal* if I was going to sell it. I didn't want to do that, I wanted to keep everything, as near as I could, to the way Joe had organised things. As the nights were really warm, I let Scamp stay in the garden. He had a lot of space to roam around and he seemed to like it out there.

I started feeling a lot better, the children had always been very supportive of me and it was a big relief not to have to pretend, or make up excuses to keep the peace. I felt as if I had been living on a knife edge, especially in the last six years, in case I said the wrong thing. I could now speak my mind without any worry. I could now talk openly about Stephen and Michael's Dad, John and my experience in the WRAC as I had never been able to do before. It was as if the five years we had been apart had never happened in Joe's eyes. He was so jealous of my life without him. It was like being on a Roller Coaster, one minute happy and the next fearful. Looking back, I can see that a lot of it was my fault really. If I had been the girl I was when I was 18 – full of life and not afraid of anything, I think Joe would have been different. If I hadn't got married or told him about Don (a mistake I made when John and I were separated), he may not have been jealous.

We had only been on our own a few months when Diane started playing up again. It was the same thing, she argued with me over everything I said, once even telling me that she wished it were me who had died instead of her Dad. Trying to make her see that she couldn't just come in and go out whenever she wanted, just brought a torrent of bad language from her. When Gary tried to tell her anything, she would swear at him and say, "You're not my Dad", and once they even came to blows, ending up with Diane's nose bleeding. She slammed out of the house, throwing our keys through the greenhouse window as she ran. Then in desperation I called the police, hoping that she would listen to someone who was not involved. When even the policeman could not get through to Diane, he found a place for her in *Linneus House hostel*. She was taken to a room she would share with lots of other people, but she left there as soon as the policeman had gone 'camping' on our front doorstep until I let her in again. Diane's friend Anne, who lived in the block behind us said she could stay at her house and I was happy with this, because she came home to see us every day and we didn't have the hassle. Diane did move a few times after that, ending up living with Caroline on Preston Road. I used to go to see them sometimes.

As the weather grew colder, I decided that Scamp should come indoors on an evening, but it didn't work. He had made the space between the living room door and the back door into his own and barked at anyone who crossed over it, especially when it was any of the children. Gary, David and I had a talk about this and realized that we were being cruel to Scamp. I put an advert in the *Hull Daily Mail* and a lady with a little girl came to see him. They seemed to get on like a house on fire, so they took him. I hoped that he would be alright with them. The next day, however, she brought him back and said that the dog seemed jealous of her other children and wouldn't let them near her. The next day a man who worked on a farm came to see Scamp and wanted to train him to work with him. I thought he would love being in the open air and happily let him go. That night, before I went to sleep, I told God of my concern for the dog, in case he worried sheep or anything, therefore having to be put down and I was told that my responsibility ended when I handed Scamp over to the other man, and that made me feel better. It was a big relief not to have that worry anymore and life once again settled down.

After having a talk with the boys one day, I decided that I would carry out Joe's promise to take them back to *Butlins*. This time, however, we would go to Skegness where there were no memories and just stay for a week. My friend Carol and her son Glen agreed to come with us. I booked for us to go the following

A Completely Different Life

May 1985.

I was happy with the way life was shaping up; Gary spent a lot of time after work with his friend Andy, who lived in the block in front of us. David had developed an interest in *Break Dancing* and with his friends he would practice every day after school, even buying his own square of canvas to carry around. The boys still had time to practice playing their guitars together though. David used to watch Mark Knopfler (the guitarist) on the television and pick up his tunes by ear and by noting his fingering. I used to love it when they came downstairs to ask me to listen to their pieces. Sometimes on an evening we would get settled in the living room and they would put on a concert for me, singing as well as playing. The song I loved listening to most was the original version of *Father and Son* by Kat Stevens. Gary would take the father part and David, of course, the son. They sang the song so beautifully together that I would also feel very sad, especially for David, having lost his father at such an early age. Joe would have been very proud to hear them.

The day before we were due to go to *Butlins*, Barbara, my friend next door came in and told me that she had found Michael pacing up and down in Feldane, not wanting to come to my house. She had brought him to the door but he still wouldn't come in. As soon as I saw him I knew that something was terribly wrong with him. His eyes looked wild and he had lost his two front teeth (Michael and Stephen had been experimenting with drugs since they were teenagers). He later told me that he was being plagued by very negative thoughts, which told him that he would be kidnapped and mutilated. When these thoughts told him that he had better kill himself before anyone else could do it, he cut his wrist. Thankfully, he realized in time and went to the hospital to have the wound stitched. Michael had also 'been told' to kill me, which, of course, he would never do and that's why he didn't want to come in. He was also adamant that he mustn't drink anything or something bad would happen.

By the time he came to my house that day, having been without water for a few days, he was very dehydrated. After persuading him to come inside, I made him have a drink of tea, telling him that if he didn't drink, he certainly would die. It took me quite a long time to make him realize this. Michael had always had confidence in me, though, because he knew, deep down, that I would never lead him down the wrong path. As he swallowed, he was terrified and was bright red and shaking like a leaf. It was a little better to get more fluids into him after that however, because he had seen that nothing happened. When I saw that he truly felt responsible for everything that was happening in the world, especially on the news or on television, I called Dr Parker. After checking the stitches on Michael's wrist, and listening to him for a while, he told me that Michael was showing classic symptoms of chronic overdosing on amphetamines. The doctor managed to get Michael a bed in *De La Pole Hospital* for the next day, so that night after giving him the sedatives and an anti-psychotic drug that the doctor left for him, I made him a bed up on the settee, sitting with him and trying to comfort him until he fell asleep, but I must admit that the thought of how dangerous this paranoia was, made me have quite a troubled, even having a fearful night myself.

Before I went to bed I rang my brother and told him about the situation, saying that I thought that we might not have our holiday after all. He told me it was important that we went and that he would come round early the next morning and take Michael to the hospital himself, so we would be able to go. The following morning, I was very nervous, not only about going, but also whether Michael would be all right. I was determined to give the boys a good holiday though, and we set off.

The Skegness site seemed a lot smaller than Filey and the weather wasn't very good. During the week we went to the cinema and to the children's entertainment, but although the three of them enjoyed it, Carol and I had a thoroughly miserable time. It just wasn't the same without our husbands and we were glad when the week was over and we could come home again. That was the last time we went on holiday.

Michael was discharged from the hospital after a few weeks, but I didn't like the idea of him going back to his flat; I thought he had more chance of getting better if he stayed with us for a while. He had to sleep on the settee, but that didn't bother him. Whilst with me Michael just sat on the settee and grew fat! I thought that to have his own flat would give him the incentive to move around. About 3 months later, I started helping him to look for flats and he found one in Cholmley Street on Hessle Road. We all helped to clean it and it was a great relief to me to have him settled on his own (I didn't know till much later, that because he didn't know the area, he hated every minute of being there. Life settled down and I started thinking about *Spiritualism* and trying to find out the truth about life after physical death. This was a subject that had always interested me, but like such a lot of other people, I was very scared of something that I didn't understand. Joe had once said that his mother was a *Spiritualist* but whenever I broached the subject, Joe told me not to 'dabble with the devil'. I had always believed that this life couldn't be all there was; according to the Bible we were promised *Eternal Life*, but I didn't understand how this would be. Attending church years ago hadn't made the truth any clearer to me either.

My brother felt the same way as I did and we decided that he would go first to find out what happens at the Spiritualist meetings that we had heard about. He rang one day, soon after, and told me he had been to the *Temple of Truth*, at the top end of Holderness Road, and said that Joe had 'come through' with a message, giving proof of his identity and saying he had been in *The Spirit Hospital* for a while, but that he was alright now. I was very excited but a little scared really, although I was keen to see for myself.

After going to that church the following week, and really enjoying the service, I decided that I wouldn't keep going there – mainly because they didn't have a toilet and with my nerves, that facility was essential to me. We then went to an 'Open Circle' held in a hotel in the centre of the town, but we both agreed that wasn't for us, either. Audrey's sister and brother in law, George and Elsie, helped to run the church in John Street. Stephen gave me George's number and I rang, asking about the services and what happened there. George was very friendly and after explaining, he told me that we would be welcome whenever we came.

Back on the home front Caroline had been having trouble in her marriage, so she brought Sarah home to stay with us until she worked out what she would do (Joe's words seemed to be coming true – he said that we would have her back within a year, but I had not realized that I would be by myself then).

A couple of days later, Chris came to see Caroline. She was very apprehensive about meeting him and asked me to stay with her. After a long talk with both of us, Chris persuaded her to give their marriage another chance. It didn't last long, however, and Chris moved back with his parents. They both filed for divorce, but told me that they didn't want to part. They thought they might get on better if they weren't married. By then it was nearly Christmas and the whole family were together once again. This time Caroline and Sarah stayed with us over the holiday and at least I knew that Sarah would enjoy being spoiled by everyone. It was in January 1986 that Diane met a boy named Ray at Caroline's, and on her birthday, March 7th; he gave her an Eternity Ring. They knew that they wanted to be together. We all liked Ray very much, it was lovely to see Diane so happy at last.

My brother and I paid our first visit to no 19 John Street at the beginning of January 1986 and we both immediately felt at home there. Not really understanding what would happen, my knees knocked nervously all through the service. I think that may have had a lot to do with the thought of having to walk to the bus station on the way back, though. My overriding thought after going there was that I also wanted to 'serve', to help as many people as I could, in any way. We started going to that church every week and I came to think of the people as my second family. My brother didn't have a car at that time so we went on the bus. He would get on at *Tesco's* in Hall Road. Someone would walk with me to the bus stop opposite *Rampant Horse* pub, so that I could catch it there. I would also be met on my way back home.

Even though I had been a church goer in my teenage years and had been confirmed by the *Bishop of Guildford* when I was in the WRAC, I still didn't understand the full significance of what it all meant. I loved the parables taught by the Master *Jesus*, advising us on how we should live our lives but that was all I knew. I was anxious to learn as much as I could about spirit and everlasting life, so I started buying lots of books, written by mediums, who 'channelled' spirit teachers. These included *Zodiac*, *White Eagle*, and *Silver Birch*. I seemed to know that this was to be my life's work for the future and I was fascinated and excited at the way they all told the same truths, although in different ways. White Eagle was my favourite and I learned a lot from his teachings. I couldn't understand some of the information I read but I learned that this was because my mind would only accept the truths slowly but surely. Every time I re-read a book, I understood a little more. On saying that though, I know that in one lifetime we may not even scratch the surface of the great lake of knowledge that is open to every person who wants to learn.

It was whilst I was reading a book by the Spirit Teacher Zodiac, that I had my first 'Clairvoyant' experience. I was sitting on a stool in front of the settee in my living room, when I was suddenly 'knocked backwards', although I didn't fall over. I 'knew' that it had been a big collie dog and immediately thought of Lassie. At the same time a voice from the direction of the door, around the level of the handle said to me "Hello Mummy". Without even thinking I replied "Hello Darling". My mind was in a spin and I said, "Oh, it's lovely of you to come, what shall I call you?" Straight away the name Mary just seemed to pop into my mind.

The book was forgotten for what seemed ages, whilst I relived the experience over and over again. Had I imagined it? What had made me almost fall backwards? The voice was so very clear it must have been real. I didn't know the sex of the baby that I had aborted 10 years earlier and I was always very upset when I thought of what I had done. Now here was this little girl calling me Mummy. I believed she had come to show me that she loved me enough to want to stop me upsetting myself. She was alive. I remembered Joe's visit in my dream, in which he also told me that he was alive. I felt as if I had wings, I was so happy.

A few days later when I was again reading, I actually 'saw' a little girl sitting to my right, playing with some dolls. She seemed to be engrossed in what she was doing and I only had a back view of her. Her hair was long, blonde and wavy. I didn't hear anything but I watched her for quite a few seconds before she disappeared. My biggest surprise at that time was a phone call from George (from church). He said that he had been watching a John Denver concert and taping it at the same time, when he had distinctly heard a voice calling Madge. At first he thought it must refer to another member of the church named Madge, but he was then told no, Madge Shep. The song that John was singing at that time was called *My Sweet Lady*. George told me he would give me a tape of it when he next saw me, but because I was eager to listen to the words, he sent it to me by post. The words seemed to be very personal to me, proving once again, that life really does go on.

> Lady, are you crying, do the tears belong to me?
> Did you think our life together was all done?
> Lady, you've been dreaming, I'm as close as I can be,
> And I swear to you our life has just begun.
>
> Close your eyes, rest your weary mind,
> I promise I will stay right here beside you.
> Today our lives were joined, became entwined
> I wish that you could know how much I love you.
>
> Lady, are you happy? Do you feel the way I do?
> Are there meanings that you've never seen before?
> Lady, my sweet Lady, I just can't believe it's true
> And it's like I've never, ever loved before.
>
> Close your eyes, rest your weary mind
> I promise I will stay right here beside you.
> Today our lives were joined, became entwined
> I wish that you could know, just how much I love you
> Lady, are you crying, do the tears belong to me?
> Did you think our life together was all done?
> Lady, my sweet Lady, I'm as close as I can be
> And I swear to you our life has just begun.

I began to think that Joe must have somehow influenced John Denver to write the song for me, and I was really disappointed to find out that it had been written in the 1970's. What I didn't know at that time, however was that spirit communication works in so many ways. People who have passed on may use a song, a spoken word, or even a feeling, to bring great comfort to someone suffering from bereavement.

I was still enjoying my work at church, now going on Saturday nights as well as Sundays. I really looked forward to talking to the different mediums who would come to take services for us, but I felt that I needed to try to get out more. I applied for a Care Assistant's position at *Desmond House*, which was a home for mentally disabled adults in Desmond Avenue on Beverley Road. After working there for about 14 months, however, I was keen to get back to secretarial work again, and I joined a temp agency. This didn't last long though because I wasn't happy with the way it worked. I wouldn't hear from the agency for quite a while and then they would ring, wanting me to go to out of the way places at very short notice all the time. It was rather unsettling for David, never knowing when I would be in, and I was spending almost as much in taxis as I was earning.

Talking to Dad one day, I found out that he had many clairvoyant experiences, although he didn't know whether to believe them or not. I made a tape of some of the Zodiac Messages and gave it to him to listen to. He told me that he would have liked to come with us to church but my stepmother Eve, would not let him do this. Any time that I brought up the subject she would emphatically say that neither she nor Dad would ever be going there, Dad did like me to tell him about what I had learned, when we were by ourselves however.

Around the April time, Diane & Ray came to see me, telling me that she was pregnant. They were both very apologetic, telling me that they had talked things over and that they really wanted to be together. I was pleased that after all our upsets Diane still knew that she could talk to me about anything. I couldn't bear the thought of her not being with us at this time, so when Gary and David came home, I told them about it and asked if they would mind if Diane came home. They both immediately said they didn't mind so long as Ray came with her, because he was the only one who could 'calm her down'. The next day, when Diane and Ray came round again, I asked them what they thought of the idea and they were both really pleased. I knew that Joe and even some other people would never have allowed this to happen, but I was my own boss now so I could make my own decisions. At least I knew that Diane would get the care she needed. I moved out of our big bedroom so that the boys could share it, and we all settled down happily.

Talking to the expectant parents one night, they told me that they were intending to get married but not till after the baby was born. I suggested that as this was their plan anyway, why not do it before, thus giving the baby a 'name'? After talking it over alone, they agreed and said they would like the ceremony to take place on August 1st so we started making the arrangements and Ray introduced us to his family. I was very pleased that they intended to stay together, although I was ready to support them if they later decided not to. The wedding was held in the *Registry Office* and my youngest sister, my friend Carol and I made the buffet for the reception, which we held at our house. It was an enjoyable day for everyone. When Ray and Diane had disagreements – which almost everyone has – I was pleased that they both felt comfortable enough to be able to sort out their differences in front of me. I never, ever took sides and just listened until they talked things out rationally for themselves.

Caroline was also pregnant at this time but she was reluctant to admit it because she was worried about telling Chris. I'm pleased to say that after telling him, she blossomed and looked really well.

Seeing an article in the paper later, telling of the *White Eagle Healing Sanctuary* and of the work done by the healers there, I wrote to them, asking if it would be possible for Dad to be able to see for a while for the rest of his time on earth. I also asked for help for myself to get better from the *Agoraphobia*. I received a really friendly letter back, explaining that my letter would be prayed upon, with the rest of the mail. They send out to the *Healing Ministers* on a night when people are in bed, relaxing. Knowing this, but again not understanding what would happen, I daren't sleep that night, wondering if 'something' would have to come into my head. Anyway, my fears were, of course, unfounded and I forgot about it.

A short while later, my brother started a healing circle at his house, on one night a week and I sat with them also. One night in meditation, I saw a massive big whale. Three surgeons in white coats and caps were operating on the one big eye that I could see. One of them said to the others "It's no good, the eye is dead underneath", and then the picture faded. My brother and I talked about this and although I knew that it could be an answer to my letter, we hoped that it wasn't an omen meaning that Dad's life was coming to an end. It made me feel happy to know that when Spirit needed to contact me for any reason, they did it easily. Another time in meditation, I saw a hand and my attention was drawn to a ring on its finger. I had never seen one like it before. It was gold and seemed to be a few rings fused together. Later I learned that this would have been a 'friendship' ring and was a sign that someone belonging to the ring was going to be very helpful to me. At church, I was invited to join their closed group and I eagerly agreed. I had only been there a couple of times when the then president, Muriel, told us that booking the mediums to take services was getting too much for her, so I volunteered to take it on. She brought me the necessary paperwork and at the next meeting said that she was even thinking of giving up her position as President, but again she thought no one wanted to take the responsibility it entailed. Marlene said she would take it on and the rest of the group said they would help in its running also, so from then, Marlene Bell became the new *President of the John Street Church*. As we are an independent church, not affiliated to the *Greater World* or to the SNU churches, we do not have a committee as such. Everyone of the group volunteered their services in the different aspects of running the church and we have never changed positions each year. This worked quite well, we still met on a Monday night, but after sitting in the meditation circle which we called our working group – designed to sent light and love to the hierarchy, for use wherever and whenever it was needed – we discussed church business. Decisions on whether to try out any of our suggestions were always made by vote and only when this was split did Marlene use her decider. This system always worked well and is still in place today.

Marlene always told us that because we were working for Spirit and if we gave of ourselves without thought of reward, we would automatically become more spiritually aware. She said that no person ever could 'develop' anyone else. Marlene would see the potential in someone and help to bring it out, although because there are so many different ways to serve Spirit, not everyone would decide to become a Medium. I also learned the importance of *opening up* to receive the spirit energies and *closing down* afterwards.

One of the girls in the group, Dora, offered me a lift home, which I gratefully accepted. Dora lived in Cottingham so she told me she would pick me up whenever we were both going to church. As she came for me the following Sunday, I noticed a ring on her finger and I almost gasped in surprise. It was the same ring that I had seen in my meditation. I marvelled at how true and caring our spirit friends were. After coming back home one night feeling really tired, I had my supper and walked up the stairs to bed. I could hear lots of voices in my head. It seemed as if women were all talking at once. I sat on the end of my bed saying "thank you for coming, but not tonight, I'm tired", and immediately the voices stopped. I have heard Marlene and other mediums say that we're in charge of our minds and if we get any thoughts or feelings that we don't like or want, we must tell whoever or whatever it is to go away and leave us in peace. If we are really emphatic it will happen.

I was grateful for having this knowledge because if I had not stopped 'them' they could have become more dominant and I wouldn't have been able to think clearly. I had heard too many stories of people accepting spirit 'messages' all day long, and thus making themselves ill when their minds become overtired. I decided there and then that I would only *open myself up* when meditating, or later, taking a service, or conducting private readings.

Back on the home front, on 26th November 1986 my first grandson Paul Richard (who also looked very much like his dad), was born to Caroline and Chris and everyone was happy to see him. I had looked after Sarah whilst Caroline was in hospital, and they picked her up on their way home. A week or so before Christmas, Dad rang me. He sounded very breathless and told me that he had had palpitations for a few days. After talking to him for a long while, I made him promise that he would ring the doctor. Hearing nothing else from him, I just presumed that he had done so and was feeling better. Dad and Eve were due to come for a visit during Christmas week so I just carried on with my preparations for the family get together we had every year.

On the day after Boxing Day my brother rang. He invited us to his house to finish off all the food that he had bought. When we arrived, he reminded me of the picture that I had seen in my meditation, showing the big whale being operated upon, and I immediately knew what he was going to say, Dad had died.

Whilst we had been on our way to his house, Eve had rung, asking him to tell us all the sad news. Mam, my sisters and their families arrived and we were all very upset, I can't describe how I felt. This was the man I had looked up to all my life. I had always turned to him when things had been going wrong, I could always rely on Dad to be the calming influence in my life and he supported me in everything I did — even when I had let him down. Eve told me later, that the doctor had confined Dad to bed about 5 days earlier. He had been trying to reach the bathroom when he collapsed with a heart attack.

Apart from getting Bronchitis every year, he never seemed to be really ill. Even after he retired from the *Blind Institute*, he still worked as the *East Yorkshire Area Secretary* to the RNIB. I think I had just imagined he would be here forever. Dad left a big gap in my life that can never be filled. A few days later, Diane went into labour and on 1st January 1987 her first baby girl; Kayleigh Louise came into the world — my third grandchild. I couldn't go to the hospital with her for the birth though; because the day before that I had put my back out and I couldn't move from the dining chair without pain. Diane always said (laughingly) that helping me in and out of my clothes and supporting me when I had to walk, started her labour.

It was a really strange time for me. Of course, I was over the moon with the birth of both the babies, whilst at the same time, being really sad about losing my Dad. Now that Kayleigh had arrived and we were overcrowded, the *Council Housing Department* gave Ray and Diane a house on Marfleet Lane. It was small but they liked it and I kept Kayleigh whilst they were cleaning and decorating the house. About a week later the little family moved into their new home, and life settled down once again for the boys and me.

We had another shock when Paul was about 6 months old. It was discovered that his leg muscles had not developed, and he had to have physiotherapy at the *Child Development Centre* in *Hull Royal Infirmary* for a few years to see if that would strengthen them. I was pleased that this condition had been discovered though, because my family had thought for a while that there was a problem.

One day when Gary was visiting Diane and Ray, he met Sally, who lived near them. After seeing each other a couple of times, they hit it off and started going out together. He was now looking happier than he had done for a long while. I applied for a position as *Deputy House Mother* at *Newland Homes* on Cottingham Road and started working there. It was shift work, mainly Friday morning till Sunday night, living in and looking after teenagers. Some of them had lived in the homes most of their lives, and others were not able to live with their families for different reasons. They were all learning how to live independently. I used to take David with me and I enjoyed the work. When the housemother was ill, or on holiday we would both live in, on weekdays as well as weekends. Gary was at home so I knew our house was safe. Part of my duties, were to make sure the teenagers could manage their housekeeping on their own and deal with any queries or problems that came up. Diane and Caroline used to visit with their children – they were both pregnant again and everything was going right for all of us and I was really happy with my life.

Thinking about how to solve my problem with going out, I decided that if I learned to drive, I would be able to get around much easier. I would be in charge when I was out and if I ever had a panic in the car, I could just turn round and come home again. I booked some lessons and after a couple of false starts I really enjoyed them.

Back at church, I had been receiving messages from mediums saying I needed to pick up my pen to write whatever thoughts came into my mind. This happened a few times and when later, in the circle, I saw a pen in my minds eye and I decided I would try it. I let my pen just rest on the paper without any pressure in my hand and asked for Spirit to be with me. At first the pen moved round and round and scribbled all over the page. Just when I was going to give it up as a bad job, I saw a word forming. It was DAD. I was very excited about this, even though the rest of it didn't make any sense. Gradually though, with lots of practice, I began to have some sort of communication. It always ended with 'Dad'. Later writings seemed to be in Joe's handwriting, finishing up with his name, and I asked the boys to come up into my room to see it for themselves. I was careful not to put pressure on the pen to prove to myself, as well as the boys, that it wasn't being guided by me. As often as I could, I would write, happy to see the words forming and I really felt as if they were both 'talking' to me.

When I told my brother about it, he was worried in case an 'unenlightened' spirit was fooling me. I was due to have a private reading with Beryl, a medium friend of his, and at the end of it I asked her about the writings. She told me that at first it had been Dad and Joe, but I was 'giving them a headache' by calling them so often. I realized from what I had later learned, that there could have also been another spirit 'entity' pretending to be them to keep up the communication. This would have also filled a need in the spirit to contact anyone on the earthplane, to let them know they were still alive.

Feeling despondent and a little apprehensive, I left the pen alone for quite a while. The next time I took it up, the writing and the content was different. The pieces were all philosophical, and signed "your family and friends in the Land of Light". At first I was really upset. I felt as if I had lost Dad and Joe all over again. These emotions soon left me though, and I marvelled at the wonderful 'lift' that always accompanied the writings. They seemed to know how I was feeling at the time and what had been worrying me over the intervening week (I had decided to only write on a Sunday morning) and they always contained really good advice, which gave me the strength to carry on.

In early 1988 I received a phone call from Caroline telling me that she and the children were in temporary accommodation in Ash Grove, after another attempt to leave Chris. She was unhappy with the room she had and the following day, I told her to bring them all to stay with me again and the same thing happened once more. Chris came asking to speak to her. He had bought a house in Hawthorne Avenue and persuaded her to return to him. I'm afraid I was a little relieved, not understanding what was really going on in their lives. Soon after that, Chris bought a house in South Street in Cottingham and they seemed to settle down happily. On 27th July 1988 Caroline, gave birth to Karen, another beautiful child who made their family complete. Jamie Lee was born to Diane and Ray on 16th September, I now had my fourth and fifth grandchildren.

Gary took driving lessons and passed after only a short time, buying himself his first car. He let me practice driving in it one day whilst he sat with me. As I was coming up to a street corner to turn left, I saw a dog, just sitting in the road. I swerved round it and came back in too sharply, I seemed to freeze. Gary was telling me to use the brake but I couldn't think. I ended up banging into a big metal fence on the corner of the street. Although there was no damage, Gary was furious with me for a while. When I got out of the car and threatened to walk home though, he relented – Needless to say, he wouldn't let me drive his car again. We laughed about it later – especially when I had said about walking home. I didn't even know where we where, never mind how to get home. I was really pleased that he didn't take any notice of me.

    I decided that I must have my own car, and I fell in love with one as soon as I saw it. It was a two year old light blue *Fiesta*, which I felt very confident in driving. I had lots of offers to take me out in my new car, but not to sit with me. I wonder why?

    At work, my House Mother fell ill and had to be away for a few weeks. David and I moved into Newland full time. As the teenagers were mostly out during the day, there was nothing for me to do after cleaning my flat. This was fine at first, but the boredom of it started to get me down. I didn't really know anyone on site and it was a long way for my friends to travel to see me. Diane and Caroline did bring their children once a week though. My job was to see that the teenagers managed their meals and to be a shoulder to lean on in case they had any problems or difficulties. There was one strict rule of Newland though, the teenagers could not bring alcohol onto the premises and must be in on time. With the house mother being away, one or two of the boys decided that they would do as they pleased and although I did report their behaviour, it did not stop them. I became more and more worried about this. The days seemed to really drag and I couldn't relax on the night, worrying what the boys were up to.

    Getting up one morning, I just felt as if I couldn't even think anymore. My whole body felt as heavy as lead. I was really frightened, so I asked David to ring George, the healer from church and he came round to help me. He got in touch with Michael, asking him to bring my car to take me home, and then rang the office and spoke to the Manager who was very nice to me and arranged for one of the other housemothers to take over. Someone called the doctor when I arrived home and he said that I was mentally exhausted and that I needed a worry-free environment and lots of proper rest. He gave me medication to help me to do this.

It was a really frightening feeling. I had never experienced my mind 'coming to a standstill' before. As the days passed, however, the strange thing was that I could cope with things going on at home, even working my brain on problems, but whenever I thought about my responsibilities at Newland, my mind would feel 'fuzzy' and all the energy seemed to leave my body. I realized that only a part of my brain had been stressed, and that made me feel a bit better. It took about 3 months for me to really feel well again and I decided that I would have to give my notice in at work because I didn't want to put myself under that stress again. After everything I had gone through with my own children, I had thought that it would have been an ideal job for me to do and I must admit to feeling as if I had somehow let myself down. It was a relief, however, not to have that responsibility anymore.

For quite a while now, I had been back at church, going to the services on Saturday and Sunday evenings, like most of the group, and sitting in our 'working group' on Mondays. I felt I was back where I belonged and thoroughly enjoyed it. Sometimes we would have *Fledglings* services, where our group members would get used to the feel of speaking from the Rostrum, either as the *Chairperson* or the *Medium*. Most of us were receiving messages

A Completely Different Life

for others, but were not yet confident enough to work on our own. During these and services taken by our own mediums, I would write down my thoughts for other people and pass them out to the congregation later. Marlene started taking me with her when she 'spoke' (another word for taking services) at other churches, and when she gave private readings to people.

Whilst being given inspirational writing one day, I had the feeling that these uplifting pieces were not only meant for me, and I knew that I must gather them together into a small book. I enjoyed doing this, and called it *Little Gems of Wisdom*. The introductory piece in the front was also given to me inspirationally and even though the book was 'home made'; we sold quite a few for one pound each to help church funds. I would also use the pieces as 'chairpersons readings', when it was my turn to take the 'chair' during services.

In the November of that year, Mam turned 80. Along with Jess, Mums partner, my sisters, Brenda and Marian, and some of our children, we had all decided to give her a little party to celebrate. We booked the room in the *Arctic Ranger Public House* on Hall Road, made a buffet and invited all her friends from her over 60s club. Brenda's daughters, Linda and Gillian put up decorations, some of which they brought and some the landlady had supplied. Mum thought Marian and Brenda were taking her for a drink; and when she walked into the pub and saw everyone there, she was really pleased. To top off the afternoon Brenda, Marian and I sang the Andrew Sisters' song, "Sisters" to her and the pride in her eyes made the day special to us as well as to her.

Some upsetting news came after Christmas. Stephen and Audrey had been having problems and they had decided to separate for a while to see how things worked out. I hoped they would be able to work out their differences because we all liked Audrey and I had never seen Stephen so happy.

I still had not managed to pass my driving test, and I was getting a bit despondent. I was not getting much practice in my car and I wondered if I ever would be able to drive on my own. My nerves had let me down all the time. Every time I failed a test it was for a different mistake. As soon as an examiner got into the car with his clipboard and I knew I wasn't allowed to talk to him, I seemed to go to pieces and make silly mistakes. After my fourth failed test I changed instructors to Ray Bullock. He was really great with me and I'm sure I understood more with his teaching than anyone else I had been with. One more failed test almost put my confidence on to the floor, but I knew that I wasn't going to just give up, even after all the disappointments I had gone through. Ray said it would make me more confident to use my own car for the lessons and the test so that made me feel better.

The day of my sixth test arrived and I was surprised and very relieved to see that I was to have one of the first lady examiners in Hull and it was to be at the *Salisbury Street Test Centre*. Ray had also told me that I would be able to speak about the moves I would make, although I would not get an answer. Following this advice made me more confident and I sailed through the test. Every time I made a move, which could have been different, I told the examiner why I had done it and at the end of the lesson I thought "If I haven't passed this time, I don't know what else I can do". When I was told I had passed, I nearly put my arms round the ladies neck, but instead I just kept saying 'Thank you'. Afterwards, as I drove round to tell Stephen and then my Mum – who lived in Earlscourt – my news, I was a bit afraid. The realization just hit me that I was in charge of this 'weapon', which could easily turn into a killer if I didn't keep all my attention on my driving. For a couple of months after that my stomach turned over whenever I saw an 'L' driver, knowing that they still had to face the TEST. The more I drove though, the more I was sure that all the time, money and effort that had gone into making me a safe driver, had been well spent. I now knew that I hadn't been ready to face the road on my own before this.

My life had really opened up, I could now go shopping, visit my family and go to church whenever I wanted without any worry. I visited supermarkets and big stores with ease — as long as I could park near the entrance — and I felt that I was really 'living' for the first time since my early twenties. I enjoyed taking the family anywhere they wanted to go as well. My car was referred to as 'Mum's cabs' and I loved it.

My Mum had always expressed interest in church (almost always saying "did they say anything about me?") which always made us laugh. Now that I was a competent driver, I started taking her every weekend and she really looked forward to going. She would always sit on the front row and try to 'boost me on' when I was a bit hesitant. With her dry humour, she soon became a favourite of lots of the people, including visiting mediums. I had gradually gained enough confidence to be able to give proof that Life goes on, without writing the messages down and was soon working for the other churches in Hull on my own. It made me feel really privileged to, at last, be able to help and comfort people, as I had been, so many times over the years. I found out that no matter how I felt before hand, either 'stomach troubles' or just being 'one degree under', as soon as I stood up, Spirit lifted all the conditions from me and it was only when the service finished that I remembered how I had felt. Marlene always told us that it was normal to feel a bit nervous before a service. It was a relief to know that most mediums feel the same.
I started to accept bookings to take the services at other churches, which were spaced out between Lincoln and Scarborough and it was a great experience to see how the other churches were

organised. Someone always came with me and I even enjoyed the travelling.

One night however, I was booked to go to *Grimsby Church* and I asked a medium friend of mine, Joan, to go with me. I knew she was learning to drive so I was confident that if I panicked, Joan would be able to take over (I seemed to get more courage when I had a 'lifeline' to fall back on, even though I have never, ever had to use it). On the way there we both sang our heads off enjoying the journey. The service went well and we set off for home confidently (both singing again). As we came into the countryside, fog started rolling in. At the roundabout which would take us to the *Humber Bridge*, I took the wrong turning and ended up on the motorway going west. By now the fog was so thick that Joan had to sit with her nose almost pressed against the windscreen looking for obstacles, whilst I literally crawled along. I had told Joan how I had thought she might be able to take over if I had panicked but she said that as a learner driver, she wouldn't be able to help on a motorway. Although I was very frightened, I sent out to Spirit for help and just 'locked' my hands onto the steering wheel. We had no idea where we were. Work was being done on this motorway and the few exit signs we may have been able to see were covered up and there wasn't anyway that I could turn off. I didn't have much money on me and I prayed I would not run out of petrol. After what seemed to be an age, we saw a sign welcoming us into Humberside – I didn't even know we had been out of Humberside! Before long we saw a sign for Doncaster and the M62. Finally arriving in Hull, we were very relieved to see that the fog had entirely disappeared. Joan knew the way from her house on County Road South so she was able to direct me back home – or so she thought. Again I lost my way and ended up somewhere near Brighton Street on Hessle Road. At a petrol station I was once again given directions and after completing a journey (which should have taken about 20 minutes) lasting about 45 minutes I arrived home safely.

It took me quite a while to settle down after this, but I realized that no matter what scrapes we get ourselves into, if we can put our faith and trust in Spirit, we will arrive home safely every time. Everyone said how brave I was, but I certainly hadn't felt it that night, although we have laughed about it since.

On the home front, Gary had enquired about joining the 'Specials', but was advised to apply for the *Police Force* instead and he was accepted. This was something he had wanted to do since he had been in Junior School. He had set his mind on this as a career and I was proud to think he was going to give it a try. On 28th December 1989 Gary and Sally were married and lived with David and me for a short while, but they naturally wanted a place of their own. For the last part of his training Gary was sent to Cleethorpes and when a police house became vacant they moved there. I didn't like the feeling of my dwindling family, but there was always something going on around me and David used to bring his friends in so it wasn't too bad. A few months later Gary found that working in the Police was not what he wanted after all. Sally was also very unhappy living away from her family so they came back to Hull, getting a house on Tanfield Grove, Bilton Grange.

I had been feeling at a loss with myself for a long time, so decided that I would offer my help to the *Danes Community Centre*, at the top of Dibsdane. This was gratefully accepted and I took up the post of Secretary. I really enjoyed the work and especially the meetings. It gave me something, outside the family to think about. I still enjoyed being the Booking/Minutes Secretary at church, and taking services, but again I didn't think I was doing enough.

Once again Caroline left Chris and moved in with me, this

time applying for a house in Feldane so she could be near us. Paul had been given callipers to help him to walk and Caroline was showing signs of strain. She contracted Yellow Jaundice and was admitted to *Castle Hill Hospital*. I couldn't cope with all the children myself, so Diane looked after Paul and Karen. Sarah, who was, by then attending Dane Park School, stayed with me. It had been discovered that Paul also had problems communicating with anyone (I always say that it seemed like a form of Autism because, when he was only about 18 months old, Paul could understand and work some things out for himself). It was recommended that he should go into Respite Care at *Newland House* on Beverley Road, to give Caroline a break. We went to see the house and were pleased with the way the staff reacted to all the other disabled children, so we decided we would see how Paul settled down there. We took him after nursery on a Wednesday and picked him up on the Friday teatime. He stayed with them two nights and the staff took him to his nursery on Thursdays and Fridays. He enjoyed being there.

Diane gave birth to Larissa Jo-ann on February 28th 1990 (my 6th grandchild) but began suffering with post-natal depression. She came to stay with me for a while. Ray used to bring Larissa to see her Mum and it wasn't long before Diane wanted to go home again with the baby.

Whilst meditating one day, I was very surprised to 'hear' the words of a poem coming into my mind and quickly picked up a book and pen. This is how it unfolded.

> *When I sit down and ponder, on wondrous things that be*
> *I thank my God o'er yonder, for giving them to me*
>
> *When I see the flowers in bloom, the birds flying overhead,*
> *And feel the cool breeze round me; I thank God for the shed*

> I smell the blossoms and the trees, and try to wonder why
> If we only live 3 score years and ten, did someone bother to try?
>
> Why should it matter if flowers bloom? Why bother to make birds sing? If we're only on this earth a while, why bother about anything?
>
> You see my friends a caring God, has thought it out before
> To let us know we're not alone, that we have been before
>
> If you stop and listen to the song that comes with each Spring
> And note that flowers and trees once 'dead', now bloom again to bring
>
> New hope and Love to all mankind, to tell us of our King,
> Who, loving all His children, gave the pleasures just for them
>
> He does not bring us money; He does not bring us wealth
> His treasures are all free for us; they're Happiness and Health

This was a new experience for me. As soon as I started writing one line, the next would already be in my mind, it was like *magic*. I couldn't wait to read my poem out to my family and friends and they enjoyed my experience also. I discovered that the poems reflected anything I had been reading about or was interested in at the time. The next one was an example.

> When you're feeling down just listen, to the voice of Love serene
> It tells us where we're going to, and maybe where we've been
>
> The voice of Love calls out to all, who live on this sceptred Isle
> Whilst you're on this Earthplane, cheer someone with a smile

So if you feel down hearted and troubles come by the score
Just think of this, the voice of Love, and they will be no more

I was thinking back to how Mum used to be in her younger days, when she loved dancing. I was given the next one, which I thought was very appropriate.

Not the quickstep, I couldn't stand it; it used to be a sheer delight,
but now I'm passed it, let me out into the night.

When I get lonely, I listen to the sounds
That used to thrill me, with the beat of raucous bands

The music came loud and the air was hot
My feet were so light but my head was not

The magic in the beat set my feet a tapping; I could really have laughed out loud. When I thought about going I was certainly flapping

My poor old feet and back couldn't stand it
I honestly don't know why I suddenly planned it

Can you see my dilemma, a heart full of prancing?
When you're past 82, should you really be dancing?

I was showing David my poems and explaining how quickly they were given, when he asked me to write one whilst he was there. This is what came.

Such a pleasant little fellow, nearly always full of fun
He likes to make folk happy when there's drawings to be done
He'll sit for hours and hours, to try to please the folk

Drawing faces, cars and letters, are the things he likes the most
If you ask him for a favour, he'll be sure to try to please
And will tell you what you want to know, not always at your ease

When he's down in the dumps he looks at Life
As one long problem, full of strife
He doubts himself and others too
Until at last the sun breaks through
Then all at once you'll see him smile
You know he's happy again for a while
If you want him to be good to you
Just try to find drawings for him to do

On the computer he's quite a whiz
But some of the problems have him in quite a tizz
He'll sit for hours and hours and ponder
Trying to work out this or that
But suddenly it all falls into place
With an excited yell he'll let you know
He's solved it and the smiles back on his face

David watched me writing quickly and was very pleased and surprised when he saw the content of the poem. It had even changed rhythm to match the rap style music that he also enjoyed when he was younger. I continued to write poems and pieces of philosophy whenever I asked Spirit for them.

Back on the home front, things were getting serious once again. Paul had started *Dane Park Primary School*, but as he could not really understand the lessons, and the school didn't have the staff or the facilities he needed, he was transferred to *Tesky King School* on Cottingham Road. In the November, Caroline was allocated a house at the bottom of Feldane and it was a great relief to both of us. I would be able to help her now, without the hassle of us all trying to share a house. David and I settled down to enjoy a relatively quiet life, I remember Joe always saying that we must try to enjoy the quiet times because we never knew when things would get hectic and stressful again.

Stephen was trying to patch up his marriage to Audrey and had started visiting her at regular intervals. She had been suffering with crippling headaches for a while and Stephen would take her medication from the all night chemists. Their Christmas had been planned, Stephen was to join Audrey, her son Arthur and his family for Christmas Dinner. On Boxing Day, he was to go with one of her other sons (also Stephen) to have dinner at Audrey's house.

As they weren't due until 12.00PM on Boxing Day, Stephen spent the morning with Arthur and his family. In the middle of the morning, Audrey's son Stephen went round and told them that he had found that his mother had died. Stephen, along with everyone else in Audrey's family, was naturally distraught and nothing anyone of us could do could console him. It was found that Audrey had suffered a massive brain haemorrhage caused by a ruptured blood vessel and we think the crippling headaches had been symptoms of this.

Chris wasn't very happy for the children to be living in Feldane, so early in the following year, he persuaded Sarah to live in Cottingham with him, and a few months later he took Paul also. Caroline was struggling to come to terms with everything that had happened and she just didn't have the strength to fight his decision although she did promise Karen that she would never let her go.

Gary and Sally had settled happily in their house and on the 17th July 1991 their first child, Adam John was born. He was my seventh grandchild and we were all very happy for them. Even

A Completely Different Life

Joe's sisters, Grace and Anne came over from York at different times to see Adam. The little family had to move into temporary accommodation for a few months however whilst the houses in Tanfield Grove were being re-furbished. As theirs was the first family to move back in after the work had been completed, the Lord Mayor visited them and the council sent photographers to record the changes to the house. They also took a picture of Gary Sally and Adam in their front garden. David and I were also there and Diane, Ray and their children walked round to join us. We all had a lovely day.

Whilst working for the *Danes Neighbourhood Committee*, a notice on the Job Vacancies board took my attention. It was for a part time Secretary with *Orchard Park & North Hull Enterprises*, (OPNHE). This was a company, based on the former site of *Sir Leo Schultz School* in Danepark Road which was setting up to give work and other opportunities to the residents of the area. There were quite a few candidates and a lady who lived opposite, (Debbie) and I were appointed and started work in October 1991 sharing the role – with Debbie working mornings and me taking the afternoons. I thoroughly enjoyed it there, helping to set up the office and compiling a register of residents wishing to join the company, taking minutes at meetings and lots of other administration work. As well as that, it again gave me a rest from worrying about the family. In January 1992, I had my eighth grandchild. Leon Joe was born to Diane and Ray. Everyone was thrilled and although they didn't know it at the time, he made their family complete.

One day not long after that, Barbara (next door) and I were talking about how, now that our families had dwindled, our houses were too big for us and that other people with big families would be pleased to have them. We decided to put in an application to a housing association to get one of the new bungalows being built in Priory Road. As Barbara had had a stroke and was disabled, I thought that she would be easily accepted. We didn't know if the fact that David was still living at home would affect my application though. Anyway, I thought it was worth a try.

Stephen met his future wife Margo also that year. She had a daughter Kerry who was about 2 years old. I was pleased for him because he had been really lonely since his wife Audrey had died. Margo moved in with him and it was great to see him being happy and to have a 'daughter' to care for.

I had been suffering with back pain, caused by a prolapsed womb after giving birth to Gary in 1966 and decided that, at long last I would do something to alleviate the situation. The result of this was that I had a hysterectomy in the November of that year. Diane came to stay with me for the first week or so, until I could manage again on my own and I soon recovered, happy in the knowledge that I was at last free from the discomfort.
In the beginning of the following year, 1993, my brother in law, Terry, who had been ill for quite a while, died. Of course we were all very sad about this.

Shortly after this my friend (Barbara next door) also died. Her passing was a big shock to me as well as her family, and I missed her very much. We had known each other since I had been at *Sidmouth Street Infants' School* with her sister Pat and I had been nursing at *Western General Hospital* with Barbara and her elder sister Val. We had been next-door neighbours since 1966 and even lived close by for the six years before that. Her husband John and I both decided later, that because it was what Barbara had wanted; we would still carry on with our intention to move to Priory Road.

I went back to work after three months convalescence and it felt great to be doing something worthwhile again. Caroline

A Completely Different Life 251

gave birth to her fourth child, a beautiful little boy named Craig on 29th April – my ninth grandchild. We were all pleased to see the little one and for a while everything seemed to calm down, although I knew it was going to be hard for her to cope on her own. Another great event was when on 19th September Sophie Ann was born to Gary and Sally (grandchild number 10). She was a pretty little thing and she also made their family complete. Everyone was very happy for them. At the end of that year, Caroline met her future partner, Stuart, and for the first time in many years, she was really happy.

For a couple of years, Mam had been complaining of pain in her back but the doctors didn't seem worried about this. She now lived on her own because her partner of many years, Jess, had died in December 1989. My sisters and I visited and helped her whenever we could. I still took her to church on a weekend, which she really enjoyed and she also liked meeting her friends at the over sixties club; especially going on holidays with them every year.

One night in October Mam rang me. She had fallen off her chair and couldn't get back up. I immediately rang my younger sister – who by then lived in East Hull – before setting off to Mam's house. She was adamant that she didn't want me to ring the doctor, but luckily, when my sister and her husband arrived, they persuaded her and Mam was taken into *Castle Hill Hospital*. Her condition deteriorated and on the 6th November 1993 she peacefully passed away. All of her children and some of her grandchildren and in laws were round her bedside on her last day and we were able to show her how much we loved her. We had taken it in turns to stay with her, my youngest sister, brother in law and I had been with her all the night, but luckily, before we went home for a change of clothes and a rest, we said our goodbye's to her. It was only a couple of hours later that my sister got the call that Mam had peacefully passed away, we were all, naturally, devastated.

I was really pleased that, after all the years that I had been angry with her, I had had the last 21 years to try to make up for that. We had both grown to know and love each other very much better in that time and I really regretted the years gone by when we had lost the closeness of the mother/daughter relationship we should have had.

Mum had always worried about how long she had left to live. Her sister had told her that because their Mum – Granny Abram – had died at 80yrs; no one in the family had lived longer than that. It made Mum feel good to know that she was coming up to her 84th birthday. Although I know without doubt that we will meet again and even laugh about these things, there is still an empty hole inside me, missing her physical presence. Sometimes though, when my younger sister or I look into the mirror, Mam's face looks back at us. I often feel that she is with me when I take services. I have the same dry humour, or clever little asides that made her so unforgettable.

OPNHE had decided that their retirement age would be 60yrs so in February 1994 I had to retire. I must admit I was relieved about this because I hadn't been feeling so well for a few months. I had been counting down the days until I didn't have to go to work anymore. Diane had to see a specialist about a problem with the veins in her womb and it was a shock to her to be told that she would also have to have a hysterectomy. She was absolutely devastated about this, at only 26yrs old, and loving children, she really wanted to have a bigger family. Diane came to stay with me for a while afterwards so that I could look after her, but again, it wasn't long before, naturally, she wanted to go home.

John (next door) had received a letter from the housing

association offering him a bungalow on Priory Road even though he was now by himself. He decided that he would take it. I still hadn't heard about my application though and I wondered if I would ever get the opportunity to move. With all the talk about moving to a bungalow, and wondering if it would be possible with him being at home, David started looking round at flats. He eventually found one in Pearson Park on Beverley Road and liked it as soon as he saw it. It was an attic flat and the floor sloped at an angle, but David liked the 'quirkiness' of that. It had a large living room and even larger bedroom, off which there was a bathroom with two doors, one leading to back to the hall. David moved in the September of that year. The flat turned out to be boiling hot in the summer and just as freezing cold in the winter.

Rattling around in my big three bedroomed house, I suddenly felt really lonely. After 35 years of having a family around me (30 of them with children at school), I was alone and I didn't like the feeling at all. I started clearing out furniture and things that I wouldn't need, even down to giving the children all the birthday cards I had kept for them since they had all been born. It took me hours looking through them all, laughing and crying to myself at all the different memories. I even managed to throw away all the birthday and anniversary cards sent to Joe and me over the years. Although I put my cards to Joe on the pile for recycling, I just could not think of parting with his to me.

 I was seeing quite a bit of Caroline and Craig, but she was going through a very hard time; coming to terms with everything that had happened in her life. Later, Craig was taken into care, but the reason for this is Caroline's story, not mine. We were all very upset about this and unfortunately at that time none of us were able to help. I used to take Caroline and Diane to see him at the foster carer's house and also one on Greenwood Avenue. At the start of 1995 I was suffering quite a bit with depression and anxiety. The children all tried to make me feel better and even stayed with me for a couple of days in turn. One day, Gary and Diane said they would feel better if I moved closer to them and asked me to think about moving to East Hull.

As I had always lived in Central or North Hull, I didn't know what to do. I had been to see John in his new bungalow on Priory Road, but thought the rooms were very small compared to the size of mine in Feldane, so I didn't fancy moving there (even if one had been offered to me). After giving it a lot of thought, I decided that I would see if it was possible to move to East Hull. I found that living in a big family house, and wanting to 'downsize', gave me lots of points and quite an advantage, so Diane and I went to the *Old Bilton Grange Housing* office in Wingfield Road and filled in an application form. The only stipulation I made was that I must have a side drive to get my car off the road. The houses in that area were all being refurbished but I didn't have to wait long before 'mine' was ready for me to move into. I had been given a house at Grange Road end of Wingfield Road. I received the letter on 6th March telling me to collect the keys on 7th (This was Diane's birthday and would also have been my 35th wedding anniversary).

The same night, we went to look at the house from the outside and I was really pleased. It was a red brick; semi detached and had double drive gates to the side of the house. There was a big stretch of open ground opposite, where prefabs had once stood. The thing I liked best though was the big bay window. In Stanley Street we lived in a small terrace and in Feldane the houses were in rows behind each other so I had never had such an open view since I had lived for a couple of years at the *Naval Wireless Station* in Grimsby.

Diane, Ray and some of his friends had all been waiting for

my house allocation and as soon as I picked up the keys the next day, they sprung into action. Although even the walls, doors and windows were new, it still needed cleaning and this was done in no time. My carpets were taken up from Feldane and laid down in the new house and some of the smaller items of furniture were taken also. That night, Diane and 'Co' stayed there to make sure that the house wasn't broken into. Caroline stayed with me on the night before I moved and as I went round putting window lock keys into drawers where they would be found by the next occupant, I thought what a contrast this night was, to the night we had left Stanley Street to move to Orchard Park. I had asked the council to put up the shutters on the windows in Feldane before we left because I had heard how kitchens, fires and other items were being stolen as soon as houses were emptied, and the 'departing tenants' were liable to pay for them.

On the 9th March 1995, only two days after I had received the keys for Wingfield Road, I left Feldane behind and happily drove away. Stuart had been with David to hire a van and they had moved the rest of the furniture. When we arrived at the new house later, all the furniture had been arranged. My brother in law put up curtain rails and did other odd carpentry jobs that needed doing. The only thing I had to do was organise cupboards and drawers. The following day Diane, Caroline and I went back to give the old house one last clean and we all said how strange it was that we didn't feel any emotion whatsoever about leaving. I had been there 29 years and the children had lived there all their lives.

I knew that I was taking Joe's love with me, and I would never forget the good times we had all shared there. The prospect of an entirely new start excited me and I couldn't wait to see what the future had in store.

CHAPTER NINE

My Healing Journey Begins

ONCE I SETTLED INTO MY NEW HOUSE I reflected upon just how lucky I really was. Although Joe had worked all his life, he did not earn a big wage, therefore, with six children to feed and clothe we were never able to save enough money to buy our own house. We were very lucky with the *Hull City Council* properties that we rented though, with the Feldane house being newly built and now this one. The *icing on the cake* was the view from my living room window of the sky, ablaze with a red glow as the sun went down. I had not seen such a sight for over 40 years. I took lots of photographs of the phenomena.

Although I confess to feeling not a little anxious when I first decided to move — wondering how I would cope with my new life — now that I had actually arrived, that feeling totally left me. Walking through the rooms, the whole house seemed warm and welcoming. I was really looking forward to seeing how the next phase of my life unfolded.

Diane's husband Ray came from a large extended family,

My Healing Journey Begins

most of whom had grown up in the area, so as Diane and I went out in my car, she was recognised and waved to. It wasn't long before people became aware of my relationship also and even when I drove by myself, they acknowledged me. I used to say that I felt like Noddy in his little red car with everyone waving to me. Even children who lived nearby would shout "Hiya Nanna" to me as they played.

The first year turned out to be very memorable, with lots of positive things happening. One day, shortly after I arrived, I took Kayleigh and her cousin Rachel with me to *Leo's* (which is now *Morrisons*) on Holderness Road. On the way back home, I had almost reached Maybury Road corner, when I felt a strange quiet sensation inside and realized that I couldn't see through my left eye. I immediately sent out to Spirit for help. As I have always had a 'lazy eye' on my right side, it had un-nerved me for a minute or two, but I knew I must get home safely with the two children. I could still make out objects with my 'lazy' eye and by keeping to the lines in the centre of the road, I managed to drive correctly and we arrived home without mishap. Luckily Diane had just come from work to pick Kayleigh up at the same time, so that was a relief to me. By that time I didn't even recognise my washing on the line and when I tried to speak, the words came out as 'gibberish'. Diane took me up to bed and called the doctor.

I was diagnosed as having had a slight stroke and when I later went for tests at the hospital, the specialist told me that he couldn't understand what had happened. He said there had been a large clot but somehow it had broken up. I felt sure that it was Spirit intervention that had saved us all that day. I was left feeling rather nervous again though; my confidence had been shattered and for quite a while I was unsure how far I could push myself.

Even though this was a bit traumatic, I still felt that it had happened for a reason. It was a 'wake up' call that I had to change my way of life. I needed to stop trying to achieve 100% in everything I did; 'beating myself up' when I could not reach the goals I had set for myself and most of all worrying about the family – even though none of them wanted me to.

I had to give up going to church for a while and I also asked if someone else could take over my medium Booking and Minute Secretary duties. This was hard for me to do after 9 years but I felt that I just couldn't take the responsibility anymore. Although others tried to take over from me, no one could commit to the job for very long and Marlene took it on, along with her Presidential duties.

At the same time, Gary and Sally had been having serious marital problems, so not long after that he came to stay with me for a while. Even after giving the relationship another chance, the split became permanent and Gary left for good, coming back to my house until he decided what to do. It was a very upsetting time for all of them, especially for Adam and Sophie. I must admit that I was relieved to have him stay for a while though, because I had become a little nervous about being on my own – although I would never have admitted that to anyone (When Joe had died, I had told all the children that I would never, ever allow any one of them to give up anything in their lives for me).

Slowly but surely, feeling almost back to my old self, I started driving again and fell back into my routine at church, which I loved. With Marlene's help and the promise from me that I would tell her if it became too much for me, I gladly took up my secretarial duties again. This was to become the norm for the next 8 years with both of us taking on the work; sometimes Marlene and sometimes me. When our church was granted charity

My Healing Journey Begins

status, the members of our group had all been made *Trustees* to the Charity. This, however, brought with it rules and lots more responsibility, which we were all pleased to accept.

At every excuse there was, Diane and I gave all the children a party. When Caroline, Sarah, Paul and Karen came for the weekend – when Adam and Sophie came, or when almost anyone had a birthday, we always had a party. The grown ups enjoyed the get-togethers as much as the children did. We had two visits from Craig before he was fostered away from Hull, and we brought everyone together again for this, although these were very sad occasions.

In the August, Caroline moved into Stuart's house and I was pleased that she was no longer on her own. We were told later that if Stuart had been able to commit to Caroline before Craig went away, he would not have had to go. Unfortunately, these had been very early days in their relationship and neither knew if it was to be permanent.

On November 2nd 1995 a beautiful blonde haired, blue eyed baby (little Stephen) was born to Margo and Stephen (my 11th grandchild). A few weeks later they were married. I was very proud to have been asked to sing at their wedding, and the landlady at the pub told us that everything had gone quiet in other rooms as well to listen (One of Stephens friends asked me if he could be my 'manager', but I laughingly told him he was 40 years too late!).

Michael had not been coping very well living in a flat by himself and we were all very concerned because, finding out that he was still buying drugs, we were afraid for his life, so early in 1996 Diane and Ray took him to live with them and he settled down very well, but his memory was distorted and he was still plagued by thoughts that he would be kidnapped and mutilated. Sometimes it would only take a snatch of an overheard conversation, a word said by someone in total innocence, or even the sight of a stationery van near him, to trigger this very distressing reaction. Anyway, we all supported him and tried to make him feel as safe as we could.

The next couple of years passed without any real trauma. I enjoyed going out shopping and visiting the family with Diane. By that time Diane was also coming regularly to the church and enjoying it. I was still receiving inspirational writings and poetry and travelling with friends or my brother to take services at churches as far away as Lincoln in the South and Scarborough in the North and was really enjoying the freedom. Learning to drive was the best idea I had ever had, because even though I dare not walk anywhere, I could at least get out in my car. Around Hull I was very confident – sometimes, even on my own.

I had always liked baking and my pastry was very good, although I must say I would never have won any awards for it. Spurred on by all the buffets we made for the family parties, Diane and I agreed to make anniversary, wedding receptions and birthday celebration food for some of Ray's family and our friends and that was enjoyable – especially when we were also invited.

Gary and Sally divorced and because of the children, Gary was devastated. For a short time, Sally would bring them to our house and leave them for a while, but not long after, the visits just stopped. By that time, Gary was working at *Dove House* as the Lottery Manager and one day, seeing that I needed something else to keep me occupied, he suggested I apply to be a volunteer there. I had an interview and was taken on to help in the General Office.

After only being there about five weeks, a vacancy came up for a part time Secretary, which I was encouraged to apply for. This I did and my application was successful.

My Healing Journey Begins

I really enjoyed the work; there was such a variety of tasks for me to do. After a few months, my main task was typing reports for the Health and Safety Manager. In my spare time, I saw an advert for a Doll's House Kit in a magazine by *Del Prado*. The parts would come every fortnight, along with full instructions for building all the furniture as well as the house. As, years before, I had helped Joe to make dolls houses for Christmas; I was very keen to see if I could build one by myself.

I seemed to always have the compulsion to do more, as if I had to prove to everyone – including myself that I wasn't 'useless'. I had always felt guilty knowing that other people had sometimes spent almost a lifetime out at work and I hadn't. I think it may have had something to do with my earlier experiences. Even at church I always felt that I had to volunteer for almost anything that came up, even if, deep down, I hadn't really wanted to.

I sent for this kit and started to build. I found out that if I placed my order with the *Del Prado* publishing company I would get a free gift of the 'House' family (as I called them). I am not altogether good at doing the basic work on anything. I always think I can miss steps out because in my mind, everything seems so easy – although it often never turns out that way (When I was learning to play the piano, I didn't want to practice the scales, I wanted to play the finished pieces. And when I started making clothes for myself and the children in my younger days I didn't see the need for pinning and tacking the work, so I skipped the tacking stage), of course I soon found out that things really needed to be done the 'right way' even if it took longer.

Anyway, I got my come-uppance on the house. After putting the downstairs walls together – as well as I thought I could – I started putting the ceilings into place and the first floor walls in. Imagine my horror when I discovered they didn't fit. I had to take it all back to scratch, send for some more walls and start again. I did get it right in the end though, even the furniture, although I was not very good at varnishing.

The finished house looked a picture, with electricity and brightly coloured lampshades in all the rooms, pretty curtains at all the windows and the staircase going up in the centre behind the front door. I enjoyed putting the 'House family' in various poses downstairs, although 'Mother house' usually ended up draped over the kitchen sink or the cooker, whilst 'Father House' lounged on the settee in the living room and the children usually ended up entertaining the baby at the kitchen table! I did have a little trouble fixing the minute screws into the tiny hinges on the doors, but after several attempts I managed it. When that particular project in the magazine should have ended after two years, they started inviting people to 'build another bedroom in the roof and a sun-lounge and playground', but by that time, I felt bad just thinking about lifting a screwdriver so I didn't bother.

The children who lived nearby would come, almost every week and ask to see how I was getting on with the house; they even brought friends who I had never seen before to look at it. David took lots of pictures and even for a year or so after, the children would come to ask if I had any photos of the house left.

As, at church we were all working our socks off to try to raise enough money for our Building Fund to buy a bigger property, I thought it would be a good idea to raffle the house to help funds (In any case, I couldn't bear to have to mend it again if it was broken by any of my grandchildren – even if I could decide who to give it to). The raffle was a great success and raised a good bit of money. Back home, Stephens divorce from Margo had become finalised. He had the custody of little Stephen whilst Margo had her own daughter Kerry. About the same time, Sally and her new husband took Adam and Sophie to live near his family in Wick, right at the top of Scotland. They couldn't have been much farther away and I thought we'd never see them again. Gary and I were really upset by this.

I started to feel unwell at work and was brought home. The doctor said it was stress brought on by, once again, pushing myself too hard, and I was prescribed anti depressant tablets. By that time my 65th birthday was not far away so I decided once again to retire.

Taking the tablets made me feel a lot better and before long I started back at church again. This time I decided that I could not manage both nights on the weekend so I just went on Sundays, except when I was taking the service on a Saturday night, although I did still take the services at the other churches. One night my brother went with me to Lincoln. It was a very rainy night and even though I was looking forward to taking the service, my confidence in my driving in those conditions was not very high. The road was so narrow and the oncoming traffic seemed so near. I persevered though and we eventually arrived. I was shaking and feeling so stressed that I had to be given healing before I could start the service, but once I started, Spirit 'lifted me', as they always do and I was able to give good evidence of survival. My brother drove home but after that I completely lost my confidence for driving long distances and haven't been out of town from that day to this.

On November 2nd 1996 my 12th grandchild, Rachel was born to Caroline and Stuart. It was great to see another lovely child in the family. When the *Social Services* found out that Caroline was pregnant, they told her that the baby would be taken away and fostered as soon as she was born, but that didn't happen. Someone did come to see Rachel a couple of months later, and they were quite satisfied that she was being well cared for, so that was the end of that worrying time for all of us. Stuart had two children from a previous marriage, Richard and Sarah, and now their family was also complete.

At church we always made sure that there was one of our own mediums to cover each service in case the visiting medium couldn't turn up. I volunteered to be the permanent Sunday cover, leaving the others to serve other churches without worry. This made me feel as if I was still pulling my weight. Pam and I had started a Thursday afternoon service, to cater for people who were not able to come out on a night and it was going very well. George said that he would take on the role of cover medium every other Thursday and as other members of our group had also been able to commit, I was only needed every fortnight. Pam was still the *mainstay*, working every Thursday and also a Saturday evening, only having time off when she was ill or on holiday.

As our congregation was outgrowing the one first floor room we had, we started looking into renting bigger premises and began to raise building funds by holding 'special' services, for which we would take a small charge along with raffles, tombolas, selling crystals and various other means. A couple of years later and after many emotional ups and downs, we found a suitable property further down the street. It was a great feeling; we would now have the whole three storied house with space to hold psychic suppers and different groups as well as storage space for the many other functions we would hold. On 13th July 1999, the day after Marlene came back from her holiday, she signed the lease. It took lots of planning, organisation, symbolic 'hair pulling', and very hard work, to bring the house up to the high standard we wanted, but the end product was very satisfying for us all. Shortly after we moved 'lock, stock and barrel' into no. 23 John Street, where we still are today. We held a *Dedication Service* on 9th January 2000, inviting people who had supported the church years before, as well as its present group members.

Realizing that we still had to work hard to cover costs and

maintenance of the church, we threw ourselves wholeheartedly into more fundraising. We held *Psychic Suppers, Evenings of Private Readings, Clairvoyant evenings, 'Special' Services* as well as different groups taken by Marlene, Rita and Gordon. Almost every evening (and some afternoons) had something going on, including *Healing* on Wednesdays. As well as raising funds for ourselves, we also held special days in aid of the hospitals in Hull, and with the help of the congregation, we collected and filled over two hundred shoe boxes for a Third World Appeal. We also put on venues for other worthy causes. It was a great feeling for us all. I started an *Awareness Group* on a Monday afternoon and it turned out to be like a dinner club as well. I, true to form however, didn't run the group for 10 weeks at a time as was normal, because no-one wanted a break, so we carried on through. My group only lasted for about 18 months though, because the usual pattern occurred and it became too much for me again. By popular demand, my brother started another group on a Monday afternoon a month or two later.

Back home, things were looking up in one direction at least. In the years since he had come to live with Diane and Ray, Michael had taken himself off all 'recreational' drugs, without help from anyone. One day he said he had just realized (what we had all being telling him for years), that the drugs were stopping his medication working, therefore causing him more mental pain; so there and then he decided to stop taking them. His psychiatrist, doctor, community nurses, as well as his friends and family were all very proud of his achievement. Not long after this Michael decided to stop smoking as well. He had even bought himself a second hand car and enjoyed going for runs out to the seaside or the country with Diane and her family. This was such a relief to me, because, in my mind, I have always had a picture of the younger Michael who was very smart, full of energy, and also enjoyed working and helping anyone who needed a hand. Over the last few years I have felt as if I was fighting a losing battle; he didn't seem to want to change and again I even feared for his life. Now, however, I didn't have that worry.

In November 2001 David, my youngest son, met his future partner Lee-Ann. When he brought her to meet me I was absolutely delighted. They were like 'two peas in a pod', not in looks but in their gentle outlook on life; both vegetarian; both very caring for other people and especially for the planet. Lee-Ann can't forget what I said to her that day. I said that I was very pleased that they had found each other, I really think they are soulmates. The icing on the cake in that situation was the birth of William, my 13th grandchild – on my 69th birthday! – February 13th 2003.

Soon after that, Diane helped Ray's family to organise a surprise party for his Nanna's 80th birthday. It was a great success and as she told me about it later, Diane said that they would never be able to do that for me, because I would never go somewhere out of the blue. After ignoring the 'turning over' of my stomach, I replied that as long as I knew where it would be and that I could feel comfortable getting there in my car, I would really enjoy it (When I go anywhere, I feel I need to have my own car so that I can 'escape' if I need to). A family conference (without me, of course) was held about this idea and my 'surprise' 70th birthday party the following February was arranged. I called it the best kept 'surprise' that never was. Naturally, I was kept in the dark about any of the plans they were making, although I must confess to trying my hardest to find out – discreetly, of course, but to no avail.

Diane had been having a lot of pain in her back, but had just been prescribed with pain-killers. On the 7th February 2004, she was finally given a body scan to find out exactly what was

My Healing Journey Begins

wrong. The result was that she had severe *Arthritis* in both her hips and her spine but was told that she was too young to have an operation as these synthetic hips have only a limited life and the surgeon wanted her to wait as long as she could before having one. Diane was still really positive about this and didn't let it get her down. I think Arthritis is something that runs through Joe's side of the family because my eldest daughter Caroline, who has had *Spondulosis* in her neck and shoulders since she was 16, is now also having a lot of pain in the base of the spine.

As Diane and I came back from shopping one day, Kayleigh met us and broke down in tears. She kept saying "Sorry Nanna", "I've let you down", I'm pregnant. All we could think of was to stop her tears. We both stood round cuddling her and trying to comfort her, telling her that we would make sure she was alright. She was only 16 years old at that time. I remembered how I had felt when Diane and Ray told me about their expected baby and it broke my heart to see her in such distress. Although the family had mixed feelings about it, we all rallied round to support her.

At about eight weeks, Kayleigh had a 'bleed' and the doctor said it was touch and go whether the baby lived or not. Evidently it was not to be this time and she lost the baby. This was the start of the worst three years of life for Kayleigh and her boyfriend Michael, although he never deserted her. In fact it was to make their relationship even stronger.

For a long time, I had been thinking about buying myself a new car for my 70th birthday and spent a lot of time looking into my financial situation to see if I could afford the repayments. I had been driving 15 years and had always had second hand cars. I felt it would really buck me up to own a brand new one. After a long time deliberating, I finally made up my mind and became the proud owner of my first 5 door Fiesta.

I had only had it a few days however when Michael, who

was opening the drive gates for me, called me over and asked me if I had seen the scratches on the car. I thought he was joking until he persuaded me to look. I was completely horrified. Someone had scratched right around the car twice. I couldn't believe that anyone could have wanted to do this to me and that is what hurt the most. Later in the day, Ray was making enquiries and a small boy told him who had done it. It turned out to be two 10yr olds who didn't even know me. Before they had come out to play, one of the boys had 'just happened' to see a Stanley knife in his hall and had put it in his pocket. They had climbed into my garden to get some stones, seen my new car and decided that they would see what it felt like to scratch it with the knife. After being told of this, both their mothers came to my house and when I showed them what the boys had done, they were also really upset. Bringing the boys round to apologize to me, they both said they would make them pay for the damage. At least I hadn't been hurt and I knew now that they didn't act out of malice. The car was soon re-sprayed and although I was sorry that it had happened, a bit of the 'shine' had been taken off my idea of a brand new car.

One day, I was looking for a book on the Internet when my attention was taken by one called *Conversations with God* by Neale Donald Walsch. There were three books in the set. On reading the description of these, I bought them – I still can't remember the one I had originally meant to buy.

I must admit to feeling a little apprehensive when I started reading; wondering how I would react if they contradicted any of my strongly held truths gained from the Spirit Teachers. I didn't need to worry though, he just expanded my beliefs. Through Neale, God's explanations fill out little snippets of information that have filtered through to us over the years. He gives answers so profound and yet so simple, to every question we have ever wanted to ask, filling in the gaps left by what the *Bible* doesn't tell us. When I thought about this, I was even more convinced how impossible it would be for the whole concept of 'God', or in other words *Life itself*; the whole of *Creation*, to be condensed into one small book.

I had been telling Gary about these books and although he also believes that Life goes on, he always said he didn't want to read them, or he was too busy. I used to leave the one I was reading on the coffee table when I went to bed, and one morning I noticed it had been moved. I secretly smiled to myself but didn't say anything. Soon after that, Gary would openly ask me if he could borrow it. It must have answered some of his questions because he also read them all. Many months later, after talking to some of his friends, he decided to start a 'Humanitys' Team' group. These were set up by Neale, joining others all over the world promoting *Spirituality*; helping themselves and each other to gain awareness of all the goodness in the world; thus helping to change the world by changing themselves. It made me feel happy to know that Gary was joining me in my search for Spiritual truth. Another wonderful surprise awaited me just after Christmas. Ever since her son Craig had been taken into care, Caroline and I have sent cards and presents to him on birthdays and at Christmas times and we have been kept up to date with his progress and photographs. Craig had started asking his Mum about his background. When he had first been taken away, Caroline and I had both written a *Life Story Book* and made a video of the family, but somehow they have been lost or mislaid by the *Social Services* department. One day we had a visit from Craig's foster carer and her supervisor who told us more about his progress. I lent them my photograph albums, which they copied and sent back to me so Craig does know who we all are.

Imagine my surprise and delight when, on a visit from Craig's Social Worker, she suddenly said "Oh Craig has sent you this" It was a card he had made on the computer. On it he had written "Merry Christmas Nanna, love from Craig. I couldn't speak for crying. This was the first time I had ever seen his writing or had any type of personal contact with him since he went away in 1995. I pray that when Craig gets older, he will want to come to meet all of us.

When my birthday finally arrived, my house was filled with flowers, cards, visitors and gifts as usual. I was excited about the evening, but a little scared because I didn't want to chicken out and disappoint everyone. I had been persuaded to go in Michael's car that night – he wasn't drinking and he said he would take me home as soon as I wanted to go. Once I had convinced myself that his car wouldn't break down, I was able to 'rise above' my fears. There were quite a lot of people there; people I hadn't seen for years, as well as my present day friends and family. Even cousins I hadn't met for about 54 years were there. One of them, Rose and her husband George live nearby and we are still in constant contact with each other. Rose has even started to come to church with me.

Although my grandson William was only 1yr old, he was fascinated by all the people there and he enjoyed trying to dance with the other children. He also had a good try to blow the candle out on his birthday cake. It was the first time in my life that I had had a party like this, I couldn't believe it. All these people had come to help me celebrate. I couldn't have felt more special if I had been a queen. After a couple of hours walking around, talking to everyone and even attempting a little dance with my grandchildren, I felt my energy draining, and soon after, I reluctantly had to leave – although this lovely memory will stay with me forever.

Diane had been suffering with her hips for many years now but had just been given pain killing tablets and told to rest. A short time later, Diane told me that Kayleigh was pregnant again. We all hoped that everything would go alright this time. She went to the hospital to have her 8wk 'bloods' taken and the next day, a nurse came to Diane's house and told Kayleigh that they had found something not quite right in the test. It could be *Spina Bifida*. Kayleigh was to go straight away for a scan. It was found that the baby had a condition called *Gastroschisis*, which meant that his bowel was growing outside his body. They were told that this baby was the fifth in that year to have this condition, and that they hadn't to worry because it could easily be rectified after birth. This was something none of us had ever heard of, but we all clung to what had been told to us and prayed the doctors would be able to put it right. As the year moved on, I started to get stressed, knowing how much work was needed to keep the church going and I didn't feel well enough to help out as much as I would have liked. I had been pushing myself again without realizing it; this time though, I felt really tired and even the enjoyment of meeting my friends and bringing comfort and upliftment to the congregation through my mediumship didn't help. After much thought I decided I would have to resign from the *Trustees* and all of the duties that it entailed. This was a decision that made me feel really sad, the church had been my second family for over 18yrs and I couldn't bear the thought of not being involved any more, yet even the journey was now stressing me out again. I had started getting panic attacks now and again during other peoples services and I couldn't even bear the thought of 'taking the chair' with the whole congregation watching me – I felt old and useless!

Staying at home for a couple of months with the worry of of

commitment taken away from me, I started to feel better again. I realized that I was missing church so much that I told my family I wanted to go back. Seeing the way I had been with myself, they all agreed it was a good idea. I was really pleased later, when talking to Marlene, she asked me if I would like to come back part time to take the Minutes of the Meetings. I jumped at the chance, and everything went back to normal again for a while. I had regained my confidence and my zest for life.

The main way through the city from east to west is *North Bridge* spanning the *River Hull*, and in October 1994 I heard that it was to close for repairs the following March – the work would take about 9 months to complete. That was not the only shock for me, because Lowgate leading from *Drypool Bridge* at the other side of the river was to be made into a one way street. I wouldn't be able to get to church that way either. The only other quick way was over a small iron bridge in an industrial area, but I had always felt nervous when travelling that way. Every time I thought about it I felt as if I had been punched in the stomach, so I just shut it out and concentrated on the happier things going on in my life.

Gary's children, Adam and Sophie used to come from Scotland to stay with us during the summer holidays each year. As Wick is so far away, Gary and Diane used to meet Sally and Chris at the halfway point in Edinburgh. This year, however, Adam asked his Mum if he could come down again at Christmas. Sally agreed even though Sophie didn't want to come back. I was looking forward to seeing Adam again, so I threw myself into all the preparations. Gary had been coming to stay with me whenever the children were down, so everyone was looking forward to the celebrations. Adam hadn't stayed before at this time of the year and he was really enjoying all the attention we all gave to each other. When it came time for him to return home, he was visibly upset. He told us he wanted to stay here and live with his Dad.

After a long talk together, when we told him the downside of being here all the time, namely that his Dad was out a lot with his work, or at University, so he would often have to stay with me but he still wouldn't change his mind. Gary made arrangements with Sally and instead of taking Adam back to Scotland, Diane and Gary went alone to collect all Adam's possessions.

Apart from my own bedroom, I have only one tiny room which I gave to Adam. Gary had to sleep on my sofa in the living room, but he didn't mind that. I loved having them both here but, as my house is too small for two extra 6'2" permanent 'lodgers', Gary made an appointment with the Council and was put onto the housing list. 2005 turned out to be very traumatic, I was really upset with the way I was and I had already decided that this year I was going to work hard at getting rid of my fears and phobias once and for all. I just wanted to be able to go anywhere, on the `spur of the moment', instead of having an endless I can/ I can't battle with myself. I was utterly fed up with being, as I saw it, weak minded for giving in to the negative feelings. Everything seemed to happen to contradict my new intentions however.

At the beginning of February, my first great grandchild, *Bradley* was born to Kayleigh and her partner Michael. We had known that Bradley was suffering from *Gastroschisis*, but the doctor seemed confident he would be alright, unfortunately, in trying to rectify this condition, Bradley sadly passed away. He had only lived 36 hours. Of course, everyone was devastated. Although we all have a strong belief that Life goes on, how do you comfort grieving parents and relatives on the loss of a longed for baby? Kayleigh, Michael and the whole family were inconsolable.

In May, Gary and Adam moved into their own house on

Tanfield Grove, near to Diane. Whilst I was sorry to see them go (they would be only a couple of minutes away anyhow), I was very pleased to get my sofa back, as well as all the space that had been taken up by their belongings. Adam still comes to my house for his dinner every day, even when his Dad is in. As he only has 20 minutes to eat, he likes the fact that I have everything timed to the minute.

One day, on their way to Bradley's grave, Diane, Ray and their two boys were stopped at the Clough Road/Cottingham Road lights when a BMW car shunted into the back of them, pushing the car right out into the middle of Beverley Road. They were not badly hurt but Diane received what the doctor called *Whiplash of the Spine*. The Arthritis damage has been accelerated and since then her pain has become progressively worse. She now needs to use a wheelchair and gets very depressed.

I became more and more stressed. Here was I, physically healthy, yet being stopped from living my life by not being able to 'rise above' these fear thoughts. My confidence was at an all time low and even the quality of my mediumship began to suffer. By the time the bridge closed on March 7th, I had decided that the only thing to do was to retire completely from the church. I was so tired after 51 years of pushing myself, and 'beating myself up' when I chickened out' of going somewhere, that I felt I just didn't want to fight anymore. I didn't know whether I even wanted (or even was able), to be a medium anymore either.

Some of the time, I would be really positive and think everything was going to be alright and the next minute I was despairing of ever being 'normal' again. Spirit was working hard to lift me, but I always seemed to slip out of their grasp somehow. I knew I must pull myself out of this downward spiral, but didn't know how to do it. Over the years I had tried many different forms of healing. They all worked for a while but never permanently. By this time, my world had shrunk dramatically. I even stopped going to the shops and visiting the members of my family who lived in the West of the city. I lost 9 lbs in weight — and as I am naturally a very slim person, this was really worrying, not only to me.

On a lighter note, my family enjoyed me telling them 'snippets' of my life and all agreed that I should put them down into a book, which could be handed down in the family. Thinking about this, I decided that this may be one of the ways in which I could come to terms with everything in my past, so I started with my childhood. As I wrote, I realized that this had been a very happy time for me, even though I had been under the illusion that it wasn't! I also discovered that I was rather a selfish person in my teens and I cringed at the memory of my deciding to join the army when Mam and Dad and Joe, hadn't wanted me to. Even my decision to get an overseas posting was against Joe's wishes and I knew that if I had stayed at home my life may have been very different. Going over the rest of it was very therapeutic for me at the time and I thought that re-living the past would, once and for all, lay the ghosts that had filled me with fear since the age of 23. I have since learned, however, that this was not the answer, but after stopping writing for a few months, determined to finish it, I started again.

One day, seeing an advert for Angel cards and hoping they might help, I decided to send for a pack. When they arrived they were not the ones I had asked for. They were Fairy cards and at first I was very disappointed. After reading about them however, I learned that the Angels are concerned with helping us remember our *Divine Purpose in Life* and giving us the courage to fulfil this important mission. The Fairies help us to 'lighten up' so we can have more fun. They teach us to manifest what we want and enlist our assistance in helping everyone on the planet, including the animals. I followed the advice given in the cards each day, but the 'down' periods were still more frequent than the 'ups', and I still felt really stressed. At the end of July, the message on the card I had chosen for that day, advised me to express my true feelings and innermost thoughts and then go outside into nature and mentally tell the Fairies all my fears, hopes and dreams, asking for their help. I didn't really know how to do this, but I thought I would give it a try.

Going through the kitchen on my way into the garden later that day, I suddenly had the urge to pick up a pen and I started writing "I used to enjoy being me, but I don't enjoy being me anymore", etc. "I want to go out without fear, not get so tired and stressed; I want to go back to church, helping people through my mediumship". Armed with my 'Blue Peter' – (one I did earlier) piece of paper, I sat down, closed my eyes and started to tell the Fairies what I had written. I know this will seem very strange, even hilarious to some people; it was to me at first, 'being away with the Fairies', but I had really started to believe that miracles can happen.

Sitting in meditation later, I remembered how, when I had been stressed or panicked at church, Marlene (our President) would ask me if I would be alright to drive home and I always replied that once I got into my car I would be fine – and I always was. Suddenly I became aware of a large 'entity' at my side that seemed to put a hand into my chest. I 'saw' something like a windmill going round very quickly. It had taken only a split second and then it was over, but I can still remember every detail. I thought "That was my heart chakra" and I realised then, that it had been made to spin faster and also that I must have 'lost heart' with everything.

My Healing Journey Begins

Very soon I began to feel very positive, I told my family that I wanted to get involved with church again and they were pleased. They all know how I regard my John Street friends as my 'second family' and how it upsets me when I can't go. I knew I had to face the places I had feared most and Gary agreed to take me to church over the iron bridge. He also asked me if any of the things that I had been so worried about had ever happened – I had to admit that they hadn't. Before we set out on our journey I was rather nervous and apprehensive but I remembered that nothing would happen and I would be alright as soon as I got into the car. I was pleasantly surprised how quickly the journey was over, and I told myself that it wasn't going to be a problem for me to get to church when I wanted to go. Even so, when *North Bridge* opened again in October, I breathed a sigh of relief that I could now go into the town the normal way.

It was very strange – going back as a member of the congregation instead of the group, but I still helped and everyone gave me a wonderful welcome. One thing I have kept on and I hope I will for many years to come is my mediumship, working for the churches.

In August, we found out that Kayleigh and Michael were expecting another baby, and whilst I was very happy for them, I could quite understand the little niggles of uncertainty that was felt by the family. We prayed that it would be 'third time lucky' for them. Their doctor made a hospital appointment for them straight away. There, the *Obstetrician* told them that Kayleigh would receive the very best care. They would 'wrap her up in cotton wool' for the first eight weeks until she had her first blood tests and they knew that the baby was safe. After this she would be treated the same as everyone else. This was a big relief to all of them, because after what had happened they had even lost faith in the hospital unit.

I turned my attention back to *Spirit Truths* again and was able to enjoy reading. Someone from Gary's group lent him a book by Deepak Chopra, called 'The Book of Secrets', and he let me read it. In the front of the book, The Dalai Lama says that he totally agrees with Dr. Chopra's view that 'if we want to change the world, we have to begin by changing ourselves' and says "this is the same message that I have always been conveying". I was very impressed, so much so that I knew I needed my own copy to be able to study it leisurely. A few weeks later Gary also lent me *The Power of Now* by Eckhart Tolle, which, it said, has already proven to be one of the greatest spiritual books written in recent times, and containing a 'power that goes beyond words'. I also bought this book.

From these two, I learned, among lots of other things, that every negative experience we have, is stored in the memory as blocked up energy, which cannot be dissolved by 'going back into the past'. These experiences show themselves in the present by our negative emotions and need to be dealt with in the present moment – in the Now. I enjoyed reading and learning (or remembering) from these two books, but somehow I didn't start to put the information into practice straight away. I always seemed to have something else to do and told myself that I would start it tomorrow, or later (I realize now, that that was a block, a sign that I really needed to get on with it.

Christmas came and went and we all looked forward to 2006 being a better year. I started putting the methods learned in the two books into practice and slowly but surely I saw a difference. At first, everything seemed to get worse; I understand that once you make a decision about something, it takes a little time for the new instructions to filter through, giving the impression that nothing has changed. It was as if I was being given lots of

My Healing Journey Begins

opportunities to practice.

It was *Dr Claire Weeks*, the wonderful GP turned Psychiatrist, (through her books and tapes about *Self Help for your Nerves*), who made me aware in the first place that I wasn't 'going mad' and that I was experiencing things that had a simple explanation in medical terms. She explains that the feelings are only the symptoms of our body's defence mechanism (Adrenalin) getting all the systems in our bodies ready to 'fight or run' from a now non-existent danger. Dr Weeks also says that the only way to overcome this is to stop, try to relax as much as possible and let the feelings wash over us, standing our ground even when the 'storm' is at its highest. Then, because we are no longer sending 'panic' signals to the body, it stops producing Adrenalin and the feelings subside. She says that once we have practiced this and learned our way through the fear, we will always be able to cope if ever we find ourselves 'sensitised' again. Dr Weekes has known people who, as soon as she explained to them the physical reason to what is happening, have left her office cured.

Over the years I have read her books and listened to her tapes and they have helped me enormously, especially during the night when I have been awakened by palpitations and feelings of unexplainable fear, sometimes even dread, without any apparent cause. They have been my lifeline. Talking to a friend I suddenly realized that these 'irrational fears' that had engulfed me for such a large part of my life, had stretched their tentacles into parts that I hadn't even realized had been affected. I felt as if I had just woken up out of a bad dream as we spoke and things had suddenly become clear.

When I came into Spiritualism almost 22 years ago, there was such a lot of mystery surrounding communication. We were told through many different sources, that 'Mediums were born, not made', which led me to wonder if they were a special breed;

privileged people set apart from the rest and I used to wonder how I dare think I was one of the 'chosen few.' There were so many rules about the 'right' way to connect with Spirit. We were told that we couldn't ask for any spirit entity to come to us; that they would contact us if they wished to. We were also warned to be on guard against unenlightened spirits who were, seemingly, all around us, waiting to 'attach' to any unsuspecting persons who had neglected to close all their chakras and surround themselves with the protection of the *White Light*. Once, many years ago, I had even spent a sleepless night wondering what 'they' were going to do to my mind when I was to receive *Spiritual Healing* that night. These forebodings were verified in a way by two friends of mine (at different times) ending up in a mental hospital because they couldn't 'switch off' the thoughts and voices they constantly heard. I was so worried that I decided there and then that I would never open the channel to Spirit, unless I was taking a service or holding a Private Reading.

When I started Marlene's group, however, she told us that we were 'in charge' of our minds and that if we had a thought, a feeling, or heard a voice that we weren't comfortable with, we had only to 'tell it to go' and it would. For a while now, I have been surprised and even worried at how young people without any what I would call 'grounding' have been able to show psychic abilities and it has disturbed me to wonder what harm, if any, they might be doing to themselves. After reading *Conversations with God* however, I have remembered that being psychic is part of our natural gift and something to be embraced.

Since starting on my healing journey, I have found out how simplistic Life really is. I know it is difficult to take in at first, but these are my truths as I see them at this moment. For a start there are no 'privileged few'. As we are all parts of *God/ Life - all Pure Creative Spirit*; we are all given exactly the same opportunities as each other. Upon entering the *Physical Universe* we caused ourselves to forget, thus allowing us to choose who we want to be, instead of who we really are. All the knowledge in Creation is locked up inside each of us and our main task on this earthplane is to open our minds and hearts to this and help others to open theirs also. It is our own choices that dictate the situations that confront us — as well as how we react to and deal with them. As we create our own Reality every minute of every day, it is again our choice whether or not we believe that anyone or anything can invade our space or put us in any danger. I now see that the cause of my years of mental pain is also simplistic and on some level, my own choice. The trouble occurred because I was alternating between 'living in the past' and anticipating a 'what if' future, even dreading the next few minutes or hours, thinking 'what if this happens' or 'that happens'.

Now, however, I have learned that, whilst on the *Earthplane*, I am the 'Actor' — not the character he's playing at this particular time. I have been caught up, most of my life, in all of this character's negative emotions, thinking that they are mine. I found that all I have to do is simply be the 'Watcher', putting my attention into the negative emotion (without analysing it) then seeing it disappear. The truth of these statements is already being given to me and I now know that nothing can ever be solved by going into the past — or dreading the future. The only time which has any power, is this moment — Now. All these new concepts do not usually become facts overnight for most people and I am really enjoying this next part of my journey as I practice all these 'ideas' more and more.

2006 has been a wonderful year on the family front, on May 16th Alexi Louise was born to Kayleigh and Michael. She is Diane's first granddaughter and my first great granddaughter. We were all over the moon. She is a beautiful perfect little girl.

For the first few days, Jamie (her uncle) couldn't look at her, he dare not let himself get attached to the baby, but when he realized that she was here to stay, he couldn't take his eyes off her. Kayleigh has lots of built in baby sitters – when she allows them to be. At the moment, both the proud parents naturally, want to take care of Alexi themselves.

Stephen has managed to regain residency of his son, Stephen junior, who has been very unsettled for the past few years.

The 'icing on the cake' for me is the written contact Caroline and I now have with Craig. We write to each other often and he says 'we mean a great deal to him and he hopes to be able to see us sometime in the future'. Looking back through all the different forms of healing that I have tried, I can see that they all point in the same direction. *Acupuncture, Hypnotherapy and Regression, Desensitisation by Injection, Emotional Freedom Therapy* (EFT) all basically help us to stay relaxed whilst being engulfed by the terrifying emotion of fear. They all take the condition 'out of our hands' so to speak and can be a very effective treatment. I have found though, that for me, there was no magic 'off switch'. For some reason, it had to be a very long and personal battle.

Listening to Gill Edward's tapes on *Living in the 4th Dimension* – growing through love and joy instead of pain and suffering, I learned that the Universe wants to give us everything our hearts desire. Jill says that if you really wanted to have or be anything, you would already have or be it. The only reason why you do not is because something, some inner subconscious thought must be blocking you.

My dearest wish is to live in the country, still work for Spirit, maybe using my *Inspirational Philosophies* more, as well as bringing comfort and upliftment to people through my mediumship. I should also like to meet a gentle man of like mind to myself to share the rest of my journey with. To do all this I need to have a lot of money, so I decided to get in touch with my 'blockage' and find out why this isn't happening. Gill says we can meet this younger part of ourselves on an inner journey or we can write a letter to it, using the hand we normally write with for the questions and the other one for the answers. The writing came quickly, as if these inner thoughts had been just waiting to 'bubble out. I felt so 'lifted' after this. I even found that I was looking forward to Karen's 18th birthday party, but I was still unsure.

I had 'been here before'. Countless times in the past I have felt very positive before an event but as the time drew nearer, the doubts and fears would engulf me. Then, by the time of the event, I had ended up making myself physically ill and would have to excuse myself from going. This time however, I looked forward to going more as the time came closer. On the day I even cooked myself a meal at teatime — this, I had never been able to do before. I really enjoyed myself, - talking to Chris' family as well as my own. I thought afterwards how great it was that we could all meet amicably after all that had happened. I arrived home just in time for the lottery results, I had won £10.00! I was over the moon.

The next morning I was reading the *Stella Polaris* magazine from the *White Eagle Lodge* and, closing my eyes for a moment, I suddenly saw a big round garden with rich green grass edged by a mass of different coloured flowers. This gave way to many different scenes with different people and I just felt I could 'burst' with happiness. It is very rare that I have 'seen' anything in my meditations, although when Spirit has needed to show anything to me, they have done so effortlessly. I have never seen so much at one time and in such bright colours before in my life. These were the three things I was asking about and I'm again really excited to find out what happens next. In meditation the next day, I didn't see anything, but heard these beautiful words:-

I am the Spark of Light that shines in your darkness
I am the Breath of Wind that cools your fevered brow
I am the beating heart that lives inside all creatures
I am the Beauty of Nature, the stillness of now

I rang Gary and as I read this to him, I was overtaken by such emotion because of the beauty of the truth behind the words. Now I know that whatever has been stopping me in my Spiritual work really has been healed. I feel as if I am on the threshold of something really wonderful. Since then, I have learned something that, for me, is a further truth.

The conditions we find ourselves in when we first leave the Earthplane are governed by our own thoughts. If we believe we will be met by our loved ones, we will be. People who think "when we're dead, we're dead", will sleep until in time, they 'wake themselves up' and are greatly surprised to find that they are still alive! Even ones who believe they are so bad that they deserve to go to 'Hell' (a place which, in fact, does not exist) are not disappointed. Their experience has been likened to looking through a window and seeing a replica of themselves, burning in a flame-filled room. The watching Spirit, of course, feels no discomfort and soon gets tired of looking at this spectacle and is immediately helped to move on. This proves to me that even the smallest detail of our lives and the Universe around us can only have been created by a loving, compassionate *Mother/Father God*, whose overriding thought is for the happiness and contentment of *His/Her children*.

I believe that we all have a task to carry out whilst we are here. This is to 'go inside', to our own Inner Teacher to find the truth for ourselves. We have to remember who we really are, not physical beings with a limited lifespan, but all miniatures of the Creator him/herself, with the same creative powers. We must then encourage others to find their own truths. In this way we are all helping to bring forward the *Aquarian Age* with all its wonderful changes for mankind.

It is amazing to me now however, as I discover further truths about the workings of Eternal Life, to realize that, somewhere deep inside, I have 'known' these things all my life without really thinking deeply about them. It's as if I can now see what had been happening to me for the whole of my life, as if my eyes are being opened for the first time. I had 'fallen into the trap' of reading a lot, taking in snippets of information but without doing the basic work of meditating or completely understanding.

Through the *CwG* books, and also God saying that he has been sending His message through many, many different channels down the years, I have been drawn back to my original path with *White Eagle's* teachings, a name, (not his own) but designed to raise our consciousness from the heaviness of the Earthplane up to the heights of the Spirit World. These were brought to us in the 1930s through the mediumship of *Grace Cook*. A short quote from this teaching says "You do not need to read books, you only need to love, to be still within, and be patient, to meditate, to observe – and the mystery school within the temple of your own being will teach all that you need to know."

I am even finding it easy to meditate now. I can see now that my mind has been like the proverbial 'excited little puppy dog' out for its first walk. It is so eager to explore all the new things that its senses pick up, so impatient to learn, that, instead of me controlling it and being in charge of my mind, it has been controlling me, taking me down all the dead end, alleys and following all the distractions that catch its eye.

I was given another piece in the puzzle of my life a couple of weeks ago. Gary brought a friend Shayna from his group, to see me and she was asking about my difficulties with going out. After speaking to her for a while and answering her questions, she told me that the `trigger' or starting point of my problems was definitely my evacuation at five years old (This verified what I had learned during hypnotherapy some years ago when I had realized for the first time the trauma that that small child went through). As well as being taken from my family without explanation, as I became tired, I just wanted my Mam and loved ones. I wanted to go home, but of course no one could take me and I was `stuck' with strangers. That afternoon I had a wonderful experience, Shayna sat by my side and took five deep breaths along with me. She told me to get into a lift and descend seven floors, when I would find myself in a garden, there seeing the small Marjorie. I actually `saw' the garden and pictured the little girl. After talking to her for a while and telling her I would never leave her, I `came back', feeling emotional but relaxed. The next day, Shayna sent a message through Gary, saying that I would greatly benefit from going down to meet my `Inner Child' again. This time, I even heard the clanging and felt the heaviness of the lift doors as I opened and shut them. I saw the young Marjorie wearing a red-flecked jumper suit that Mam had knitted me. I even felt the texture and heaviness of the pleated skirt as I sat by her side. I told her that we had had many different adventures together, some happy and some not so happy. As I said the latter I felt a dull pain in the side of my head and a loud `voice' cried no, no, no! Putting my arms round her, I waited for her to quieten. I found she was sitting on my knee and I was singing `Hush little baby' to her. Getting up later, I said "You don't really want to stay here by yourself do you? Do you want to come with me?

Suddenly she seemed to fling herself at me. I could see her arms and feel the weight of them round my neck, her legs tight round my waist, so much so that, for a few seconds, I actually wondered what I would do with her when I got back out of the lift! Again I felt so much better afterwards and Shayna said I have made a big healing breakthrough.

Now, after all this time, I am finally beginning to understand the wisdom in all the truths which have been opened to me. It was as if I could `talk the talk', without `walking the walk', so to speak, or learning some of the anatomy without understanding the physiology. Looking back over the times when I have been frozen with fear about going out, it is as if I can actually see, for the first time, what was happening. I had let this little puppy dog take charge again, running wherever it wanted to go; filling me with foreboding about `what ifs' and `Oh my God's', taking me onto a journey into the imaginary outcomes of situations that never, ever materialised.

Things are now going well with me, however; I have learned (well almost), to step out of the `Mum mode' and let my children solve their own problems (They have been good naturedly trying to get me to do this for years). I am beginning to take great strides in my fight against fear. Already I am going to the supermarket by myself – something I hadn't done for many years. On Sunday, I even went at a time when there were lots of other people there – and I still didn't panic! I know without a doubt that things can only get better. As I see the results of my efforts, I grow more confident and stronger all the time. Even my physical, as well as mental strength seems to have improved such a lot. I don't get half as tired as I used to and my housework gets done in half the time (whenever I feel like doing it!).

Caroline has been diagnosed with a degenerative condition in her spine and although it was upsetting for her to be told she will never be able to work again in the *Caring Profession*, she is staying positive and looking forward to starting a *Counselling* course. Diane has finally been put on the list to have her hip operations which will, as she puts it, give her her life back.

I had never been able to understand why I had to *do it the hard way* or *take the scenic route* on my journey, but now I am beginning to see that if, by writing this book and reliving the events, I can help even one person through my experiences, it has all been worthwhile.

I also think the time was never right for me to benefit from the different forms of healing earlier, but now, however, I feel sure that it is. I am constantly getting proof that, if I can only remember that I am not the negative thought, feeling or emotion, threatening to engulf me, and just `watch' it (without trying to analyzing it), I am rewarded with a wonderful sense of peace and happiness after it has died away. With Gary's help I have learned such a lot about myself in the last few months. Although I didn't know it at the time, most of my life has been in co-dependent relationships, starting with my first marriage to John. I learned to push my feelings down. I dare not speak my mind in case I upset him and made him angry with me. When living with relatives, I always tried to make sure I didn't get in the way (in case they asked me to leave). When I married Joe, I was always felt he was more important than me because he had been good enough to `take on' my children. When he told me off, I was always terrified that he was going to tell us to go. I again pushed my feelings down all the time. Whatever happened, especially when I was trying to go out and when I had to go into the *Psychiatric Hospital* and I was so very frightened, I daren't let my feelings come to the front of my mind, telling myself not to be so silly and that everything would be alright – I told myself off a lot in those days. When our babies died I felt that I must

My Healing Journey Begins

not go to pieces because I would upset everyone more. I had to be strong to keep us all going. Even when Joe died, I just pushed my feelings down, telling myself that he was out of his mental pain now and I had to be strong for the children. It has only been in the last couple of weeks that I have admitted feeling angry and cheated because it had happened. I was only 50 years old at the time. Joe was always telling us to 'look after our bodies because it was the only one we had', but he didn't look after his own!

Now I take one day at a time. Memories sometimes bring painful emotions which I allow to engulf me, without reliving the memory, until at last the emotion subsides into peace. I can sometimes even catch myself slipping backwards or forwards in time, and quickly bring myself into the present moment more and more often. A couple of days ago I suddenly realized that I no longer 'hear' the critical thoughts that have been my constant companion for as long as I can remember. This has been a traumatic battle for me — trying to think of positive thoughts to counteract these. I have never been so quiet inside. I am not saying that I don't slip back into fear sometimes, but not at all as often as I used to. Now though, I know how to deal with it. When I do have to go out anywhere, I take the journey in my mind at first. I see myself calmly and confidently getting there, doing what I have to do and getting back safely. Then I feel ten feet tall.

The healing journey I am undertaking is a wonderful experience and I am making new discoveries all the time. I can sometimes even 'enjoy' the bad times, knowing that they don't last long and bring a wonderful sense of achievement afterwards. I am really grateful to everyone who has helped me — and is still helping me. Being totally relaxed and at peace with my life is something I despaired of ever achieving, but it is happening.

Before I finish I must relate the latest step. Through Gary's group once again, I have been led to the work of *Esther and Gerry Hicks*. Gerry is the 'questioner' and Esther 'channels' a group of loving entities calling themselves Abraham. They tell about the *Law of Attraction* (that which is like unto itself is drawn), which is the most powerful law in the Universe and when we say birds of a feather flock together, it is this law that we are talking about. Abraham say that this law must be understood before anything we are living — or anything we observe anyone else living — can make any sense. Through their teachings I have learned that no matter how dark, how disillusioned and even scary my life had become, I can start to alter it, not by going over past events, but by simply changing my thoughts. As I read, I experienced an immediate feeling of relief and hope for the future; the feeling of being in control returned. Although I know it will take a lot of work it is impossible to analyse my thoughts all the time, so I have to take notice of my emotions, how I feel about different circumstances.

In the Foreward to the book, 'The Law of Attraction', Neale Donald Walsch (Author of Conversations with God) says "Have you ever wished that life came with an instruction book? Well, now it does. Typing the final few words of this part of my life's story is bringing mixed emotions. In one way I am pleased that I have managed (with a lot of help from family and friends) to remember all the facts, but in another way I feel as if I am letting go of a big part of myself and it feels a little emotional. I know with absolute certainty though, that this 'blanket of fear' will never be able to take complete control of my life again. Now I am enjoying the sunshine of my freedom and stepping confidently into the future with Joy, Gratitude and Appreciation.

Printed in the United Kingdom
by Lightning Source UK Ltd.
127876UK00001B/79-87/A